The Life of Beetles

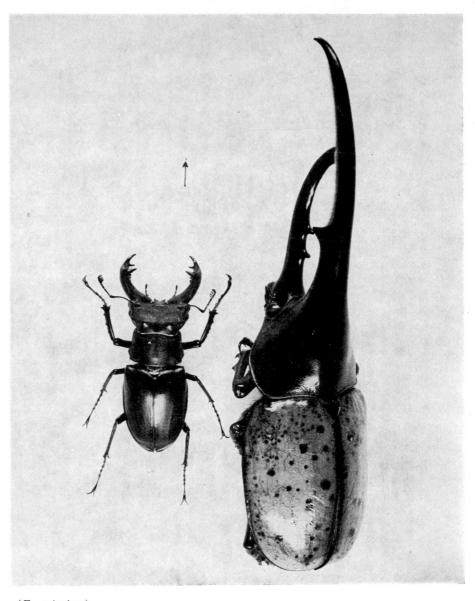

(*Frontispiece*)
Top left: Ptiliolum fuscum (Ptiliidae); 0·7 mm; *bottom left: Lucanus cervus* male (Lucanidae): 56 mm; *right: Dynastes hercules* male (Scarabaeidae): 145 mm. (Courtesy of the Manchester Museum.)

The Life
of Beetles

Glyn Evans, B.Sc. Ph.D.
Senior Lecturer in Zoology, University of Manchester

Foreword by Dr R. A. Crowson
University of Glasgow

London   George Allen & Unwin Ltd
Ruskin House   Museum Street

Printed in Great Britain at the Alden Press, Oxford

FOREWORD

When it is considered that beetles are one of the most familiar and popular groups of insects, with an extraordinary diversity in habits and modes of life, that many of the species are economically important, and that a number of them have been favourite subjects for twentieth-century laboratory researches in biology, the scarcity – at least in the English language – of good modern general works on them may seem surprising. Dr Evans, himself a decidedly learned academic entomologist, with a long-standing interest in beetles and author of some important functional anatomical studies in the group, has made a bold attempt to fill this conspicuous gap in entomological literature – and I think the resulting book will go a long way towards achieving this aim.

He writes in a clear, direct style, avoiding unnecessary technical terminology, so that his book should be intelligible – and interesting – to anyone with the most elementary biological knowledge. If his work serves to draw the attention of a wide public to the particularly interesting features of the order Coleoptera, one of Dr Evans's main purposes will have been fulfilled; its second, perhaps equally important aim, is to broaden the minds of those laboratory experimentalists who may already be working with beetles, leading them to study the more specialist coleopterological literature. A third group of people who should benefit from Dr Evans's work is composed of the relatively small but active band of amateur beetle collectors, whose field activities and observations may gain new dimensions of interest from reading him. Finally, there are the ecologists and Pleistocene or Quaternary palaeontologists, who are increasingly using beetles as ecological indicators – these too should benefit from reading this book.

R. A. CROWSON
Department of Zoology
University of Glasgow

AUTHOR'S PREFACE

Today, more people have leisure than ever before, and so it ought to be possible for the ordinary reader to delve into quite a specialised subject provided it is presented with a minimum of specialist jargon. This is not possible in some sciences, but many aspects of biology can be simply explained, and this may account for the large number of excellent books in this field that have appeared in the last few years. They include several insect natural histories which present a great deal of interesting information and yet do not assume a technical background. However, there is no similar treatment of beetles in English, yet they comprise one quarter of the species in the animal kingdom. This book deals with the lives of beetles in a straightforward, but not oversimplified manner. It attempts to interest both the reader of general natural history and those student Coleopterists who have already started collecting beetles and are also looking for more background information. Of course, the danger of aiming at two targets is that one may hit neither; nevertheless, the beetles are such a huge and fascinating segment of the living world that the effort is well worth making. If this brief survey gives the impression of a bewildering, seemingly endless range of adaptations, it may be somewhere near the truth. It is precisely because beetles convey this impression that they interest naturalists and biologists; for the opportunities that they offer for further research are also well nigh endless.

GLYN EVANS
University of Manchester

ACKNOWLEDGEMENTS

I am happy to be able to thank my colleagues, Dr R. R. Askew, J. Gordon Blower and Colin Johnson for their useful criticisms of various chapters, and I am especially grateful to Dr R. A. Crowson for his comments on the whole manuscript. Obviously, remaining errors are my own. I am also grateful to Dr A. R. David and Dr C. E. Nield for their help and I would particularly like to thank my wife for typing most of the manuscript. Mr Les Lockey has kindly taken the photograph for the frontispiece.

Many of the illustrations in this book have been redrawn from other works, and I am indebted to the following publishers for permission to use the figures noted below:

Academic Press, New York, for figures 46 and 47; American Association for the Advancement of Science for figure 45 (right); Blackwell Scientific Publications for figure 32; Clarendon Press, Oxford, for figure 52; Entomological Society of America for figure 44 (left); *Entomologist's Monthly Magazine* for figures 4D, 17D & E and 33D; Frederick Warne for figure 27; *Heredity* for figure 58; Hutchinson University Library, London, for figure 51; Institute of Biology, London, for figure 49; Istituto di Superiore Agricole, Laboratorio di Entomologia, Bologna, for figure 37; Masson, Paris, for figure 36 (left); McGraw-Hill, New York, for figure 59; Melbourne University Press for figure 38; Payot, Paris, for figures 20A–C and 36 (right); Royal Entomological Society of London for figure 34; Royal Society of Edinburgh for figures 15, 17J, 18 and 35; Royal Society of London for figures 8E & F and 10; Sociedad Mexicana de Entomologica for figures 20D–H and 40; Weidenfeld & Nicolson for figures 50 & 53; Zoological Society of London for figure 42.

I would also like to thank the authors concerned, who are acknowledged in the appropriate legends. The author's work referred to is quoted either in the Bibliography, or in the following list:

Figure 8E & F after Dennell, *Phil. Trans. Roy. Soc. B.* Vol. 231 (1942), p. 247.

Figures 15 & 35 from Evans, *Trans. Roy. Soc. Edinb.* Vol. 66 (No. 5) (1964), p. 91.

Figures 17J & 18 from Evans, *ibid.* Vol. 64 (No. 14) (1961), p. 297.

Figure 19 (bottom) after Balduf, *The Bionomics of Entomophagous Coleoptera*, (St. Louis, 1935), 220 pp.

Figures 20A–C and 36 (right) after Paulian, *Les Coléoptères*, (Paris: Payot, 1943).

Figure 21 after Fernando, Ph.D. Thesis (University of Manchester, 1963).

Figure 24 after Riley, *Trans. St. Louis Acad. Sci.* Vol. 3 (1877), p. 544.

Figure 36 (left) after Jeannel in Grassé, *Traité de Zoologie*, Vol. IX (1965), p. 771.

Figure 37 after Grandi, *R. Inst. Super. Agr., Lab. de Ent. Bol.* Vol. 9 (1937), pp. 33–64.

Figure 38 after Ewin in Britton, *The Insects of Australia* (C.S.I.R.O: Melbourne University Press, 1970).

CONTENTS

J. B. S. Haldane was once approached by a distinguished theologian to ask what inferences one could draw about the nature of the Creator from the study of His creation. He replied with his usual extreme terseness, 'An inordinate fondness for beetles.'

(I am indebted to Professor A. J. Cain for this anecdote, which was recounted to him by Professor Haldane.)

CHAPTER 1

Introduction: An Age of Beetles

We live in an age of beetles, and beetles are almost everywhere. In fact, one animal in every four is a beetle, and nearly 300,000 species have already been described. There are almost 3,700 species in Britain, yet the average man-in-the-garden may only notice the ladybirds on his rose-trees and the black beetles under old bricks. Again, beetles are probably the commonest insects in collections, after butterflies and moths, yet although we cannot miss seeing flies, bees and butterflies on a summer's walk in the country, the beetles are mainly noticeable by their absence. These apparent paradoxes reflect a characteristic of the beetles as a group, the fact that beetles do not flamboyantly force themselves upon our attention, but rather hide just beneath the surface of things.

Many of the features that have enabled the beetles to become such a successful group of land animals are shared with other orders of insects, and we must first ask which characters of insects have enabled them to form nearly three-quarters of the world's animal species. Small size is one of the most obvious features of insects; although this has prevented them from doing vertebrate-type jobs, it has allowed them to take advantage of many smaller occupations, and of course, these are innumerable for animals with the ability to go almost anywhere on land and to eat almost anything that they find there. This food includes nearly every animal and vegetable material from grass roots to solid timber, and from stored grain to stored museum specimens. Some beetles can even eat such unlikely foods as opium, strychnine and deadly nightshade.

In a successful small animal the total body mass of a species is broken up into a large number of small individuals. Small, that is, when compared with most vertebrates, although large insects are bigger than many of the smaller fish, frogs, birds or mammals. However, the relatively small size of most insects enables them to use food which would be overlooked by most vertebrates, and to shelter in crevices impossible for larger animals. The disadvantage of small size is that many physical forces which can be disregarded by large animals now become dangerous. At the size of the smallest insects – about a third of a millimetre in length – directed flight is impossible and air must be 'rowed' through. Or again, a water drop on a cabbage leaf becomes an inescapable trap if the surface film has been broken into. Insects, therefore, are small enough to use the myriad of niches left untouched by large vertebrates, but not so small as to be restricted to a few types of habitat.

In common with other arthropods, insects have a strong, external skeleton. Thus not only are points of attachment provided for the muscles, but a tough shell protects all the soft parts. This seems to be the most efficient type of skeleton for the insectan size range. It could not be used by large vertebrates because the shell must be moulted if growth is to occur, and a large, soft-bodied animal would be very vulnerable between moults. An additional mechanical advantage of an exo-skeleton is that many parts consist of cylindrical structures which are very resistant to bending or distortion, but are sufficiently flexible to minimise fractures as a result of blows. The reasons for this lie in the structure and formation of the exo-skeleton. The basic materials are protein and chitin which together form the cuticle. The chitin is composed of long-chain molecules, and being soft and flexible is ideal for the joints between the hard parts of the cuticle. These hard parts, the sclerites, are formed by a process akin to the tanning of leather, whereby the soft chitin is reinforced by a hard, tanned protein.

The outer layer of the cuticle is usually covered with a wax layer which helps to waterproof the skeleton. This is most important in a land animal, and is necessary to solve the same problem that the reptiles overcame in evolving from the amphibia. Other devices for water conservation include closing mechanisms on the spiracles and methods for resorbing water from waste food in the rectum. The minimising of water losses has enabled some insects, especially beetles, to live in very dry places such as deserts. Conversely, their waxy cuticles have allowed other insects to live in very wet situations for, in a completely aquatic habitat, the water-repellant property of hairs on the cuticle enables an air store to be obtained and carried.

Land insects have a unique method of breathing which has many advantages over a system involving lungs and special oxygen-carrying blood corpuscles such as that found in mammals. In insects there is a direct method of carrying air and oxygen to individual tissues and cells. This is via the network of tube-like tracheae which ramify internally from the external body openings, the spiracles. In small insects, the movement of oxygen inwards, and of carbon dioxide outwards, takes place mainly by diffusion. Large and active insects help this process by pumping movements, as a diffusion system becomes inefficient above a certain size. In an outsized insect, no pump could be efficient enough and so this method of breathing also sets an upper limit to the size of insects.

One noticeable feature of insects is the very large number of individuals in some species. The total numbers of a single species of ant, midge or greenfly must be astronomical. This reflects a capacity for rapid reproduction which, besides making up for the deficit of a high death rate, also gives insect populations and communities a considerable degree of flexibility. It means that the damaging effects of a hard winter on a community can soon be made good, and that new habitats can be colonised rapidly without draining the parent population. This capacity for rapid reproduction is best seen in such insects as aphids, although it is also reflected – though at a less fantastic rate – in the ladybirds which prey upon them.

Perhaps the most obvious character of many insects is their ability to fly. Flight lifts many insects out of the range of their predators, and enables them to seek out new sources of food or shelter. It also allows the very rapid infiltration of a species into a new area. The finest insect aeronauts include the dragonflies and the Diptera, and the beetles cannot match these in their conquest of the air. Although many beetles make use of this most important faculty in order to distribute themselves, and to gain access to new food sources, none hunt aerial prey or move with the precision of hoverflies. Beetles are not masters of the air but of the surface of the earth, and as this surface has an incredible number of niches, so are there vast numbers of species of beetles.

I have considered some of the advantages that beetles obtain by being insects, but why should so many insects happen to be beetles? To answer this we must find out which particular insectan characters have been elaborated so successfully by the beetles. What makes an insect a beetle? The definition usually given is that a beetle is an insect with a life history consisting of egg, larval, pupal, and adult stages, which has biting mouthparts, and in which the front pair of wings are modified to form wing cases almost always meeting in a straight line down the middle of the back. Unfortunately, this definition misses out the characteristic element of 'beetleness' which in most cases enables one to recognise a beetle immediately. The impression of 'beetleness' is mainly due to the strong cuticle, the sclerites of which give the beetle an armoured appearance. The cuticle of the head, thorax and elytra may be especially thick and strong. If a beetle is trodden on when walking upon soft ground, it is quite likely to be pushed unharmed into the mud, whereas another insect would be crushed. The weakest point is usually the central junction of the wing cases which bursts open long before the rest of the skeleton is injured. In many wingless ground beetles, this has been prevented by the fusion of the elytra centrally. The great strength and toughness of the cuticle of beetles is probably due to its detailed structure.

19

In section, the cuticle is seen to be composed of a series of horizontal lamellae. Within the lamellae, bundles of fibres form a meshwork, always crossing at the same angle. Thus, an immensely tough and flexible skeletal structure is produced, rather like a sheet of lamellated fibre-glass.

Although most beetles have mouthparts adapted for biting, there is a wide variety of feeding methods, and different species may deal with the same type of food in quite different ways. However, the jaws and maxillae are always recognisable as such, and the drastic mouthpart modifications seen in bees or butterflies are rarely found in beetles. Some predators may have very similar mouthparts to scavengers or herbivores, and these may all be members of the same family. Thus adaptations to different diets do not always require large changes in the shape of the mouthparts. Clearly, such a versatile pattern of mouthparts must have a considerable evolutionary potential.

The adaptability of beetles to a wide variety of diets, coupled with their generally hidden habits, has led to the invasion of many specialised habitats such as fungus and decaying vegetation, carrion and dung. A fact which has helped the beetles to exploit these with perhaps greater efficiency than even the flies, is that both larval and adult beetles tend to live and feed in the same places. With the flies, most of the feeding is done by the larvae. This contrast is partly due to the long life of adult beetles, and partly to the frequent modification of both larval and adult mouthparts for the same diet. Although the adult is the fully winged distributive phase, it can still spend most of its time within the larval habitat, thanks partly to the efficiency of its protective wing cases.

Beetle larvae are much more diverse than the adults. As they are not concerned with distribution and reproduction, they can concentrate on their tasks of feeding and growth. Thus the shapes of the mouthparts and the body, and the sizes of the antennae and legs all depend on how and where the food is obtained. A predatory ground beetle larva has strong, slender legs for fast running but in a root-feeding wire-worm, smaller legs for slower movements are quite sufficient, and a weevil larva which spends its whole life in a hazelnut is legless.

As with the adult, the adaptability of the beetle larva has led to the exploitation of almost every attainable food source. Plants are used from the roots to the fruits, and from the bark to the heart-wood. Some larvae will only eat the developing seeds whilst others search out plants that are dead or decayed. Carnivorous larvae may specialise on mites or snails, or even eat tadpoles and small fish. However, relatively few beetles have become parasites. In some beetles where the larval habitat changes several times during a single life cycle, corresponding changes of larval form are brought about by hypermetamorphosis (see Chapter 3). In the beetle pupa we again see the overall influence upon the order of hidden habits. The pupa is almost always enclosed in a cell, frequently in the soil, and is only rarely exposed, as in the ladybirds.

The picture of the Coleoptera that emerges, therefore, is of a group of insects that is both physically and physiologically tough. It is not a group which has specialised in a particular habit such as parasitism or social life, but one which has retained a sufficiently unspecialised body form and function to enable it to occupy an enormous variety of habitats. The most obvious feature of the group is its unobtrusiveness, and the development of elytra to protect the folded wings is both adaptive to, and symbolic of the hidden life.

How can one treat a group as large as the Coleoptera in a small book? It can be only by concentrating on the more general problems of their ways of life. This book does not attempt to deal with lists of beetles found in different habitats, nor explain how to identify various species (for this, see Appendix); instead, it tries to provide some answers to the more obvious questions about the group.
For instance:

What are beetles, and what range of variation do they cover?
How do they breed, and what are their different types of life cycle?
What do they eat?
How do they protect themselves?
How do they fit into their environment, i.e. what is their ecology?
How do they influence mankind?
Finally, how did this successful group evolve?

Each of these questions will be considered in turn in successive chapters. Each chapter will illustrate a different aspect of the most obvious attribute of beetles – their variations on a single theme. This implies that beetles are a well-defined kind of insect with a characteristic common structure which gives them an easily recognised 'beetleness', yet superimposed upon this single theme is an immense range of variations. This is the most outstanding feature of beetles as a group, and this book will emphasise the point by describing a variety of beetle activities. We shall see that beetle diversity does not consist merely of structural modifications; it encompasses variations of breeding habits, types of larvae, kinds of food, methods of concealment or offence, and a myriad ways of fitting into an environment that already contains a host of other creatures.

CHAPTER 2

Beetle Forms and Body Functions

This chapter tries to answer some of the most basic questions asked about beetles, in particular:

What are beetles?
How do they differ from other insects?
What differences are there between different kinds of beetles?
How many beetles are there, and how big are they?
How are beetles constructed?

Answering these questions will involve defining beetle structure and its range of variations, dealing briefly with the classification of beetles, and then considering the organisation and operation of the beetle body. I shall deal with these topics in turn, as follows:

1 The characteristic features of beetles;
2 The range of forms;
3 Classification;
4 Size and numbers;
5 The cuticle;
6 The organisation of the body.

1. The Characteristic Features of Beetles

The most important characteristics that enable beetles to be distinguished from other insects are as follows:

(a) Beetles are insects which have a life history of the type: egg – larva – pupa – adult.
(b) The mouthparts of the adults are almost always adapted for biting; a pair of biting jaws (mandibles) are always present, and they usually point forwards ('prognathy', see fig. 1) rather than downwards. In the

remote ancestors of beetles the mouthparts pointed down, towards the ground. In beetles, the axis of the head has been swung upwards and forwards into line with the body axis. To protect the exposed throat and neck region, a plate behind the mouthparts on the underside of the head – the gula – has been developed (fig. 7).

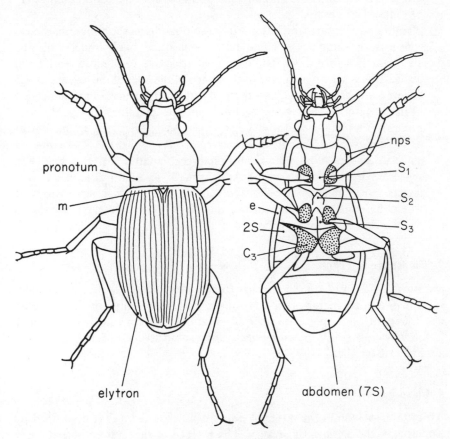

Figure 1. *Left: Upper surface of a ground beetle*
(m – mesoscutellum.)
Figure 2. *Right: Undersurface of a ground beetle*
(C_3 – third coxa; e – epipipleure of elytron; nps – noto-pleural suture; S_1 – prosternum; S_2 – mesosternum; S_3 – metasternum; 2S – second abdominal sternite; 7S – seventh abdominal sternite.

(c) The middle region, the thorax, is obviously divided into a large, freely movable prothorax, and a meso- and metathorax which are more or less fused with the abdomen.

23

(d) The first pair of wings (mesothoracic) has been transformed into wing cases (elytra) which cover the folded (and usually functional) second pair of wings. The elytra usually cover all the upper surface of the beetle behind the prothorax, and meet in a straight line along the middle of the back. In some beetles the elytra are greatly reduced in size, and in a few species they are absent. Similarly, the hind wings of certain beetles may be reduced or absent.

(e) A rather odd feature which is not quite so obvious as the above characters concerns the hind legs. These have been tilted back underneath the abdomen of a beetle so that they tend to move in a more horizontal plane. This is due to a change in the shape of the base of the leg, the coxa; this now runs from the side of the body transversely across the underside of the metathorax to reach a second, inner articulation (fig. 2). In some beetles (Adephaga) the hind coxa either has a very slight movement or is immovable although in others (most Polyphaga) it has a limited angle of swing. A possible evolutionary explanation for this has been suggested by Crowson for the Adephaga. If ancestral Adephaga were insects living in the narrow spaces under bark, or in holes in logs, it would be easier to push with the hind legs if they were tilted back to operate near the plane of the body.

2. The Range of Forms

Superficially, the Coleoptera appears to be a more homogeneous group than some of the other major orders. However, within the limits of their 'beetle-ness' there are an immense number of variations of form and size. The range of forms is most easily shown by illustrating some diverse species taken from a variety of families (fig. 3).

3. Classification

All systems of naming plants and animals are based on that developed by Linnaeus in the eighteenth century. The essence of this system is that every animal species has its own Latin name which is distinct from the name of every other species. In fact, the specific name is a pair of Latin names: that of the genus (with a capital initial letter) followed by the specific or trivial name (with a small initial letter). In print, the specific name is written in italics; it is often followed by the name of the author who first described it. Thus: *Carabus violaceus* Linnaeus or *Carabus violaceus* L., or if this species has already been referred to: *C.violaceus* L. Sometimes the authority may appear in parentheses, thus *Calosoma inquisitor* (L.). This means that Linnaeus used the trivial name to describe this species, but it has now been placed in

24

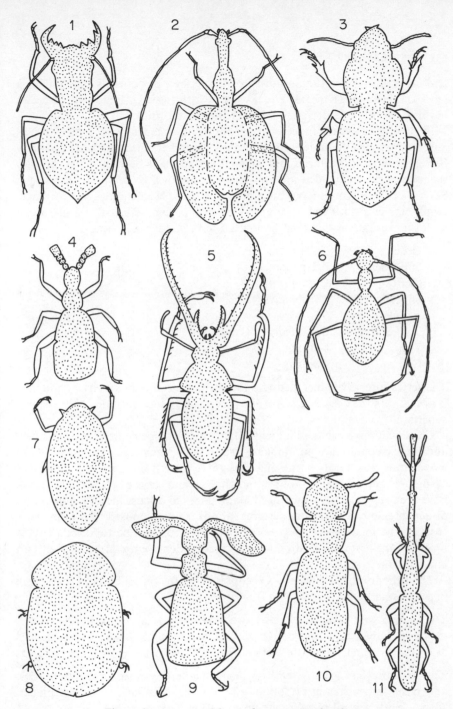

Figure 3. *A range of forms from various families*

1: *Mantichora*, 70 mm (Carabidae-Cicindelinae); 2: *Mormolyce*, 60 mm (Carabidae); 3: *Pasimachus*, 37 mm (Carabidae); 4: *Claviger*, 2 mm (Pselaphidae); 5: *Chiasognathus* (male), 70 mm (Lucanidae); 6: *Paranthrophlus*, 7 mm (Silphidae – cave species); 7: *Gyrinus*, 7 mm (Gyrinidae); 8: *Cassida*, 8 mm (Chrysomelidae); 9: *Paussus*, 12 mm (Paussidae); 10: *Creophilus*, 20 mm (Staphylinidae); 11: *Rhyticephalus*, 60 mm (Brenthidae).

another genus. Since the authority of a species can be easily checked in a work of reference (Kloet & Hincks for British insects), for brevity, species in this book will be referred to without their authorities.

In classifying a beetle, species are grouped into genera, genera into families and families into the order of Coleoptera. However, since there are so many beetles, many subcategories and supercategories have been invented. Species themselves can be divided into subspecies, varieties, geographical races, etc. Several of these groups have their own particular latin endings, for instance, family names always end in -idae. These groups can be listed as a hierarchy with the word endings most frequently used *italicised* as follows:

Order	Coleoptera
Suborder	Adephaga
(Series	Carab*iformia*)
Superfamily	Carab*oidea*
Family	Carab*idae*
Subfamily	Carab*inae*
Tribe	Carab*ini*
Genus	*Carabus*

The series category is included to show its place in the hierarchy although it is not used in the classification of the Adephaga, which includes only a single superfamily, Caraboidea.

Classification depends to a great extent on the judgements of the classifier, and the Coleoptera are an immense group with many awkward decisions to make; thus it is hardly surprising that there have been many differences of opinion about the major groups, and that several ways of classifying beetles have been suggested. It would need many pages to discuss the advantages and disadvantages of the various systems, and it is not proposed to do this here. Instead, the modern system proposed by Crowson will be followed. This is probably the first classification to have made extensive use of both adult and larval characters.

The primary division of the Coleoptera is into four suborders, two large and two small.

The *Adephaga* ('ravenous eater') are the second largest suborder. They include mainly carnivorous beetles with large jaws, long, slender antennae and 5-5-5 jointed tarsi. Most are 'ground beetles' but a large group is aquatic.

The *Archostemata* ('first, stem' beetles) include the most primitive beetles, and have some characters found in both the Adephaga and Polyphaga. They include several early fossils up to 280 million years old.

The *Myxophaga* ('slime eaters', i.e. algal eaters) are a small group of very small beetles recently separated from the Polyphaga.

The *Polyphaga* ('eating many' things) are the huge suborder which includes all the rest of the beetles. They are a very diverse group.

Some of the characteristics used to separate the suborders are illustrated in fig. 4.

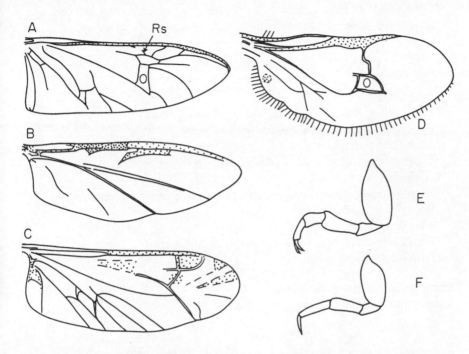

Figure 4: *Some major differences between the suborders: wings and larval legs*
A: Adephaga – wing of Carabid (O – oblongum; Rs – Rs vein); B: Polyphaga – Staphylinoid wing (*Philonthus*); C: Polyphaga – *Dascillus* wing; D: Myxophaga – *Lepicerus* wing (after Crowson); E: Adephaga (Carabidae) – side view of larval leg; F: Polyphaga (Staphylinidae) – side view of larval leg.

Crowson has defined all the superfamilies, families and many subfamilies of the Coleoptera by keying them out in his book on beetle classification. Since it is not possible to summarise adequately Crowson's detailed study in this book, an outline classification will be given which merely lists the suborders, series, superfamilies and some of the more important families. This should be used mainly for reference, and to check commonly used beetle names with the latin names of their families, etc.

27

OUTLINE CLASSIFICATION
(Non-British families are marked thus *)

Suborder 1: ARCHOSTEMATA
1 superfamily of 2 families plus several fossil families

Cupedoidea
*Cupedidae: The most ancient beetle family; wood feeding larvae
*Micromalthidae: 1 species with a very complex life cycle

Suborder 2: ADEPHAGA
1 superfamily of 10 families

Caraboidea
*Rhysodidae: un-Carabid-like beetles of dead wood
*Paussidae: include un-Carabid-like ant guests
Carabidae: ground beetles
*Trachypachidae: ground beetles related to water beetles
Haliplidae: water beetles
*Amphizoidae: non-swimming water beetles of fast-running streams
Hygrobiidae: screech beetles (aquatic)
Noteridae: water beetles
Dytiscidae: carnivorous water beetles, diving beetles
Gyrinidae: whirligig beetles

Suborder 3: MYXOPHAGA
1 superfamily of 4 families of small beetles

Sphaerioidea

Suborder 4: POLYPHAGA
6 series of 19 superfamilies of about 150 families

Series 1: *Staphyliniformia*
 1 *Hydrophiloidea*
   e.g. Hydraenidae: primitive vegetarian water beetles
   Hydrophilidae: vegetarian (or scavenging) water beetles and some dung
       beetles
 2 *Histeroidea*
   e.g. Histeridae: include predators often found in carrion
 3 *Staphylinoidea*
   e.g. Ptiliidae: minute, feather-wing beetles
   Leptinidae: ecto-parasites and commensals
   Anisotomidae: often found in fungus
   Scydmaenidae: tiny beetles of soil and leaf litter

28

Silphidae: carrion feeders, predators, etc
Staphylinidae: rove beetles
Pselaphidae: tiny beetles of soil and leaf litter

Series 2: *Scarabaeiformia*
1 *Scarabaeoidea*
e.g. Lucanidae: stag beetles
*Passalidae: bessy-bugs, patent leather beetles
Trogidae: carrion feeders
Geotrupidae: dor beetles, dung beetles
Scarabaeidae: chafers and dung beetles
2 *Dascilloidea*
Dascillidae
Rhipiceridae: partial endo-parasites
3 *Eucinetoidea*
E.g. Helodidae

Series 3: *Elateriformia*
1 *Byrrhoidea*
Byrrhidae: pill beetles
2 *Dryopoidea*
e.g. Heteroceridae: mud burrowers
Dryopidae: terrestrial and water beetles, aquatic larvae
Elmidae: clinging (rather than swimming) water beetles
3 *Buprestoidea*
Buprestidae: jewel beetles
4 *Elateroidea*
e.g. Elateridae: click beetles and fire-flies; larvae are wire-worms
5 *Cantharoidea*
Drilidae: include snail-eating beetles
Lampyridae: glow-worms and fire-flies
Cantharidae: soldier and sailor beetles
Lycidae: mainly distasteful tropical beetles

Series 4: *Bostrychiformia*
1 *Dermestoidea*
e.g. Dermestidae: skin, larder, bacon beetles; museum beetles
2 *Bostrychoidea*
Anobiidae: furniture beetles, wood-worm and death-watch
Ptinidae: stored-products beetles, spider beetles
Bostrychidae: wood-boring beetles
Lyctidae: powder post beetles

Series 5: *Cucujiformia*
  1 *Cleroidea*
    e.g. Cleridae: chequered beetles, ant beetle
    Melyridae: include flower haunting beetles
  2 *Lymexyloidea:* include larval wood borers
  3 *Cucujoidea*
    There are traditionally two major groups of these:
    (a) Clavicornia
    e.g. Nitidulidae: pollen beetles
    Rhizophagidae: bark beetle predators
    Cucujidae: include stored-products beetles
    Cryptophagidae: fungus beetles
    Byturidae: includes the raspberry beetle
    Erotylidae: fungus beetles and ladybird-like beetles
    Coccinellidae: ladybirds or lady-beetles
    Endomychidae: ladybird-like beetles
    Lathridiidae: fungus beetles and stored products beetles
    (b) Heteromera
    e.g. Cisidae: fungus beetles
    Mycetophagidae: fungus beetles
    Tenebrionidae: darkling beetles, desert and stored-products beetles;
            mcal-worm larva
    Tetratomidae: fungus beetles
    Pyrochroidae: cardinal beetles
    Scraptiidae: flower haunting beetles
    Rhipiphoridae: partly parasitic beetles
    Oedemeridae: flower haunting beetles
    Meloidae: oil beetles and blister beetles
  4 *Chrysomeloidea*
    Cerambycidae: timber beetles; longhorns or longicorns
    Bruchidae: pea and bean 'weevils'
    Chrysomelidae: leaf beetles, tortoise beetles
  5 *Curculionoidea*
    e.g. Anthribidae: weevils with some primitive features
    Attelabidae: include leaf-rollers, British oak and hazel weevils
    *Brenthidae: giraffe beetles; weevils with some primitive features
    Apionidae: clover weevils
    Curculionidae: most weevils, snout beetles, bark and ambrosia beetles

Series 6: *Stylopiformia*
  Stylopoidea
  2 families of stylops

4. Size and Numbers

The size range covered by beetles includes both some of the largest and some of the smallest insects. The heaviest insects are probably beetles, but as they are compact animals, the body lengths of the largest beetles are less than those of some long, slender stick insects. Most of the size range covered by the Coleoptera is shown in plate 1 (frontispiece), where three beetles chosen from the upper and lower ends of the size spectrum are shown at their natural sizes.

The biggest beetles are mainly Scarabaeidae and Cerambycidae. Some of the largest Scarabaeidae are found in the Dynastinae which are often called rhinoceros beetles because of the huge horns of many males. *Dynastes* includes hercules beetles (in particular, *D.hercules*) and *Megasoma* – elephant beetles (in particular, *M.elephas*). These are mainly South American, but the Asian Dynastids include large atlas beetles such as *Chalcosoma atlas*. The largest Cetoniinae are the African goliath beetles (*Goliathus* spp.) *D.hercules* males may reach a length of 16 cm ($6\frac{1}{2}$ inches), but half of this is the length of the horn. *M.elephas* and *C.atlas* may both reach about 12 cm ($4\frac{3}{4}$ inches) but they have shorter horns, and the body of *M.elephas* can be at least as big as in *D.hercules*. Similarly, the largest goliath beetles may be longer than 12 cm (e.g. *G.goliathus* with several sub-species), and as the males have still shorter horns than the Dynastids, the body may be bigger than that of any other beetle.

The Cerambycidae are not so stout as the Scarabaeidae, and they have relatively longer and narrower bodies. Thus they are not usually as heavy as the largest Scarabaeidae although in a few cases they may be longer. One of the largest species is *Macrodontia cervicornis* from the Amazon region, which is usually between 12 and 15 cm in length, although Arrow has stated that it may reach a length of 7 inches (nearly 18 cm). As in the Scarabaeidae, the largest Cerambycidae show a very wide individual variation in size in some species. This is true of what is probably the largest Cerambycid, *Titanus giganteus*, which is also found in the Amazon basin. This is usually of about the same length as *M.cervicornis*, but larger specimens have been stated by Reitter to reach as much as 20 cm (8 inches) in length. This would also be one of the heaviest beetles. Unfortunately, most of these specimens have been found dead floating in the Amazon tributaries, and little is known of the habits of the species.

At the other end of the size scale, the smallest beetles belong to the Ptiliidae, and are less than 1 mm ($\frac{1}{25}$ inch) in length. Many common species lie between 1 mm and 0·5 mm ($\frac{1}{50}$ inch). Several North American species are about 0·4 mm ($\frac{1}{60}$ inch) in length, and some species may well be smaller. *Nanosella fungi* is often quoted as the smallest beetle at 0·25 mm ($\frac{1}{100}$ inch), but the status of this species is uncertain and the original record seems to need verification. Perhaps it is not surprising that in such an enormous order of insects, there is still much uncertainty about the upper and lower limits of size.

The number of species of beetles in existence today is even more difficult to determine than their size limits. Because there are so many, even the number of species in museums is difficult to estimate, let alone the number of species in nature. Some beetle catalogues are many years out of date, and many more species have been described since their publication. If the text-books of entomology published over the last hundred years or so are con-

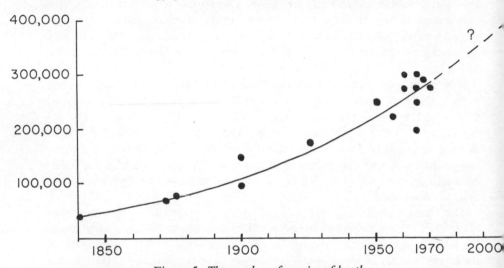

Figure 5. *The number of species of beetles*
The graph shows how the estimates of the number of species of beetles described or in collections has steadily increased over the last 130 years. The estimates are nearly all taken from entomological textbooks.

sulted, it can be seen that estimates of the numbers of species have risen rapidly over the years (fig. 5). The most authoritative recent figures are those of Arnett and Britton. In 1967 Arnett gave the number of beetles catalogued as 219,409, and the estimated number of species in nature as 290,119, whilst in 1970 Britton estimated that there were about 278,000 known species of beetles. These are the best-informed guesses, but they may well be conservative ones. On existing figures, one in four of all animal species described are beetles. It has been suggested that as many as half of all the different species of insects may prove to be beetles, and that only a fraction of the insect species in existence have already been described. Recent museum work supports the latter assertion; it is not just an over-enthusiastic speculation; in fact, Williams has used a statistical technique to estimate that there may be as many as three million species of insects in the world. One third of this number – one million – would probably be beetles.

The Coleoptera have been divided up by Crowson into about 170 families. The size of these families differs considerably, however, and over 200,000 species have been estimated to occur in the nine largest families. These are listed below with Arnett's and Britton's estimates of their probable numbers:

		Arnett (1967)	*Britton* (1970)	
1	Curculionidae	50,000	60,000	1
2	Staphylinidae	28,000	27,000	2
3	Chrysomelidae	25,000	20,000	4
4	Carabidae	20,000	25,000	3
5	Cerambycidae	20,000	20,000	5
6	Scarabaeidae	18,000	17,000	6
7	Tenebrionidae	17,000	15,000	7
8	Buprestidae	15,000	11,500	8
9	Elateridae	10,000	7,000	9

As a comparison, there are about 4,500 species of mammals, and about 40,000 species of vertebrates.

5. The Cuticle

The cuticle of an insect is both its outer skin and its skeleton. It is a tough, waterproof covering which protects the soft, inner organs and provides a rigid frame from which the body muscles can operate. In adult weevils and jewel beetles the cuticle resembles thick, armour plating, but in many beetle larvae it is thin and flexible, although still very tough. As in armour, there are a series of close fitting plates – sclerites – which are joined together by a flexible material, the arthrodial membrane. Both sclerites and membranes are different versions of the same cuticle. The cell layer which forms the outer living skin of an insect is the epidermis, and this secretes the non-cellular cuticle. In section (fig. 6), the cuticle can be seen to consist of three main layers: a very thin outer epicuticle lying above an exocuticle and an endocuticle. All layers are penetrated by minute canals and glandular ducts which carry some of the materials used to build the cuticle.

The two basic materials of the cuticle are chitin and protein. Chitin is a substance made of long-chain molecules which is closely related to cellulose, the substance out of which the cell walls of plants are built. In cellulose, the chains consist of linked units of the sugar glucose. In chitin the sugar units include nitrogen, and the chains consist of linked units of glucosamine. Thus chitin has a fibrous structure; it is very tough, but not hard. In its pure form, it is best suited to form the arthrodial membranes, but not the hard sclerites. The sclerites contain chitin impregnated with protein which undergoes a

33

kind of tanning; this process is very similar chemically to the process of tanning soft mammal skins to produce leather. The exocuticle contains mainly the tanned protein – sclerotin, whilst in the endocuticle it is untanned. Like chitin, the protein consists of long-chain molecules. The hardening process is achieved by cross-linking these chains with the aid of a tanning chemical. Thus the sclerite contains both chitin and sclerotin. Sclerotin is very hard, light and strong, and resistant to bending and compressive forces; chitin contains a series of tough fibres which gives the cuticle great tensile strength. It is the mixture of these two components which gives the cuticle its resemblance to fibre-glass. It also closely resembles bone and plywood in its strength, lightness and hardness.

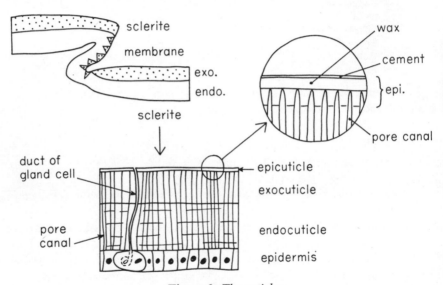

Figure 6. *The cuticle*
Longitudinal sections to show the structure of the various parts of the cuticle. (Partly after Wigglesworth.)

The cuticle is not only a skeletal structure, it is also a waterproof coat. In some heavily armoured beetles (e.g. some Tenebrionidae), the layer of sclerotised cuticle may be sufficiently thick to prevent some water loss from the body by evaporation. However, these beetles and most other insects need a more efficient waterproofing mechanism, and this is the function of the epicuticle. This very thin outermost layer is itself made up of several layers of different materials One of the most important is a wax layer which consists of a single sheet of densely packed molecules. It is protected by an outer-most layer of 'cement' which forms a thin, hard coat over it. Even so, such a thin coat is rather delicate, and soil-living larvae such as wire-worms inevitably scratch and damage it. However, soil is normally a very damp environment, and so the larvae are not likely to dry up and die.

6. The Organisation of the Body

There are three major regions in an insect body:

The head is that part of the animal which 'meets the environment first', and so it includes the mouth and mouthparts, the major sense organs and the 'brain'.

The thorax is the middle of the insect. It contains the centre of gravity, and the organs of movement – the wings and legs – are located on either side of this point.

The abdomen is the hindbody which contains many of the essential organ systems, for instance, much of the digestive system and the reproductive organs.

A brief explanation of the main body functions can best be made by considering each of these regions in turn.

A. THE HEAD

(i) *The Mouthparts* (fig. 7). The head is a nearly cylindrical capsule of hard cuticle which protects the soft internal organs. The head capsule is narrowed behind where it is joined to the prothorax by the membranous neck. In front it holds a series of mouthparts adapted to deal with the particular food of the beetle.

These mouthparts are:

The labrum (the upper lip);
A pair of mandibles (the main jaws);
A pair of maxillae (the accessory jaws) and maxillary palps;
The labium (the lower lip), the labial palps.

The undersurface of the labrum roofs over the mandibles, and leads back into the mouth, to form the roof of the foregut. The upper surface of the labium forms a tray underneath the maxillae, and its upper surface leads back to the mouth to meet the lower wall of the foregut. Thus the mandibles and maxillae form the movable sides of a cavity lying in front of the mouth. In this cavity, a piece of food which has been seized or cut off by the mandibles is chewed before it enters the mouth.

Nebria brevicollis is a carnivorous beetle in which the mandibles are used to seize its prey. Pieces of food are detached by the sharp tips of the mandibles and then cut up with the basal (molar) regions. The maxillae close as

35

the mandibles open, thus keeping the food in place, and they are also used to rake the food back into the mouth. Once in the mouth, a muscular pharyngeal pump forces food along the foregut. In carnivorous beetles that feed upon more liquid substances the mouthparts are thickly fringed with hairs. I shall consider the working of these more specialised mouthparts in Chapter 4.

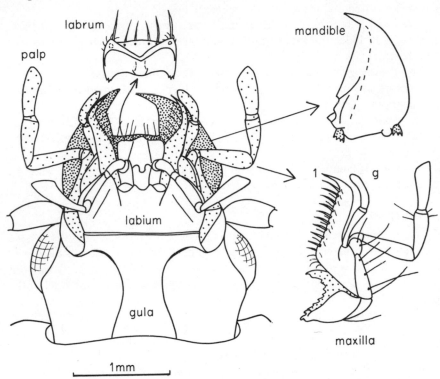

Figure 7. *The head and mouthparts*
The undersurface of the head of the predaceous Carabid, *Nebria brevicollis*, showing the structure of the mouthparts. (l – lacinia; g – galea.)

In herbivores (fig. 8), the mandibles are less sharply pointed. They are built for cutting and crushing vegetation (as in chafers) rather than for piercing prey. In beetles which eat hard substances such as wood, the mandibles are either very large and powerful as in timber beetle larvae, or they may be very small and hard as in adult weevils.

(ii) *The Sense Organs.* Although insects are complex animals, they are small, and must make the best use of their limited resources. There are several devices which simplify the link-up between the sense organs and nervous

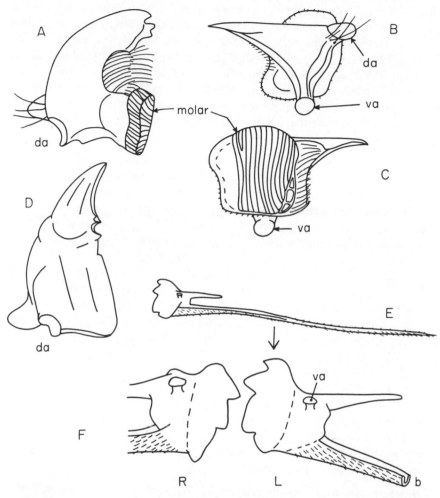

Figure 8. *Mandibles of herbivores*
A: Upper side of the left mandible of a chafer (*Phyllopertha horticola*, Scara-baeidae); B: Side (external) view of same mandible; C: Internal view showing the grinding surface; D: Left mandible of a timber beetle larva, upper side (*Rhagium bifasciatum*, Cerambycidae); E: Left mandible of a weevil, ventral view (*Sitophilus granarius*, Curculionidae); F: Enlarged view of right and left mandibles of the above weevil (da – dorsal articulation of mandible; va – ventral articulation of mandible; b – pharyngeal bracon – this is a long extension of the inner corner of the weevil mandible which helps to move food up the long snout). (E and F after Dennell.)

37

system. For instance, a sense organ stimulates a nerve cell directly and not through a modified epithelial cell as in a mammal, i.e. one cell does the work of two in an insect. Again, the insect may have relatively few sense organs. In a fly's leg Dethier found only 500, although specialised structures like the antenna can have many thousands. Another problem is that although the mammal has a soft, flexible skin which contains millions of microscopic organs for touch, heat, pain, etc., insects are encased in suits of armour which must be pierced by their sense organs to gain facts about the outside world. Thus almost all the insect sense organs (except the eyes) are basically hairs or pits in the cuticle.

Touch and body position: The basic touch sense organ is a hair (seta) which arises from a socket in the cuticle to which it is attached by a flexible, cuticular membrane. If the tip of the seta is touched, and thus moved, the nerve cell at its base is stimulated to send impulses to the nervous system. Of course, the touch receptor may be more complex, and either involve more nerve cells or be composed of many hairs in a clump. This latter type of receptor is commonly found in the joints of legs, where the coxa meets the body, or on the neck membrane. It tells the beetle the position of its own legs or head in relation to its body, which can use this information to sense the direction of gravity. Positional information is also gathered from sense receptors in the muscles which send out impulses when they are stretched. The stress receptors found in the cuticle are usually minute oval plates or domes which respond to tension or compression. They are particularly common in the legs, for instance, where they are aligned on the long axis of a leg. Other stretch receptors may be cord-like structures stretched across a joint (chordotonal organs). Many of this type of sense organ are gathered together to form Johnston's organ between the second and third segments of the antenna. This enables movements of the main part of the antenna to be accurately recorded, whether they are due to stationary objects, other animals, or air currents (including sound waves).

Hearing: The touch-sensitive hairs on the surface of a beetle will also respond to the small, regular vibrations of the air caused by sound waves. Even so, it is doubtful if a beetle can 'hear' in the same sense as we do. Beetles do not usually possess an ear of the sort found in grasshoppers and crickets, and although vibrations in the air can be sensed, beetles are more sensitive to vibrations in the ground which they feel through their legs (probably via chordotonal organs in the ends of the tibiae). Some Carabidae, including species of *Carabus* and *Pterostichus*, have been shown to be rather insensitive to sounds, although they will respond to a range of tones up to a pitch about two octaves above middle C. Beetles more sensitive to sounds include species of *Geotrupes* and *Melolontha*, and they are particularly sensitive to the highest octave of the range of pitch mentioned. They also react to very high-pitched pure tones. These are not common in nature except, for instance, as components of sudden noises transmitted through the ground; it may be because of this that it is important for the beetle to be able to detect them.

Taste and Smell: These sense organs also include many hair-type receptors together with other types of receptors such as pegs, which are found particularly on the antennae, palps and legs; they are not touch sensitive, but by responding to dissolved substances form the chemical senses of taste and smell. Taste receptors usually need to come into direct contact with a substance, but smell receptors may react to very small numbers of molecules which may have travelled a great distance from their source.

The kinds of tastes perceived by water beetles (where 'taste' and 'smell' are probably very similar) have been demonstrated by the difficult task of training the beetles to approach or avoid particular tastes. Thus *Dytiscus marginalis* and *Hydrophilus piceus* have been shown to distinguish between tastes which we ourselves find obviously different, such as sugar, salt, acid and quinine (bitter). Also like ourselves, they cannot distinguish between some closely related substances such as the sugars sucrose and glucose. On the whole, they seem to be like man in having four main categories of taste: sweet, salt, acid and bitter substances.

Smells also play an important part in the life of a beetle, and most smell receptors are found on the antennae, although some are also present on the palps. In many beetles, the sense of smell is important in locating food, and it may also be used to bring opposite sexes together, as in bark beetles. The intensity of a smell is important, for an attractive odour may become repellent at high concentrations, although an initially repellent smell remains repellent. A particularly important 'smell' is that of water. Humidity receptors are also found on the antennae. It is not known how these work, although they seem to respond to the drying power of the air. However, the response of the beetle to water is very obvious. This may be seen in an orientation to water from a distance, the avoidance of a low or a high humidity, or the aggregation of individual beetles in the humidity they prefer. In some stored-foods pests such as *Tenebrio molitor*, *Tribolium castaneum* and *Ptinus tectus*, fairly low humidities are preferred, but after being dried their preference is (not surprisingly) reversed. Many beetles prefer high humidities, especially soil beetles. Species of the wire-worm *Agriotes* are so sensitive to moisture changes that they can distinguish between relative humidities of 95% and 100%.

The Antennae: (fig. 9) They arise from the front of the beetle's head; they carry many of the tactile, heat sensitive, olfactory and humidity receptors, and

39

house the complex Johnston's organ between the second and third segments. Beetle antennae are usually 11-segmented, but some segments may be lost or fused together in certain cases, and they are extremely variable in form. They may be long and slender (Carabidae, Cerambycidae) or clubbed and elbowed (Curculionidae) or with sense organs concealed between the club

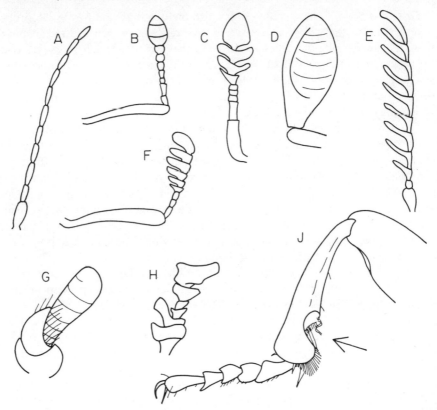

Figure 9. *Antennae and an antennal cleaner*
A: Carabidae (*Carabus*); B: Curculionidae (*Otiorrhynchus*); C: Hydrophilidae (*Hydrophilus*); D: Paussidae (*Paussus*); E: Elateridae (male *Corymbites*); F: Lucanidae (Female *Lucanus*); G: Gyrinidae (*Gyrinus*); H: Meloidae (Male *Cercoma*); J: Right leg of Carabid (*Abax*), anterior surface to show the antennal cleaner (the arrowed notch) at the base of the tibia.

segments (Anisotomidae) which may be flattened to form plates (Scarabaeoidea); they may be designed to break the surface water film (Hydrophilidae) or be strangely twisted (Meloidae) or even formed into handles for easy transport by ants (Paussidae).

Because of their importance as sense organs the antennae are frequently cleaned, and this is performed by the mandibles and front tarsi. Many beetles have evolved special cleaning organs on the front tarsi or tibiae, and these are especially well developed in Carabidae and Staphylinidae (fig. 9).

Eyes and Sight: The importance of sight varies amongst different species of beetles. In soil beetles it is not as well developed as in daytime hunting beetles, but it is important in most beetles as a means of avoiding enemies.

All eyes work on the same basic principle. A pigment is present which absorbs the energy of light and transforms it to chemical energy; this is

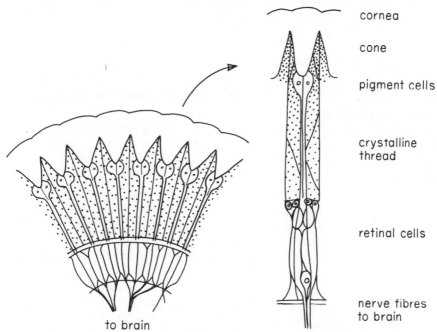

to brain

Figure 10. *Section through the compound eye of the glow-worm, Photuris (Lampyridae)*
Left: longitudinal section of part of whole eye; *right:* longitudinal section of a single ommatidium. (After Horridge.)

eventually transformed into the electrical energy represented by an impulse in a nerve cell. In structure, however, the compound eye of an insect is very different from our own. With the exception of a few blind cave-dwelling or semi-parasitic species (and some oddities) all adult beetles have compound eyes. In a few Dermestoidea and Staphylinoidea, dorsal ocelli are also present. These are simple eyes set between the large compound eyes. Simple eyes are present in most beetle larvae where they are set in the positions of the adult compound eyes.

The compound eye (fig. 10) is constructed of many simple eyes (ommatidia) bunched together. It is thus relatively large, but as it is built externally of cuticle it does not need accessory structures such as eyelids and tear glands. The cuticle over each ommatidium is transparent, either forming a lens which lies above a crystalline cone, or extending inwards to form the cone itself. This carries the light down to a transparent rod, the rhabdom, which is formed by the inside edge of a ring of retinal cells. In *Photuris*, Horridge showed that slender crystalline threads form light guides which lead inwards from the cones to a very well-developed layer of retinal cells. It is in these cells that light produces a signal which is carried by the optic nerve to the brain. Each ommatidium is at least partly surrounded by a ring of pigment cells which can be used like the iris of a vertebrate eye to reduce the glare of daylight on the sensitive receptor cells.

It is much easier to demonstrate the structure of the insect eye than to say what an insect actually sees. In theory, each lens of each ommatidium will produce a small, inverted image. However, these images would all be very small, and greatly distorted; it is likely that the ommatidia only register how much light is coming from that part of the visual field at which they are aimed. Since the compound eye is nearly hemispherical in some cases, and all the ommatidia converge upon its centre, the ommatidia each point at a slightly different part of the visual field. Thus, the eye probably produces an image composed of many spots of light which together form a 'mosaic' picture. A nineteenth-century attempt to demonstrate a single, non-mosaic picture resulted in a famous photograph taken by Exner (and reproduced by Imms) through the outer parts of the eye of a glow-worm. However, Horridge has recently shown that in living *Photuris* this image could not be received by the retinal cells, and would probably not be formed. Where a beetle larva has several simple eyes, it may well form a simple mosaic image. Many Adephaga have six simple eyes on each side of the head, and in *Cicindela* larvae these are larger than usual, as each large lens covers several cells.

Insects can recognise simple patterns. This has been clearly demonstrated in honey bees, but water beetles can also be trained in similar ways to link a pattern with food. However, it is usually more important for an insect to react to movement than to forms and patterns, and the compound eye is especially good at this. In fact, it is more efficient in detecting flicker-type movements than the human eye. The distance at which the insect eye perceives recognisable information seems to be much less than for many vertebrates. *Cicindela* larvae recognise prey at up to about 2 inches distance, and even the adults with their huge compound eyes only recognise prey up to about 5 to 6 inches away. Vision over these short distances appears to be adequate for small animals with short nerves and rapid reflexes. However, movements of large objects, (e.g. entomologists) at distances of several feet may often cause an insect to flee.

Many insects can see colours. The spectrum for these insects seems to range from blue-green to ultra-violet, although beetles have not yet been shown to see ultra-violet. Several beetles have been shown to be especially sensitive to yellow-green and blue-green light. This applies not only to glow-worms which produce light of these colours, but also to species of *Dytiscus*. The firefly *Photinus pyralis* uses red flashes. It seems likely that crude colour vision is present in beetles but there is probably much variation between species.

B. THE THORAX

The thorax (figs 1 and 2) is the three-segmented middle region of the beetle which provides attachments for the legs and wings. The first segment – the prothorax – is characteristically large in beetles. Its roof – the pronotum – is usually a single broad plate which overlaps the neck and part of the head in front, and the origins of the elytra behind. The elytra arise from the mesothorax and form strong wing cases to protect the second, functional, pair of wings. In most beetles the elytra can be locked into place, and the suture between the elytra is not the line of weakness that might be expected. The mesoscutellum forms part of the locking device, and this small triangle is usually the only part of the mesothoracic roof to be visible from above. The functional wings arise from the large metathorax, and when not in use are folded under the elytra. Where the elytra are short, as in Staphylinidae, the wing folding may be rather complicated.

In contrast to the prothorax, which is freely movable on the mesothorax, the meso- and metathorax are bound closely together, as is the metathorax to the abdomen. This gives the beetle its characteristic appearance from above with the mobile prothorax forming a middle region between the head and the elytra, which cover the hindbody.

Walking and Running: The sides of each thoracic segment, the pleural regions, give rise to a pair of legs. A leg in the adult beetle (fig. 11) consists of five parts: a basal coxa to which is pivoted a small trochanter which is partly united with the large femur; to this is hinged a thinner tibia which is jointed to a segmented tarsus – the 'foot'. The number of elements in the tarsus is never more than five; the variations in different species are useful classificatory characters. The shape of the legs in a beetle is closely adapted to its way of life. Since this may be running, swimming, burrowing, boring, tunnelling, climbing, or just clinging, there is obviously much variation and this will be considered in Chapter 5.

The basic function of an insect's legs is walking and running; how is this accomplished? Before answering this question we can first ask another. Why are there six legs? The first point is that mammals have two pairs of legs because their fishy ancestors had two sets of paired fins. The arthropods that gave rise to insects may have had many pairs of legs, as do modern centipedes. Now, it is obviously useful to be able to run fast for both escape and attack, and a common way of gaining speed is to have long legs. In a many-legged animal with long legs, a major problem is to prevent interference between each leg's field of movement, i.e. to stop tripping over its own feet. This problem has several solutions, one of which is to reduce the number of legs. The minimum number at which good stability is maintained seems to be six; it is still possible to raise half the legs in walking and still be supported by a stable tripod. One might expect better stability if the pairs of legs were widely separated. This might be true of a static insect, but in a fast moving insect it would give rise to stresses which would cause the insect

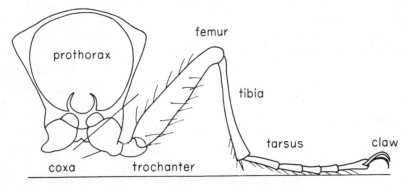

Figure 11. *Fore leg of a tiger beetle*
The fore leg of *Cicindela* is shown attached to the prothorax which is drawn in transverse section. The coxal axis is shown as a straight line.

body to buckle or undulate from side to side; also, the centre of support would fluctuate widely, and both of these effects would lower the running efficiency. The solution seems to be to have the pairs of legs set close together in a short thorax. Their fields of movement can still be separate, their bases are too close together to allow undulations of the body, and they all support the body near its centre of gravity. Thus the beetle with its six spindly legs is the logical solution to a rather different set of problems from those facing a walking vertebrate.

We can now return to the question, how does the beetle walk? If successive frames of ciné film are examined, or the beetle is made to walk over smoked paper in order to leave tracks, the sequence in which the leg movements are made can be observed. In normal walking, and running, the legs are moved alternatively, right side and then left side, in the sequence: R1, L2, R3;

L1, R2, L3; R1, etc. The first three legs may move almost together, followed by the second three legs. Thus the beetle is always supported by at least a tripod, i.e. by 3, 4 or 5 legs whilst 3, 2 or 1 legs are moving. Since the legs move alternately and not in pairs there are no wide variations in support about the centre of gravity. Again, the leg behind is put down just before the one in front is raised, and there is always a very slight delay before stepping.

There is no sudden transition from walking to running, it is all a single process. Speed in a particular insect can be increased by (a) decreasing the duration of a pace; (b) decreasing the relative time of the back stroke to the forward stroke (the back stroke is the pushing movement with the tarsus on the ground); and (c) increasing the angle over which the leg swings. Most of the power for these movements comes from muscles lying in the thorax and attached to both the basal parts of the leg, the coxa and the trochanter. In most beetles, the swing of the coxa is restricted to turning about a single axis (fig. 11), although the fore coxae of higher Staphylinidae are very mobile. The hind coxae of Adephagid water beetles cannot move at all and in ground beetles they have a very restricted movement. Thus the swing of the hind legs in Adephaga is almost entirely from the trochanteral pivots. This restriction is compensated for by their having more freedom of movement at the trochanteral–femoral joint than is found in most Polyphaga.

The speed at which insects can run depends upon their size and temperature; since they are cold-blooded animals, they will have nearly the same temperature as their surroundings. The fastest insects recorded (see Hughes) were fairly large cockroaches of about 30 mm (1½ inches) in length which ran at about 120–130 cm/sec., (approximately 3 m.p.h. – or about 40 body lengths per second) This was at a temperature of over 30°C. (86°F.), i.e. very hot. The fastest running beetles are probably tiger beetles sprinting over short distances of a few centimetres. These have been timed at 60 cm/sec. in the case of a 15 mm beetle at 21°C. (70°F.) This is about 1⅓ m.p.h. (also about 40 body lengths per second). If this seems slow, remember the small size of the insect. It is equivalent to a racehorse 8 feet long travelling at over 200 m.p.h.

Flying: The second major function of the thorax is to house the flight mechanism. The two pairs of wings arise from the top of the sidewall (pleuron) of the thorax, where it meets the thoracic roof (notum). The first pair, the elytra, vary a good deal in different beetles (fig. 12). They usually have longitudinal grooves, or striae, on the upper surface which are separated by interstices (fig. 1). The elytra meet in the midline at the suture, where longitudinal grooves in their edges help the wing cases to lock together (fig. 12). The outer margins of the elytra (epipleura) are bent downwards to make a good fit with the strong sternites of the abdomen. All these elytral features may be absent in some beetles. In Staphylinidae the elytra are very short, in oil beetles (Meloidae) they appear to fit badly, and overlap, and in *Atractocerus* (Lymexylonidae) the elytra are very reduced and cannot cover the wings. In male Stylopoids they are reduced and peculiarly modified to form

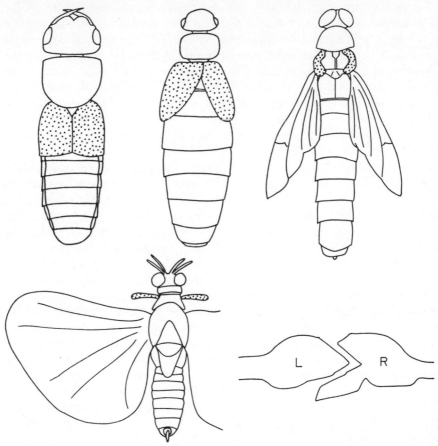

Figure 12. *Elytra*
In these views of the upper surface of four beetles, the elytra is shown stippled. *Top row: Staphylinus, Meloe,* and *Attractocerus* (Lymexylonidae); *bottom left:* A stylops; *bottom right:* transverse section through the sutural region of the elytra in *Cicindela* to show the elytral junction (L – left elytron; R – right elytron).

balancing organs rather like the halteres of true flies (Diptera). They are completely absent in some female beetles such as glow-worms, Drilids and the Scarabaeoid *Pachypus candidae*.

In order to raise the elytra the front end of the mesonotum is pulled forwards and downwards, and this tips up the locking catch at the back end

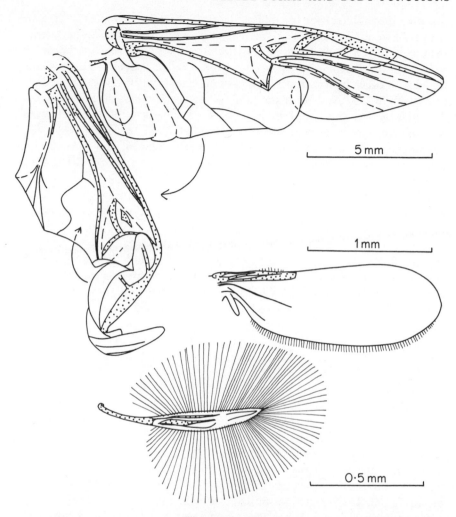

5 mm

1 mm

0·5 mm

Figure 13. *Wings*
Top: Wing of *Cicindela* to show the beginning of folding as it is swung towards the body; *middle: Atomaria* (Cryptophagidae); *bottom: Acrotrichis* (Ptiliidae.)

(the mesoscutellum) and frees the elytra. A small arm at the front end of the elytron is then pulled downwards and inwards; the elytron swings on its pleural fulcrum which lies just behind this arm, so that the main (back) part of the wingcase is raised and swung upwards and outwards. This exposes the more delicate hind wings which are folded in order to be concealed beneath the elytra. The methods of folding differ somewhat from beetle to beetle, but generally the wingtip is folded in and the outer third of

47

the wing then folded over (or under) the more basal part (fig. 13). The wing is opened by the movement of small sclerites at its base, and these sclerites then lock it open ready for flight. Beetles also differ from one another in the patterns of their venation. All beetles have a rather reduced venation compared with other insects, but it is most complete (and therefore presumably primitive) in the Archostemata, and Adephaga and such Polyphaga as *Dascillus cervinus* (fig. 4). Many Polyphaga have fewer veins and their wings are sometimes termed 'cantharoid' or 'staphylinoid'. In small beetles (e.g. Cryptophagidae), the number of veins is greatly reduced, and in very small beetles such as the Ptiliidae, the wing is merely a strap bordered front and back with a row of long hairs (fig. 13).

When a beetle is in flight, the elytra are turned to point forwards and upwards and probably act like aeroplane wings to give the beetle some lift. Indeed, in at least some species (e.g. rhinoceros beetles) they give lift by beating through a small angle in phase with the wings. In one group of efficient fliers, the Cetoniinae (rose chafers and goliath beetles, etc.), the front end of the epipleuron on each elytron is cut away so that the elytra can be lowered and nearly closed whilst the beetle is in flight.

The actual flight mechanism, which causes the wings to beat, is basically similar in all the largest and most advanced insect orders, and is a most ingenious system. It is also very complex mechanism, and only a brief idea of how it works can be given here; several clear accounts are readily available (e.g. Wells; Chapman). The flight 'motor' is provided partly by muscles of the metathorax which do not attach directly to the wing bases, and partly by direct muscles. The metathorax is an elastic, distortable box to which each wing is pivoted at the upper corner between the pleuron and the notum (fig. 14). The wing in the 'up' position is stable. When the dorsal longitudinal muscles (running the length of the metathorax) contract, the notum is raised (in contrast to flies, where it becomes more domed). This forces the wing bases to move upwards, thus pivoting the wings downwards about their pleural fulcra. The direct wing muscles, attached to the wing bases, assist in pulling the wings down. When the wings have swung down to a horizontal position, their bases lever out the pleural walls of the thorax slightly. Since the thorax is an elastic box, the pleural walls resist this pressure by pushing inwards on the wing bases; thus the wings are unstable in this horizontal position. As they are already moving downwards, the wings continue until they reach a second stable position in the 'down' position, where the pleural walls have moved inwards after forcing the wing bases all the way upwards. Thus the wings 'click' over from a stable 'up' to a stable 'down' position. The process is reversed by the dorso-ventral (noto-sternal) muscles which produce the up beat.

In small insects, such as some midges, the wing beat is very rapid, up to a thousand times a second. In most beetles it is much slower, although it may be nearly two hundred times a second in some species. If the relationship of one nerve impulse to every muscle contraction is to be maintained the upper limit is between fifty and a hundred beats per second, as above this rate ordinary muscles (like leg muscles) would not have time to relax between impulses and thus be ready for another contraction. In many higher insects very rapid wing beats are possible and a new kind of muscle has been evolved, in which the contractile stimulus is provided by the muscles themselves. We have seen that as a contracting muscle moves the wing base from the first stable to the unstable horizontal position the elasticity of the thorax takes over, and the springiness of the thoracic walls moves the wing base to its

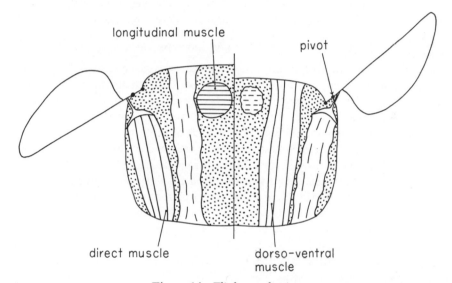

Figure 14. *Flight mechanism*

A diagrammatic vertical section through the metathorax of a beetle to show how the main flight muscles move the wings. On the left, the dorsal longitudinal muscle and the (vertical) direct muscle are shown at the end of their contraction cycle, having pulled the wing downwards. On the right, these muscles have relaxed, and the dorso-ventral muscle is shown at the end of its contraction cycle, having pulled the notum down and so forced the wing upwards.

second stable position. As the thorax takes over, all tension is suddenly taken off the contracting muscle, and this switches it off for a moment. But in the second stable position the opposing muscle is stretched, and it now takes over, i.e. contracts. As the wing clicks back to the stable position, this muscle is switched off in turn, and a rapidly oscillating system for beating the wings is set up. It still needs regular nervous stimulation to keep it vibrating, but it can produce more wing beats a second than nerve impulses fired into it.

The details of the wing's tilt, etc., are provided by smaller muscles attached to the wing bases, and these accessory systems enable the insect to man-oeuvre in flight. Manoeuvrability is great in insects such as flies, but it is usually much less in most beetles. We see this in the rather blundering flight of chafers and dor beetles, and even in some small Staphylinidae such as species of *Oxytelus*. Joy suggested that the common *O.tetracarinatus* is frequently one of the irritating 'foreign bodies' that sometimes enter the eyes of cyclists. In spite of lacking agility in the air, many large beetles are powerful and determined fliers. Chafers can often be seen flying around tree-tops on summer evenings, and their tropical relatives such as the African goliath beetles have similar habits. Capturing these huge beetles is a difficult task, but one effective method is to shoot them down with a shotgun using dustshot cartridges.

Some beetles are able to glide in a similar way to birds or dragonflies. This is obviously a more economical way of flying in terms of fuel (food) reserves used than is flapping flight, although gliding is probably only used for short periods. The stag beetle has a lock on the wings to enable them to remain outstretched for gliding. Small insects have rather different aero-dynamic problems to large ones, and this is reflected in the structure of their wings. The unusual strap-shaped Ptiliid wing has already been mentioned (fig. 13), and other minute insects such as Chalcid wasps also have a wing with reduced venation. Horridge suggested that this reduced venation may allow the wing to twist passively between up and downstrokes, rather than be ac-tively twisted by wingbase muscles. He also suggested that since air may be a relatively viscous medium for a very small insect, these odd wings may be adaptations which allow the insect to 'row' its way through the air, rather than fly in the ordinary sense.

Breathing – Tracheal System: Like all engines, the flight motor of beetles needs fuel to burn. The fuel consists of carbohydrates derived from the food. They reach the muscles via the blood system which bathes all the organs of the body. This blood space is characteristic of insects and is in contrast to the closed system of vessels which carry both food and oxygen in our own bodies. The major closed vessel in an insect is the heart, a chambered vessel lying just below the dorsal wall of the thorax and abdomen. This pumps blood forwards towards the head, and it is then circulated down to the legs and to the ventral and posterior regions of the body. Oxygen is not carried by the blood, but is taken directly to the various tissues by a network of air tubes, or tracheae. Fresh air enters and stale air leaves the tracheal system via a series of opening – spiracles – in the pleural walls of the body. The first spiracle lies between the prothorax and mesothorax, and the second between the mesothorax and metathorax. These are followed by up to eight spiracles lying in the abdominal segments.

The spiracles usually have some sort of closing mechanism which is particularly important in controlling water losses, since the danger of drying up is a major hazard for small terrestrial animals. The spiracles open into the main tracheal trunks which run the length of the body. These are cross-linked, and have many branches to supply the various organs. The trunks and the larger branches are strengthened with spirally wound ridges of cuticle, but as the branches subdivide, and become smaller and smaller, this strengthening becomes unnecessary and is lost. Oxygen reaches the tissues, and carbon dioxide is removed from them by a process of gaseous diffusion which requires no muscular effort. However, this process works efficiently only over small distances, and in larger insects – especially actively flying ones – muscular pumping is also necessary.

Nervous System: We have already noticed the economical way in which the sense organs link up with the nervous system, and have also seen that relatively little nervous stimulation may be needed to keep the large, indirect muscles of the flight motor oscillating. Economy seems to be the keynote of the relationship between nerves and muscles in insects. In a mammal each muscle receives many nerve fibres which supply all the individual, muscle fibres, which can thus be stimulated to contract. The tension produced by the muscles depends upon how many of its component fibres are contracting. This system is unsuitable for small animals like insects because since the size of individual nerve and muscle fibres cannot be much reduced, their number must be. Thus to provide smooth variations in tension with a relatively small number of muscle fibres, a different type of innervation is necessary. In an insect, there may be as few as two nerves to a muscle system as, for instance, in the leg of a cockroach. Stimulation of a muscle by one of the nerves produces the normal or 'fast' contraction. The other is a 'slow' nerve in which repeated impulses are necessary to cause contraction. Since the amount of tension depends on the frequency of these impulses, a smooth variation in tension is possible.

The position and shape of the nervous system of beetles is much as in other insects. It is basically a ladder-like system of pairs of linked ganglia (masses of nerve cells) lying on the floor of the body cavity. The ganglia in the head are divided into two groups. Those above the level of the mouth and pharynx are fused to form the 'brain', and receive nerves from the antennae, labrum and eyes. The ganglia below this level are fused to form the suboesophageal ganglion, and they innervate the mandibles, maxillae and labium. These head ganglia are linked together on either side of the oesophagus, and the

51

suboesophageal ganglion is linked through the neck to the first thoracic ganglion. There is usually a ganglion (or a pair of ganglia) in each thoracic segment, and they are connected by nerves to the legs, wings and wing muscles, etc. The hinder end of the nervous system is more variable. In a few beetles (e.g. some Cantharoids, many larvae) there are seven or eight abdominal ganglia which end in a rather larger ganglion that represents the fused ganglia of the hindermost segments. In other beetles more fusion of the ganglia has taken place, and any number of abdominal ganglia between one and six may be present (e.g. *Atomaria*, where all the abdominal ganglia are united). Some Scarabaeidae show a much greater degree of fusion than this as they have some of the thoracic centres fused up with those of the abdomen. A few chafers (e.g. *Serica brunnea*) actually have all the thoracic and abdominal ganglia fused together, and the ventral ganglia have all coalesced in Scarabaeid larvae.

C. THE ABDOMEN

This legless region behind the thorax is the third major part of the beetle's body. Its segmentation can be seen from below (fig. 2), although its roof is usually covered by the elytra. The strongly sclerotised sternites form the floor of the abdomen; they join the metathorax where the hind coxae are attached, and the first visible sternite often forms the back of the coxal cavity. Although the first, second and third abdominal tergites (nota) are easily visible if the elytra and wings are removed, the first few sternites are fused together and somewhat modified. The first sternite is reduced to forming merely the front rim of the second sternite, and this is often fused up with the third (although part of it remains separate in the Adephaga and Cantharoidea). At the back end of the abdomen the hinder segments are telescoped together and modified to form the male or female genitalia. The last clearly unmodified segment is usually the seventh, but occasionally the eighth. In some beetles such as chafers, the end of the abdomen projects beyond the elytra to form a 'pygidium'.

The abdomen contains almost all of the reproductive system and its associated genitalia, and these will be discussed in the next chapter. It also contains parts of the nervous system and tracheal system and much of the digestive system – the alimentary canal.

The Alimentary Canal. Food is conveyed from the mouth through the foregut to the midgut, where it is digested and absorbed, and waste materials are then carried by the hindgut to the anus to be voided. The fore- and hindguts are both lined by cuticle, and cannot do more than absorb a certain amount of water. The job of the foregut is to process the food for digestion by the midgut, and to stop any large pieces of food, which might be damaging,

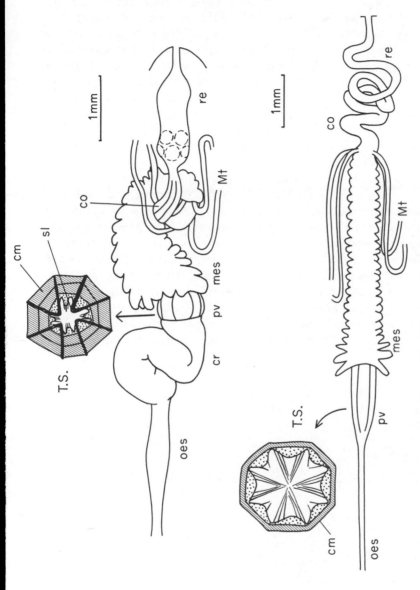

Figure 15. *Alimentary canals of predators*

Diagrams of the alimentary canals of *Nebria brevicollis* (Carabidae) *above*, and *Philonthus decorus* (Staphylinidae) *below*. In each case, a transverse section of the proventriculus is also shown (cm – circular muscles; co – colon (hind gut); cr – crop; mes – midgut; Mt – Malpighian tubule; oes – oesophagus; pv – proventriculus (gizzard); re – rectum (hind gut); sl – sclerotised ridge). (From Evans, 1964.)

from reaching the delicate midgut. From the mouth, food passes through the muscular pharynx and the oesophagus into the crop and gizzard. The crop is a thin-walled food store which is found in many beetles, especially those taking occasional, large meals. Many predators come into this category, for instance, *Nebria* (fig. 15), which has a grinding and filtering gizzard. In beetles where feeding is more continuous, or the food is mainly fluid, the crop is absent and the gizzard has a simple filter of hairs (e.g. *Philonthus*, fig. 15). Crushed and filtered food is passed through a valve from the foregut to the midgut, where the walls secrete a battery of digestive enzymes (which some predators can regurgitate onto food in the mouth). The delicate digestive and absorptive surfaces of the midgut are protected by the peritrophic membrane; this is a sheath which is thin enough not to hinder the exchange of fluid materials.

At the entrance to the hindgut, there is a ring of either four or six Malpighian tubules which are the excretory organs of insects, equivalent to the kidneys of a mammal. They lie in the blood space of the body cavity where they extract waste materials from the blood and pass them into the hindgut. The end of the hindgut, the rectum, stores waste products before they are voided from the body. It may also have the important function of water conservation. Thus Carabidae have special rectal ridges to resorb water from the waste matter, and in many other beetles this transfer is effected by having the free ends of the Malpighian tubules bound tightly against the hindgut. Some beetles have rectal (pygidial) glands opening beside the anus, but as their function is normally defensive they will be discussed in more detail in Chapter 5.

CHAPTER 3

Reproduction and Life History

The basic questions concerning growth and reproduction are:

What are the breeding habits of beetles?
What are the young stages like?
Where are they found and how do they grow?

There are two main 'themes with variations' described in this chapter.

Firstly, different beetles breed in a fundamentally similar way, for the eggs must always be fertilised internally; however, there is a great variety of differences between males and females, and a similar variety of ways in which the sexes are mutually attracted.

Secondly, the egg-laying mechanism and a life cycle which includes larval and pupal stages are common to all beetles; however, there are many places in which eggs may be laid, and larvae and pupae can be of many different sizes and shapes.

Thus, I shall discuss the following topics:

1 The differences between the sexes;
2 Courtship and mating;
3 Egg laying;
4 The life history;
5 How the life cycle is controlled.

1. The Differences Between the Sexes

It is very difficult to determine the sex of some species of beetles without examining the genitalia, but in many species some external differences can be seen. These may be very slight, or they may be as profound as in the Stylopoidea where the male is free-living and the female is in most cases a larva-like parasite. Size is a common sexual difference. In most Carabidae and some Cerambycidae males tend to be smaller than females, whilst in the Scarabaeidae, the situation is reversed. Before egg-laying, the abdomen in female beetles may be obviously distended, as in many Carabidae. In Staphylinidae, the different shapes of the hindermost abdominal sternites are more permanent sexual features (e.g. *Philonthus decorus*, fig. 16). A more easily visible difference is seen in many weevils, where the shape of the abdomen

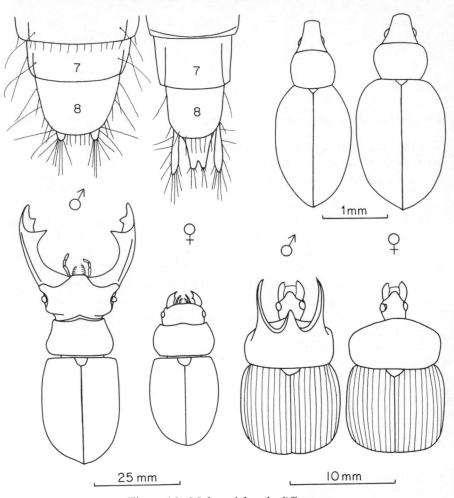

Figure 16. *Male and female differences*
Beetles are viewed from above in all cases. *Top left:* seventh and eighth abdominal segments of male and female *Philonthus decorus* (Staphylinidae); *top right:* male and female *Barypithes araneiformis* (Curculionidae); *bottom left:* male and female *Lucanus cervus* (stag beetles, Lucanidae); *bottom right:* male and female *Typhaeus typhoeus* (minotaur beetles, Geotrupidae).

56

(and elytra) in the female is often more convex than the rather narrow male abdomen; this can be seen in the common soil and litter weevil, *Barypithes araneiformis* (fig. 16). Another frequent sexual difference in weevils concerns the snout, which may be longer in the female – which uses it to drill a hole for eggs – than in the male (e.g. *Curculio nucum*, the nut weevil). This kind of difference is also found in the Brenthidae, such as the New Zealand 'giraffe weevil' *Lasiorrhynchus barbicornis*. In this case, however, the male snout is very elongate and has terminal antennae, whilst in the female it is a more business-like boring instrument with the antennae set back half way along the snout.

The female beetle sometimes differs quite markedly from the male. In *Dytiscus*, the female elytra are heavily ridged in contrast to the smooth elytra of the male. Some female beetles have lost both their wings and elytra, and must be discovered by their active partners. Occasional examples of this sort occur in a number of families, for instance, *Pachypus candidae* in the Scarabaeidae. A more familiar example is the glow-worm, *Lampyris noctiluca* (Lampyridae). In the Drilidae, the contrast is even greater, as the active males are much smaller than their sedentary, wingless females. The most extreme cases of this type of modification are found in the Stylopoidea, where in contrast to the small, active male, the female is an internal parasite which is not very different in structure to its larva.

It is probably more common for the male beetle to be transformed in some way in contrast to the more 'normal' female, and this modification can affect almost any part of the body. For instance, in the timberman (the Cerambycid, *Acanthocinus aedilis*) the male antennae are enormously long, up to four times the length of the whole body. In the oil beetles, *Meloe*, the male antennae are kinked and flattened in the middle to help the male maintain its hold on the female during mating. Clasping modifications of this sort are frequent, but more usually involve the legs. In many male Carabidae and Staphylinidae the front legs are equipped with special adhesive hairs which form pads underneath the tarsi. These clasping organs are best developed in male *Dytiscus*, where the basal three tarsal segments are greatly widened and form a circular clasper which contains enlarged adhesive organs. Another remarkable difference is seen in the front legs of the male harlequin beetle, *Acrocinus longimanus*. In this South American Cerambycid the legs are extraordinarily elongated in comparison with those of the female; the same type of modification is found in male chafers of the subfamily Euchirinae.

An odd difference in tarsal segmentation occurs in some Cucujoids such as the Cryptophagidae, for in some genera the males have lost one of the segments in the hind tarsi. This gives them a 'tarsal formula' of 5-5-4, instead of the normal 5-5-5 which is found in the females.

In addition to the antennae and legs, the mandibles may also be used as claspers if they are large enough. This is true both of tiger beetles, where both sexes have similar mandibles, and of stag beetles, where the mandibles are greatly enlarged in the male (fig. 16). Other kinds of male adornments are found in a great variety of other beetles. One of the commonest is the presence of protuberances or horns on the head or prothorax. For instance, in some species of the small Staphylinid *Bledius*, the males have a median prothoracic horn which projects forwards above the head. Horns of this sort are occasionally found throughout the Coleoptera, but they are most dramatically developed in a number of big beetles. In the Scarabaeoidea, the males frequently differ from the females in being large, or more brightly coloured, or more richly endowed with horns or enlarged jaws. Amongst the Geotrupid dung beetles, the British minotaur beetle, *Typhaeus typhoeus*, shows this well (fig. 16). The female closely resembles those of the dor beetles, *Geotrupes* spp., but in the male a small prothoracic horn which projects forwards over the head has large horns on either side of it. In the very rare English scarab, *Copris lunaris*, the male bears a large, recurved horn on its head.

The giants of this group are found in the Dynastinae, and some of these large tropical beetles show the same sorts of modifications as the British Scaraboids. In the American elephant beetles (*Megasoma* spp.), the males have both a cephalic horn and three prothoracic horns. The male hercules beetle (*Dynastes hercules*) is one of the largest of all insects, but nearly half of its length consists of a single huge horn extending forwards from the prothorax over a large cephalic horn (frontispiece). In the far less conspicuous female these are absent. The male atlas beetle (*Chalcosoma atlas*) not only possesses huge thoracic and cephalic horns, but is larger and has a shining, metallic green colour which is lacking in the small, dull female. Similarly, the male *Hoplia coerulea* of southern France is a beautiful blue and silver in contrast to the dull brown female. As Arrow has pointed out, in cases where the male is huge and horned and the female is small and unadorned, especially in the dung beetles, the work of nest excavation is carried out by the female with little or no help from the male.

Amongst British beetles, the most spectacular sexual difference is seen in the stag beetle, *Lucanus cervus*. In this species, the male is usually larger than the female, and has huge, antler-like jaws, whereas in the female the jaws are much smaller, but are of more use for biting (fig. 16). Although some males may reach nearly three inches in length, their size is very variable and small individuals may be smaller than the females. In these small males, the jaws are not only absolutely smaller, but are also relatively smaller than those of the large males. This difference in the relative size of an organ which is dependent on the absolute size of the individual is known as allometry, and is found in many kinds of animals.

58

The reproductive organs of an insect, the testes and ovaries, lie in the abdomen. Their basic construction is similar in most animals, and only the details differ. In the male, sperm are produced by each testis and are then carried by a duct, the vas deferens, to a sperm storage reservoir, the seminal vesicles. From here, they can be ejected through an ejaculatory duct which carries the semen to the copulatory organ, the penis. In the female, eggs are produced by the ovaries. They are carried down the egg ducts, oviducts, to a median oviduct which is expanded farther back to form the vagina. Sperm are placed by the male organ, the aedeagus (of which the penis is the final section), into the vagina or into a small pocket off the vagina, the bursa copulatrix. It is usual for the female to have a sperm storage organ, the spermatheca, which is used to keep the sperm until the eggs mature, when sperm can be released at the correct time.

This basic pattern is also seen in the Coleoptera. In the male, the detailed variations concern the form of the testis and the glands associated with the male tract. The two major suborders differ in these respects, for in the Adephaga each testis is a simple coiled tube whereas in the Polyphaga the testis is composed of a large number of separate follicles (fig. 17, A and B). The accessory glands, which supply the various materials needed by the sperm (such as a spermatophore to contain the sperm in some species) are very variable in number and position. They have been divided into two sorts termed ectadenes and mesadenes. The male genital tract ends in the aedeagus, which is the male intromittent organ. It is extruded from the abdomen during mating, and afterwards it is retracted into the body by telescoping the various parts so that they occupy as little space as possible. To facilitate this, the aedeagus consists of a complex series of sclerites, membranes and muscles, through the middle of which runs the sperm duct. At its base there is a ring of sclerites composed of a basal piece which usually supports a pair of sclerites – the parameres – which act as sensory appendages. This basal ring surrounds a median lobe, or penis, which is extruded through it during mating. The penis is a sclerotised tube which contains membranes such as the internal sac, which has further sclerites. During mating, the internal sac and its sclerites are everted so that the sperm duct is carried right into the female tract. The shape of the aedeagus is normally a very constant character for any particular species of beetle, and it is often used by specialists to help define species. However, there are considerable aedeageal variations between different species, and the aedeagii of different families or superfamilies may be quite different in shape (fig. 17, C–F).

In the female (fig. 17, G and H), each ovary consists of ovarioles which are composed of lines of developing eggs. The number of ovarioles differs greatly from beetle to beetle. Robertson noted that the number varied between four and forty in the Adephaga; in the Polyphaga there may be as many as

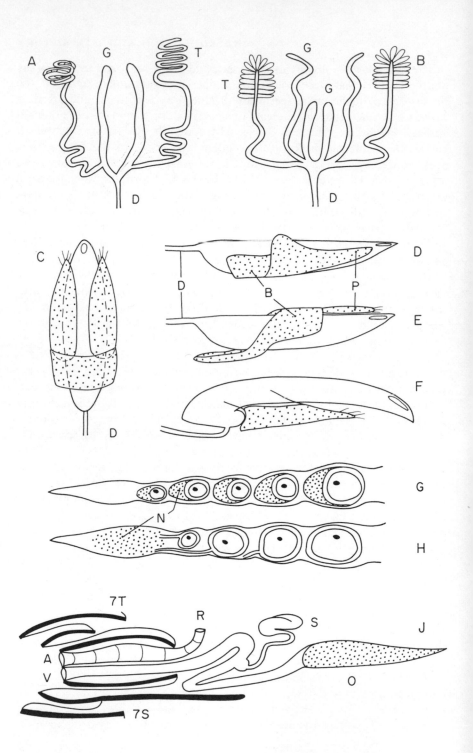

two hundred as in the Meloidae, or as few as one as in the Scarabaeinae (=Coprinae). In these dung beetles there is only one ovary which has this single ovariole. The ovariole numbers in most superfamilies are rather variable, although in the Scarabaeoidea there are often six, while the Curculionoidea almost always have one or two. The spermatheca, which often has an associated spermathecal gland, leads into the vagina by a long, thin duct. The spermatheca is often strongly sclerotised, and like the aedeagus, its characteristic shape in a particular species may be a useful aid to the identification of the species. The main differences between the Adephaga and Polyphaga are in the structure of the ovarioles. In the Adephaga, the developing egg cells alternate with groups of nutritive cells (polytrophic condition). In the Polyphaga, these nutritive cells are all grouped at the apex of the ovariole (acrotrophic condition). The egg is eventually passed down the oviduct to the central part of the female tract which ends in the female opening. This is surrounded by a series of telescoped-up sclerites (fig. 17J) which are extruded for egg laying.

2. Courtship and Mating

The first step in the chain of events which leads to the fertilisation of the eggs by sperm is the coming together of the sexes. This meeting may happen by chance, for example when the Carabids search for food at night on the surface of the woodland floor. During the breeding season, there is often a considerable increase in their activity which leads to more encounters between males and females. In many species it is unlikely that opposite sexes will frequently bump into one another in this way, for the beetles may live in a less homogeneous habitat; this could be dense vegetation or particular kinds of trees which are widely separated in a forest. These beetles usually have some sort of 'assembling' method which will bring the sexes together. A common mechanism of this sort is the secretion of a particular chemical substance by the female. This substance has a smell which is only attractive

---

Figure 17. *Reproductive organs*
A: Male reproductive organs in the Adephaga. (T – testes; G – accessory gland; D – ejaculatory duct); B: Male reproductive organs in the Polyphaga; C: Aedeagus–trilobe type (e.g. Byrrhoid) seen from below; D: Aedeagus – trilobe type (e.g. Byrrhoid) seen from side; E: Aedeagus – Cucujoid type seen from the side; F: Aedeagus – Caraboid type seen from the side (B – basal piece; P – paramere); G: Ovary with developing series of eggs – Adephagid type; H: Ovary with developing series of eggs – Polyphagid type (N – 'nurse' or nutritive cells); J: Longitudinal section through the end of the abdomen of a female beetle (*Atomaria ruficornis*) (A – anus; O – ovary; R – rectum (hind gut); S – spermatheca; 7S – seventh sternite; 7T – seventh tergite; V – female opening). (C, D and E based on Crowson; J after Evans, 1961.)

to the male beetle, who searches actively until he discovers its source. This is known to happen in some chafers. The scent is detected by the antennae of the male, which in some species have longer lamellae (plates) than in the female. This kind of difference is also seen in male Elateridae and Buprestidae, where the antennae are often more elaborately pectinate (comb-shaped) than in the female.

In some beetles the scent is given out by both sexes, and is better described as an assembling scent rather than as a sex attractant. This is found in the khapra beetle, *Trogoderma granarium* (Dermestidae), which is a pest of stored products such as grain and flour. A particularly interesting side effect of the scent is that it acts as a repellent for one of the beetle's competitors, the flour beetle *Tribolium castaneum*. An assembling scent is also present in many bark beetles. The chemical is produced by the intestine of *Ips confusus* and is a very effective attractant; Wood and his colleagues found that the beetles showed a detectable response to extracts of the chemical diluted to the equivalent of the amount of chemical produced by one male in one third of a second. The importance of the chemical messenger (or pheromone) produced by a bark beetle seems to be that it not only evokes the mass colonisation of a tree, but it enables the males and females of a particular species to recognise and 'home in' on one another, even when other closely related species are attacking the same tree.

Scent is probably the commonest means of bringing the sexes together for mating, but other types of signal are used. Sounds can be produced by some beetles, for instance, death-watch beetles are known to tap the walls of their tunnels. In the American plum weevil, *Conotrachelus nenuphar*, sound is also used during the mating period although it is apparently not an essential preliminary to mating. Both sexes stridulate by rasping the last abdominal tergites against the undersides of the elytra, but in each case, Mampe & Neunzig found that the rasping only attracts the opposite sex.

The 'mating call' that we can most easily appreciate in beetles is light, which is produced by glow-worms (Lampyridae), by fire-beetles and fire-flies (Elateridae, Lampyridae and Phengodidae). In several Lampyrids the female is wingless, and signals her presence to the flying male by a flash of light, or a steady glow. In the British glow-worm, *Lampyris noctiluca*, the female may climb to a low 'lighting site' in the late evening, for instance, in the bottom of a hedgerow; or it may stay amongst the cut grass of a hayfield where it is concealed by day but visible at night. The female gives out a continuous glow from light organs on the underside of the end of her abdomen, and this is twisted to allow the light to be easily seen from above. The male flies slowly and fairly close to the ground. It produces very little light itself, but is attracted to the female's glow. When it passes above a female, it folds its wings and drops. Its aim is remarkably good, for Schwalb found that if the females were placed in glass cylinders six inches tall and only one inch wide, 65% of the males fell into them, and the other 35% dropped less than eight inches away.

In countries where fire-flies of many species are common, the recognition of the right female by the right male is more difficult. In North America, which has several closely related species, there is often an exchange of flashes between male and female. The males flash their signals as they fly around and the females reply on perceiving them. For instance, in *Photinus pyralis*, Buck noted that the male gives out a short flash every 5·7 seconds. When these rhythms have been synchronised, the male lands and mating occurs. In *P. consanguineus*, however, the male signal is two short flashes two seconds apart, and this is repeated every four to seven seconds. The female replies with a one second flash after the male's signal. These signals are characteristic enough for beetle collectors to use torches at night to imitate the male's flashings, and so discover the females when they respond.

The frequency of signalling is not the only way a male distinguishes the female of his species. Schwalb studied both *Lampyris noctiluca* and *Phausis splendidula* in Central Europe, and found that the colour, brightness, size and pattern of the lights are also important. Both these glow-worms emit a yellow-green light. When an imitation light was used to decoy *Lampyris* males, it had to be very like the *Lampyris* female's light in colour, size and pattern; only the colour could vary slightly. In *Phausis*, however, the males were less choosey, and actually preferred bigger, brighter and especially bluer decoys. This has been called a 'supernormal' response. It is interesting to find that although in *Lampyris* there is a 1:1 ratio of males to females, in *Phausis*, the males are relatively abundant with a 5:1 sex ratio. Perhaps it does not matter too much if some of these excess males are diverted from their duty by the bright lights.

When the male has discovered the female beetle, he usually displays some sort of courtship behaviour. This not only enables the pair to check that they are the same species, but stimulates the female to accept the male's advances and thus allow mating to occur. There are two main phases in this courtship behaviour. Firstly, the male and female make contact. The male 'identifies' himself, and attempts to mount the female. Secondly, having mounted the female, he must stimulate her to respond in such a way that mating can then take place. The sexual behaviour patterns shown by beetles are very diverse, with much variation from species to species. The male beetle often makes a series of movements with his antennae such as waving, shaking, tapping or even hitting the female with them. The legs may be similarly used, and these movements may be accompanied by bobbing of the head, or the vibration of another part of the body. Many male beetles also use the jaws to bite or gnaw at the female, or alternatively, this may be the

63

female's reaction to the male. It has been suggested that this gnawing behaviour is derived from a need of one partner to taste the other and so check its species. In some beetles, this need is catered for by the production of special secretions by the male. In species of *Malachius* (Melyridae) the males have a variety of secretory organs. When the products of these have been eaten by the female, she becomes receptive to the male. Thus the male secretions actually elicit an important part of the mating behaviour in the female.

In most beetles, the male seems to pair with as many females as possible, that is, he is polygamous. In only a few species is there a more permanent relationship between the sexes, as in the Sexton beetles (*Necrophorus* spp.) and some dung beetles. The relationship in bark beetles varies with the species. Species of *Scolytus* are monogamous. The female bores the tunnel, and the first mating takes place on the bark nearby, or just inside the tunnel. Later, however, the male excavates a nuptial chamber where further mating can occur. Species of *Ips* are usually bigamous, and the male constructs the nuptial chamber off one of the egg galleries which each female bores. Other species of bark beetles are polygamous, and the borings contain a single male with up to several dozen females.

When the courtship behaviour has been successfully completed, mating follows. It has already been noted that male beetles have evolved a variety of clasping devices to hold onto the female. This enables the male to insert his intromittent organ, the aedeagus, into the vagina of the female and eject sperm. The pair of beetles usually stays coupled with the male sitting on the female whilst clasping her, but in some species the male may descend after the initial coupling, and the beetles then remain linked end to end only by their genitalia.

The complexity of the mating process, and of the structures involved, may be the price a land animal must pay in order to transfer sperm safely.[1] In water, many animals merely shed sperm and unfertilised eggs near one another at about the same time (i.e. fertilisation is external). Davey has suggested that the aquatic ancestors of insects shed a packet of sperm (spermatophore) into the water with the eggs. With the colonisation of the land, it is probable that in primitive insects the spermatophore remained outside the female, but its long neck allowed the sperm to reach the spermatheca. In higher insects, for instance in beetles, copulation provided a more elaborate and effective means of ensuring that the sperm reached the spermatheca. Some beetles, such as the Scarabaeidae and Tenebrionidae, still produce a spermatophore but this is inserted right inside the vagina, and probably acts as a plug to hold in the sperm. Other beetles, including Cerambycidae and

[1] However, there may be other reasons. Parker has emphasised the importance of intrasexual selection – the competition between males to fertilise eggs of a particular female by putting their sperm as near the eggs as possible.

Curculionidae, do not produce spermatophores but have developed a long, narrow tube, the flagellum, at the end of the aedeagus. This tube is apparently inserted into the base of the spermathecal duct, and thus a single, narrow duct is formed between the testes and the spermatheca (fig. 18). Not all those beetles which transfer free sperm have a flagellum, however; some species are intermediate between the two main types.

The rest of the structure of the aedeagus is mainly concerned with holding itself in the female genital opening, and keeping the system distended to allow sperm to be pumped along the inner duct. The detailed structure of sclerites and muscles varies considerably from one species to another. Some

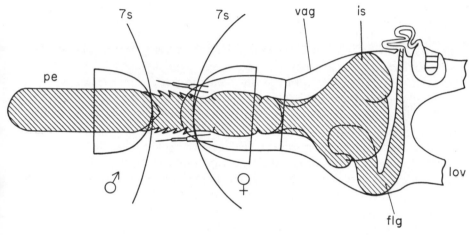

Figure 18. *Diagram showing how copulation occurs*
The everted aedeagus (shaded) is shown inserted into the female system. In this species (*Atomaria ruficornis*) the male tract ends in a long, thin tube, the flagellum, which deposits sperm at the base of the female sperm store, the spermatheca (flg – flagellum; is – internal sac of penis; lov – oviduct; pe – penis; 7s – seventh sternites of male and female beetles; vag – vagina). (From Evans, 1961.)

of the posterior abdominal segments have been modified to help guide the intromittent organ, and to enable it to be properly everted and retracted. It has been suggested that some of these elaborate systems of sclerites enable the aedeagus of a particular species to act as a 'key' which will only fit its particular 'lock', i.e. the female system. It is obviously true that the male and female systems are co-adapted to fit together, but in some species there are only very minor differences in the genitalia; it seems more likely that it is specific patterns of behaviour and different pheromones, etc., which ensure that the right male mates with the right female.

3. Egg Laying

In a few beetles, the female apparently lays the eggs at random in the soil, but this is very uncommon. It happens in some oil beetles (Meloidae), though not in the related blister beetles, and also in a few predaceous soil beetles such as some Staphylinidae. Most beetles give the eggs at least a minimum of protection by laying them in cavities in the soil, or under stones or bark. In oil beetles, the number of eggs laid may be very large, up to several thousand. This is in contrast to some Scarabaeidae, particularly dung beetles such as species of *Scarabaeus* and *Copris* which lay very few eggs – sometimes only one. Many beetles excavate a hole of some sort, to receive the eggs. This applies not only to soil- and litter-inhabiting species, but also to aerial forms such as chafers and Cantharids. The end of the abdomen in the female can often be extended in a telescopic manner, so that it can act as an egg-laying tube, or ovipositor. In the burrowing Staphylinid *Bledius*, a special tunnel, or a series of alcoves off a main tunnel, is constructed for the eggs. The exact form depends on the particular species, but it is normally blocked by sand to protect the eggs after egg-laying.

The great majority of female beetles, if they do no more, at least place their eggs near the food of the future larvae. This is very easy for herbivorous beetles; for instance, Chrysomelid leaf beetles usually glue their eggs to a leaf or stem, and chafers put their eggs into a hole in the soil near roots. It is nearly as easy for some predators. If the prey is sedentary, the larvae will be assured of food if the eggs are laid nearby. This is true of ladybirds which eat aphids, and to a lesser extent of blister beetles (e.g. some *Epicauta* spp.) which feed upon the egg pods of locusts. It is a small step from this situation to actually placing the eggs in the larval food. This is also characteristic of many herbivores. Weevils are particularly well equipped to do this, for the female uses her rostum (snout) to drill a hole into the larval food plant, and then protrudes the end of her abdomen into it to lay the egg. This is most obvious in the long snouted weevils such as the nut weevil, *Curculio nucum*. Some leaf-eating weevils enclose their eggs in the larval food supply by rolling up the leaf, for instance, species of *Attelabus*, *Apoderus* and *Deporaus*.

Beetles that tunnel through wood in the adult stage are clearly well placed to put their eggs right inside their food supply. This applies to bark beetles, where the female cuts an elongated egg gallery and then carves out a series of egg niches in the walls. When the larvae hatch, their feeding activity produces a series of tunnels at right angles to the main egg gallery. Since some species are monogamous and some polygamous, and egg galleries are cut in various directions in relation to the trunk, the resulting patterns sculptured under the bark are characteristic of the various species of beetles (fig. 19). A few carnivorous beetles also place their eggs right inside the larval food. This only applies to semi-parasites such as the Anthribid *Brachytarsus*. In this case, the female beetle puts her eggs into the body, or egg chamber, of a scale insect by means of a hole she has gnawed in the cover of the scale.

Obviously, the placing of eggs inside the food has the added advantage of protecting them from chance predators. Ways of protecting the eggs have also been evolved by some beetles which lay eggs outside the food, however.

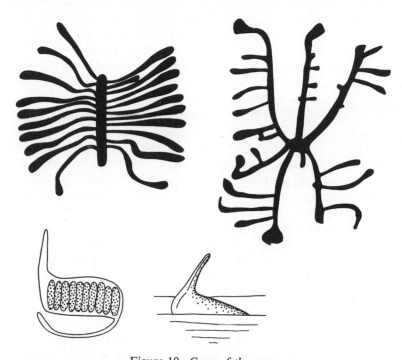

Figure 19. *Care of the eggs*
Top left: larval feeding galleries (on either side) of *Scolytus scolytus* in Elm; a monogamous species with a single adult gallery in the centre; *top right:* larval feeding galleries of *Ips acuminatus* in pine; a polygamous species with female galleries radiating from a central mating chamber; the larval feeding galleries arise from the sides of the female galleries; *bottom left:* vertical section through the egg cocoon of *Hydrophilus piceus* (after Balduf); *bottom right:* position of cocoon floating in water.

This is true of several Chrysomelidae. The tortoise beetle, *Cassida*, covers her eggs with a secretion which forms a protective cover over them. Other leaf beetles have a slightly different type of egg case. Some species take up each egg after it is laid and rotate it with the back legs in a cavity under the back

67

end of the abdomen. In this way the egg is given a coating which includes faecal material, and it is then laid down next to a series of eggs all cemented down in a solid egg mass. Some weevils also make use of faecal material to cover the eggs. One of the most elaborate cocoons is produced by a number of Hydrophilidae. In the great silver water beetle, *Hydophilus piceus*, the female makes it out of silk produced by the Malpighian tubules. The silk cocoon is carefully woven to contain the batch of eggs, and then attached to a floating leaf or twig. One end is extended upwards above the water surface like a periscope (fig. 19). This may ensure an air supply to the eggs but is more likely to be a 'tail-piece' at the end of the silk production. Some Hydrophilids actually carry the cocoon around with them. Balduf noted that in *Spercheus* and *Helochares* the female swims with it beneath the abdomen and attached in front to the hind legs. This is an interesting parallel to the way in which the cocoon is carried in wolf spiders.

Some of the beetles which do not lay their eggs inside the larval food make a 'nest' to protect the eggs and larvae, and provision this with the larval food. In *Bledius*, the female provides the sand tunnel with a culture of algae, and in the wood-boring ambrosia beetles (see chapter 4) the female infects the tunnel with a culture of fungi. This type of behaviour is best seen in the Scarabaeoidea, where a great many species make some sort of provision for their larvae. In some species this labour is entirely carried out by the female, as in many of the giant species of Dynastinae (Scarabaeidae). Arrow has pointed out that it is because of this that the males in genera such as *Dynastes*, *Chalcosoma* and *Megasoma* have been able to evolve their enormous horns. In Dynastids such as *Strategus* in which the males have smaller horns, both sexes co-operate in digging the nesting burrow. Manee found that the American *S.antaeus* dug a vertical shaft down to eight inches beneath a pile of loosened soil. A horizontal chamber was excavated at the bottom and it was provisioned with pieces of decaying oak leaves, upon which a single egg was laid. Decaying vegetation, fruit or humus are commonly used as the larval food by Dynastids, although a few use dung. Zwölfer has noted an unusual case of dung provisioning. Two species of the Australian weevil *Tentegia* collect marsupial dung and bury pellets of it with their eggs to provide the larval food.

Dung is by far the commonest larval food in the Geotrupidae and the Scarabaeidae–Scarabaeinae, which are the two main groups of Scarabaeoid dung beetles. The Scarabaeid *Onthophagus taurus* was one of the dung beetles studied by Fabre. The male has a pair of slender recurved horns on his head, and does not help the female in digging. It is the female alone who bores a shaft beneath sheep dung, and excavates a chamber at its base to hold the mass of dung which she brings down to it. A fairly large cavity is left for the egg, and the chamber is sealed with dung. Dung beetles have well-developed teeth on the fore legs to assist them in digging, and Arrow made a study of these teeth in the males of many species to see if wear could be detected, and thus show whether they help the females in digging. In *O.taurus* few males showed any signs of tibial wear – as would be expected from Fabre's account, but in an Indian species, *O.bonasus*, the same proportion of both males and females showed tibial wear. Thus in the latter species, co-operation between the sexes would be expected, and further evidence for this is the fact that both sexes had similarly developed horns. This type of co-operation is well known in the Geotrupidae. In Britain, it is found both in the dor beetles (*Geotrupes* spp.) and in the minotaur beetle (*Typhaeus typhoeus*). *Geotrupes stercorarius* digs tunnels 18 inches to 2 feet beneath cow-pats, and removes huge quantities of dung in providing its next generation with food. The female does most of the excavation of the tunnel and then digs brood chambers either at its base, or laterally from the main shaft (fig. 20). The male digs out the mass of dung and takes it down to the female, who kneeds it into sausage-shaped masses to stock the brood chambers. Both males and females have powerful legs with spiny tibiae, the first pair of legs having particularly long teeth. In Geotrupidae, the head is relatively small compared with that of many Scarabaeidae, but the jaws are large and help the legs in burrowing.

In the Scarabaeid, *Copris lunaris*, the male is also active in stocking the large brood chamber. Here, the large quantity of cow-dung collected is moulded by the female into a wide 'cake' of which part is then cut out by the female and worked with her legs into a smooth ball. The top of this ball is hollowed out to receive an egg, and is then built up so that the egg is enclosed by walls of dung; the egg lies in an air cavity – the hatching chamber – which communicates by a pore with the brood cavity. The dung containing the egg in its hatching chamber is then a pear-shaped object with smoothed-off walls. In about three months of work, seven or eight of these 'pears' are made, and the parents remain with their brood after the larvae have emerged. They repair damaged cells and apparently prevent the growth of moulds. Halffter & Matthews found a rather similar pattern of behaviour in the Mexican *C.armatus* (fig. 20), although the female may remain alone with her brood.

Some Scarabaeidae dig nests and feeding burrows some distance away from the source of the dung, and have overcome the transport problem by turning the dung into a ball which can then be rolled to the selected site. A good example of one of these pill-rollers is *Scarabaeus sacer*, the sacred beetle of Egypt and the Mediterranean region. Such species often make many dung balls, but most are used as food for the adult beetles, and this feeding activity is described in Chapter 4. When it is collecting dung for its larvae, Fabre noted that the sacred beetle selects moist sheep dung rather than horse dung (which the adult often eats); and if the nesting burrow is not far from the food source, the beetle may not roll it there in a ball, but carry it to the burrow in small quantities. The female alone excavates the nest in this species. The large brood chamber is constructed only a few inches below soil level. Inside this cavity, the female makes first a dung ball, and then turns this into a smooth 'pear' in a similar manner to *C.lunaris*. The outer layers of the pear form a tough rind which prevents the food, or the larva, from drying up in the hot Mediterranean summer.

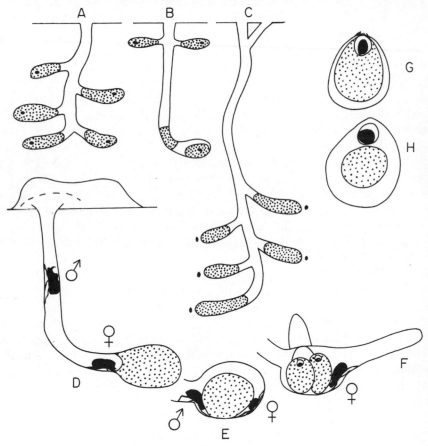

Figure 20. *Egg burrows of dung beetles*
Dung stores are stippled; eggs and adults are shown black. A: *Geotrupes stercorarius* (Geotrupidae); B: *Geotrupes vernalis* (Geotrupidae); C: *Typhaeus typhoeus* (minotaur beetle, Geotrupidae); D–F: *Copris armatus* (Scarabaeidae): Three stages in the preparation of the larval food mass; G: *Malagoniella violacea* (Scarabaeidae). Outer clay coat shown; H: *Phaenaeus palliatus* (Scarabaeidae). Outer clay coat shown. (A–C after Paulian; D–H after Halffter & Matthews.)

At this point, it may be useful to summarise the different types of nesting behaviour shown by dung beetles. The following account is based upon an extensive survey of the natural history of dung beetles belonging to the Scarabaeinae which has recently been made by Halffter & Matthews.

A Dung on the surface is eaten by larvae *in situ*, e.g. most Scarabaeidae–Aphodiinae.

B Dung is nearly always buried by adults for larvae, Geotrupidae and Scarabaeidae–Scarabaeinae.

1. The egg(s) are laid directly in a food mass packed into the end of (or a branch of) a burrow dug under, or near, the dung source: Geotrupidae, e.g. *Geotrupes* and *Typhaeus*, Scarabaeinae, e.g. *Onthophagus* and *Oniticellus*.

The following beetles are all Scarabaeinae:

2. The egg is laid in a sphere or 'pear' specially modelled by the female and given an outer coat of soil. The sphere is made underground under or near the food source. Parents do not stay with the larvae in the brood chamber. The egg may be enclosed in a hollow ball of clay which lies in the food mass as in *Gromphas*, or both egg and food mass may be enclosed together in a clay shell, in separate compartments as in *Phaeneus* (fig. 20) and *Heliocopris*.

3. A large underground chamber, which is made under or near the food source, is first stocked with a large mass of dung. This is then compacted and divided into several ovoids in each of which is laid one egg. These are not usually coated with a clay shell, because the female (or both parents) stay in the brood chamber during all or part of the larval development e.g. *Copris* (fig. 20) and *Synapsis*.

4. A ball of food is made on the surface at the dung source and then rolled away for some distance before the egg is laid. The ball is usually buried, when it may be coated with clay as in *Malagoniella*, or with soil or a dung–soil mixture as in *Scarabaeus*, *Gymnopleurus* and some species of *Sisyphus* and *Canthon*. In *Nesosisyphus* and some species of *Sisyphus*, the brood ball is coated with clay on the surface and not buried.

There are also a number of variations on these themes, but this gives some idea of the range of nesting behaviour patterns shown by one section of the Scarabaeoidea.

It has been noted above that the parents (or at least the female) in species such as *Copris lunaris* stay with the young after the larvae hatch, and carry out 'maintenance work' on the larval cells; the parents (or the female) finally emerge with the brood. In this behaviour one can see the primitive beginnings of family life, although the adult beetles have little direct contact with their progeny. A brief contact between the female and her larvae is

71

found in several species which protect their eggs until the first stage larvae emerge. This is seen in a number of Chrysomelidae, particularly in Cassidinae, and it is even known in the Carabidae, where *Pterostichus multipunctatus* acts in a similar way. Direct contact of a more significant kind between adults and their larvae is found in the Passalidae, a Scarabaeoid family which inhabits rotten wood in the warmer parts of the world. Family groups of these beetles have been found in which the male and female are associated with a number of larvae. This association was first reported by Ohaus from Brazil at the end of the nineteenth century. He believed that the adult Passalids were the parents who fed their larvae upon predigested food. He also suggested that chirping sounds were made by the larvae to keep the family together. Passalid larvae have highly developed sound producing organs. The back legs are greatly reduced and act as scrapers upon ridges found on the bases of the second pair of legs. (This capacity for sound production is also found in the larvae of *Geotrupes* and some other Scarabaeoids. The third pair of legs is not so drastically reduced, but has spines that rub against the bases of the second pair.)

Since the time of Ohaus, the evidence for parental care in Passalids has been rather conflicting. However, this may merely reflect a wide range of habits in a large group of mainly tropical insects. In the North American *Popilius disjunctus*, it was found by Pearse and his colleagues that although older larvae could be reared on rotten wood, newly hatched larvae needed food prepared by the adults, and when separated from these they did not survive. Ohaus described what is possibly a similar situation in another South American beetle, the Tenebrionid *Phrenapates benetii*. In this species there was also an association between adults and larvae. The parents made a long tunnel in balsa wood and cut a series of lateral niches in which eggs or larvae were found. The niches also contained loose wood fibres upon which the larvae were feeding, and these may have been provided by the adults.

The habit of parental care in beetles is probably best known in the case of the sexton or burying beetles, *Necrophorus* species. The details of this behaviour were worked out by Pukowski, and a good recent account has also been given by Ling. The British species are all black beetles with bright orange bands on the elytra, except for the entirely black *N.humator*, and the extremely rare *N.germanicus*. Adults are drawn to the carcase of a small mammal or bird by their acute sense of smell from a distance of up to two miles away. The first beetle to arrive will attempt to drive off any small animals of another species, and any of its own species if they are of the same sex. It will accept a member of the opposite sex, and together these will try to drive off any other pairs of the same species. This happens during the reproductive period when the corpse is buried rather than merely used for food by the adults. The corpse is buried remarkably quickly, particularly if it is laid upon light soil. Earth is dug away from beneath the carcase and a narrow shaft is sunk beneath it. The carcase is then pulled into the ground from below. If parts of the body protrude and prevent this, they may be cut away by the powerful jaws of the beetle. As it is pulled down, the carcase is skinned. This apparently difficult operation is aided by the narrow shaft which helps to roll the flesh into a ball and shear off its outer covering. The flesh is buried between four and nine inches down, where it is housed in a spherical 'tomb' or 'larder' large enough for the beetles to walk round it.

After mating has taken place, the male leaves, but the female stays until the larvae are part grown. The eggs are either laid in separate niches around a central chamber, or a curved egg gallery is constructed with egg niches on either side of it. The female waits in the central chamber until the eggs hatch and the larvae emerge. The larvae are apparently attracted by smell to the female and the food store. When they reach the ball of flesh, the female bites a hole in it so that they can enter. To start with, however, the female feeds the larvae individually with regurgitated meat which is partly digested. When the larvae are old enough to feed themselves, the female leaves. The larvae eat the meat stored for them, but leave a hard skin or rind on the outside of the ball. This may prevent them from drying up in the same way as with many dung beetle larvae. The behaviour seen in a few beetles such as *Necrophorus* and the Passalidae has been called 'sub-social'. It involves an association between one or both parents and the larvae, and in particular, the direct feeding of the larvae by the female. The more complex behaviour of this type which is found in wasps, bees and ants can be termed truly social behaviour.

4. The Life History

Beetles are like bees and butterflies in having a life cycle of the type:

adult → egg → larva → pupa → adult

The larval stage is the feeding and growing period of the beetle's life, whilst the pupal (or chrysalis) stage is seemingly a quiescent period which shows very few signs of external activity. In fact, the activity is internal, for in the pupa the larval structure must be changed to that of the adult beetle with wings and elytra, etc. The pupa is the stage which allows this complete metamorphosis from larva to adult to occur. The larval period is not a single stage but a series of stages or instars. This is necessary because the presence of the external cuticle, which can be only slightly stretched, means that the larva must moult this in order to grow. Thus there are a series of successively larger larval instars. The number varies, but in many beetles there are three, as for instance in most Carabidae, although there may be as many as fourteen instars in some Elateridae (fig. 21).

The beetle egg is usually a simple ovoid. As in other insects, the egg is often surprisingly large in relation to the adult because it contains a large quantity of yolk to nourish the embryo. The latter is surrounded by an egg membrane (the vitelline membrane) and an outer shell, the chorion. This outer shell is tough and flexible rather than hard as in a hen's egg. In beetles it is normally smooth and not sculptured as in butterflies or bugs. The chorion has a wax layer inside it to deal with the water conservation problem, and there are sometimes other layers. For instance, in some water beetles the chorion is thin and the embryo secretes a tough, chitinous cuticle around itself.

All these layers, particularly the outer shell, must be ruptured on hatching to allow the first instar larva to escape. This escape is partly due to biting by the mandibles, and partly by body movements aided by small spikes or spines – the 'egg-bursters'. Van Emden found that the egg-bursters usually occur on the front of the heads of larval Adephaga. In the Polyphaga (except for the Hydrophilidae and a few other species) they are normally thoracic or abdominal. Gardiner has shown how these work in many Canadian Cerambycidae. In some timber beetles, the opening and closing of the mandibles tears a hole in one end of the egg. To gain purchase, the body is forced against the side of the egg, and the spines on the thorax and abdomen prevent it from slipping. Thus Gardiner preferred to call these 'hatching spines' rather than egg-bursters. In other timber beetles, waves of muscular contraction pass along the body so that its spines are rubbed against the side of the egg shell and tear a longitudinal slit. The larva enlarges this and then bulges out through it. The two methods are connected with the method of egg laying. It often happens that the egg is laid loosely under bark or on the surface of the tree, and here there is plenty of room for the larva to hatch by the second method. Where the egg has been firmly buried in the tissue under the bark, the emerging larva must leave through the end of the egg, since there is only room to move forwards, into its food.

Beetle larvae almost always have a basic structure consisting of a strongly sclerotised head, three similar sized thoracic segments which usually bear legs, and a series of eight or nine similar abdominal segments. In most species the mouthparts are adapted for biting as in adult beetles, but they may be rather simpler. This also applies to the larval antennae and the eyes, where up to six ocelli replace the compound eyes. However, the larvae are at least as varied in their structure and habits as the adults. Just as in adult beetles, the larval mouthparts are adapted to their particular kinds of food. In predaceous larvae such as many Carabidae, Staphylinidae, Hydrophilidae and Cantharidae, the mandibles are large and sharp-pointed and lack a

74

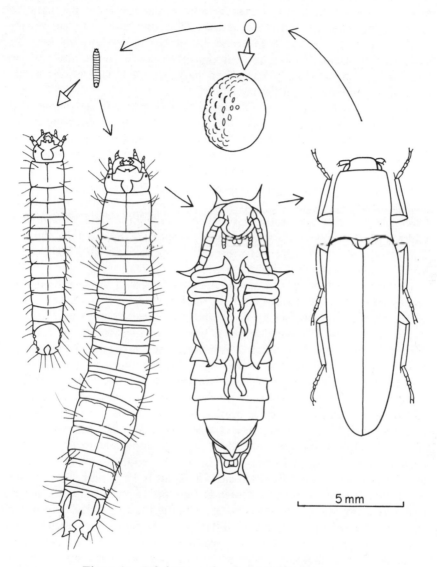

5 mm

Figure 21. *Life history of a click beetle/wire-worm*
The life cycle of *Athous haemorrhoidalis* (Elateridae). Only the first and last (14th)
instar larvae are illustrated. Open arrows indicate enlarged diagrams of the egg
and the first instar larva. (After Fernando.)

basal molar region. In *Dytiscus* and *Lampyris* they are channelled to facilitate external digestion. Some herbivores have the molar regions of the mandibles enlarged for grinding, and the jaws may be strong enough to cut through hard, woody roots or stems. In timber beetle larvae, the jaws are large and extremely powerful. Indeed, as in many other beetle larvae, the jaws and head are the most strongly sclerotised parts of the larva and the head is dark brown in contrast to the pale body.

Another obvious way in which beetle larvae vary is in the shape of the body and the development of the legs. These characters reflect the activity or lack of activity of the larva, and this in turn usually reflects the nature of the food. Carnivorous larvae in the Carabidae and Staphylinidae are active hunters which can pursue their prey. Thus the body is relatively slender but well sclerotised, the legs are well developed and there is often a pair of 'feelers' at the back as well as the antennae at the front. These posterior feelers are the cerci. Again, the last segment bearing the anus is often turned underneath to act as a 'leg' (or pseudopod) supporting the tip of the abdomen. This active type of larva has been termed 'campodeiform' after the primitive insect *Campodea* which it slightly resembles (fig. 22).

Very similar campodeiform larvae are found in both the Caraboidea and Staphylinoidea. If one looks closely at the legs, however, it can be seen that six segments are present in Caraboids and only five in Staphylinoids, because in the latter larvae the tibiae and tarsi have fused together (fig. 4, E and F). This difference is a fundamental one which separates the Adephaga and Polyphaga, and shows that superficially similar types of larvae can be evolved by different groups of beetles in response to similar ways of life.

Although campodeiform larvae are characteristic of most of the Adephaga, including the carnivorous water beetles, in some species the larval form has been modified. For instance, tiger beetle larvae (fig. 22) are sedentary insects which live in burrows, and their legs are important in holding on to the tunnel wall. The abdomen bears a pair of hooks dorsally which also help to prevent its forcible removal. The head is large and shield shaped, and closes the entrance to the burrow. Less active types of larvae are also found in many families of Polyphaga including the Elateridae (wire-worms, fig. 21), Cantharidae and Coccinellidae (fig. 22). Some herbivorous larvae are fairly sluggish, and of these the scarabaeiform larva has a characteristic form. This occurs in a few groups besides the Scarabaeoidea, but it is typical of the chafers and dung beetles. Apart from its head, a chafer larva (fig. 22) is much less strongly sclerotised than a Carabid larva, and its long, slender legs are adapted for clinging rather than running. The larvae is C-shaped and has a swollen abdomen in which all its faecal material is stored. It is a root feeder, and like other underground larvae it is usually whitish, and has spiracles with filter plates to keep out soil particles.

The most highly modified larvae are the apodous (or nearly apodous) types (fig. 22). These are characteristic of enclosed situations where very little activity is required; thus they are mainly wood borers and weevils, but they also include some parasites. The wood borers include the Cerambycidae, Buprestidae and Curculionidae–Scolytinae. In all these larvae the head capsule is strongly sclerotised and the jaws are often large and

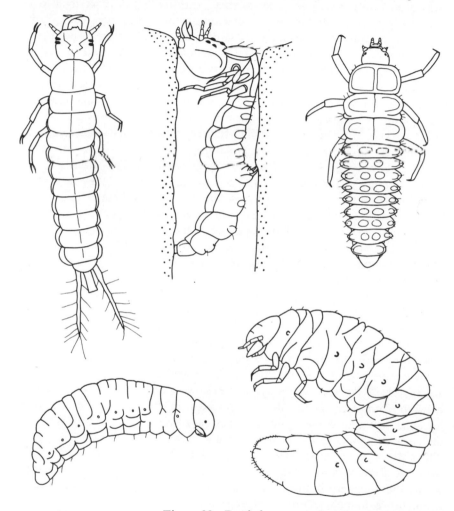

Figure 22. *Beetle larvae*
Top left: Carabidae (*Nebria* from above); *top centre:* Carabidae (*Cicindela* from left side shown in its burrow); *top right:* Coccinellidae (*Coccinella* from above); *bottom left:* Curculionidae (weevil larva from right side); *bottom right:* Scarabaeidae (chafer larva from left side).

77

extremely powerful. Reduced legs may be present in many Cerambycid larvae, but they are of little functional value and in the Lamiinae they are usually absent. Apodous larvae gain purchase for moving by pressing projections on the upper and undersides of the abdominal segments against the tunnel walls. Buprestid larvae have a widened prothorax which presumably acts in a similar way. In most of the Curculionoidea, legs are completely lacking and only a very few species (e.g. Anthribidae) have vestigial ones. Weevil and bark beetle larvae are very similar in appearance, being rather short, white grubs in which the only hardened part is the small head. Like timber beetle larvae, they are almost always hidden in their food supply, but they are usually much less active than the Cerambycidae. In those rather unusual predators which lead a semi-parasitic life, some instars are apodous, and these will be mentioned when their complicated life cycles are described.

In summary, we can observe (following Imms) that there is a gradation of larval types from active, free-living hunters to sedentary, enclosed grubs. The former have well-developed antennae, mouthparts, legs and cerci; they usually have several ocelli, and are well armoured. The latter have very small antennae, reduced mouthparts and no legs or cerci; they lack ocelli, and apart from the head, the cuticle is soft. In between these extremes come the modified campodeiform types (sometimes called eruciform) such as chrysomelid larvae, which have small legs and soft bodies but which are moderately active, and the less active scarabaeiform types already mentioned. Many of the peculiarities of larvae are protective, and some of these will be described in Chapter 5.

We have noted that many beetles have three larval instars. Paulian has observed that beetles fall into two broad groups; those species with three larval instars in which the number is very constant, and those with more than three instars in which the actual number may be more variable. The first group includes many Caraboidea, Staphylinoidea, Scarabaeoidea and Curculionoidea. Many of the Elateroidea, Cantharoidea and Dermestoidea are found in the second group. In these species, the number is usually between four and about fifteen, although in the Dermestid *Anthrenus fasciatus*, as many as twenty-nine instars have been recorded. In this species the normal number is six for the male and seven for the female. This sexual difference is seen in other Dermestidae; for instance, in *Dermestes lardarius*, there are four instars in the male larva and five in the female. In species where the number of instars is variable, this variation may depend on temperature, humidity, food or other external conditions.

The last instar must pass through a pupal stage before the adult can emerge. We have seen that the reason for the pupa in higher insects is to bridge the gap between the unlike structures of the larva and the adult. The biggest difference between these two stages is the presence of wings and

78

flight muscles in adult insects. These adult structures do not suddenly appear in the pupa, they are usually present as rudiments in the larva. Beetles are often more alike in their larval and adult stages than, say, flies, and whereas the fly's body is almost totally reconstructed in the pupa, the beetle's body is merely rebuilt and many larval structures are used. The rudimentary wings are present in the last instar larva although they are inside out. On moulting to form the pupa, the wings are everted and most of the other adult structures then become visible. The eversion of the wings outside the body provides enough space for the muscular system of the adult flight mechanism to be formed, and much of the rest of the adult structure at the same time.

Before the last larval instar pupates, there is usually a change in its behaviour. It stops feeding and may leave its food supply altogether. Leaf and stem feeders often drop on to the soil and burrow beneath the surface, whilst predaceous Carabid and Staphylinid larvae tunnel under stones or into the litter. At the end of its burrow, the movements of the larva hollow out a pupal cell and the larva becomes quiescent. This is the prepupal stage, just before pupation occurs. Some Carabid larvae burrow six inches or a foot, or as much as several feet into the ground to pupate. This puts the larva (and thus the pupa) into a region of more constant temperatures and humidities, and out of reach of many enemies. Water beetles, both Dytiscidae and Hydrophilidae, usually leave the water and burrow into the soil of the waterside to create a pupal burrow. In the case of Scarabaeid dung beetles, the pupal chamber is lined by a hard, smooth layer of faecal 'cement' applied by the anus of the larva. Some root-feeding chafer larvae use the same technique to line a pupal chamber of soil or plant material. A few larvae actually construct a cocoon, although this is rare in beetles. A variety of beetles from several different families, especially Staphylinidae, Ptinidae and Chrysomelidae, have this habit and usually have special glands to secrete the cocoon material. In *Lebia*, a secretion of the Malpighian tubules is used.

The purpose of all these prepupal habits is to provide protection for the inactive pupa. The pupa in its pupal chamber is usually capable of some movement, particularly a flexing of the abdomen, but this is very restricted. Apart from protection, another factor is important in determining the pupal position. The pupa must be located near enough to the surface for the emerging adult to escape. This is particularly important in wood borers, where the larva spends its life surrounded by a very hard food substance. Before pupating, the larvae of Cerambycidae, Buprestidae and various Curculionidae all bore outwards to the surface, and either make a pupal chamber just below the wood surface, or bore straight out and then make a temporary stopper of chewed wood. Some Cerambycid larvae make a white, limey cap with which the adult can fairly easily deal. In these cases the larva pupates with its head end outwards as the adult would not have enough room to turn round in the cell, and its jaws must be ready to cut its way out.

Most beetles have an 'exarate' pupa (fig. 21). This means that the appendages are not stuck down to the surface of the body and the pupa is free to move slightly. This sort of pupa is characteristic of a hidden position, usually inside a pupal cell. It is usually supported within this cell on long setae which thus allow some ventilation and so prevent the growth of moulds and other fungi. A few species have a pupa in an exposed position, for instance, on the surface of a leaf as in ladybirds. Here, the limbs and wings

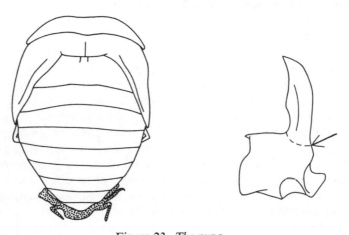

Figure 23. *The pupa*
Left: an obtect pupa (Coccinellidae) viewed from above. The remains of the last larval cuticle are still attached to the rear end of the pupa; *right:* mandible possessed by adult Otiorrhynchine weevil (Curculionidae) whilst still in the pupa. The incisor region has a line of weakness at its base (arrowed) which enables it to be shed after the adult has cut its way out of the pupal cocoon.

are all soldered to the body, and the pupa itself is strongly glued down. This has been called an 'obtect' pupa (fig. 23) and it is found in some Chrysomelidae and Staphylinidae besides the Coccinellidae. In an obtect pupa, the last larval skin may still remain attached to the end of the abdomen, and help to fix the pupa to its substrate. In the exarate pupae of certain Dermestidae, the last larval skin is also retained, and gives some degree of protection; it splits along the back to disclose the pupa, but is not shed. Since obtect pupae are exposed, it is not surprising that they have a number of devices to protect themselves. The usual method is camouflage or a resemblance to inanimate objects. For instance, ladybird pupae on the upper surfaces of leaves are often marked to resemble bird droppings. Hinton has described some ingenious devices on the surfaces of Chrysomelid pupae to protect them against very small scavengers or predators. He called these 'gin-traps' to describe the way some intersegmental regions snap together if triggered by a small marauder.

We have already seen that the first major problem for the newly formed adult beetle is emergence from the pupal cell. (This problem does not arise in obtect pupae which are not hidden.) Beetles normally wait in the cell until their cuticle has partly or fully hardened. They then use their jaws to cut their way out. A few beetles have special devices to help emergence. For instance, in the Otiorrhynchine weevils, the small mandibles of the adult have long, projecting incisor regions which are used to cut a way out of the cocoon. The whole of this incisor region then breaks off and is shed after emergence (fig. 23).

Beetles do not all have the straightforward life cycle described above. In some beetles the life history is more complex, especially where different types of larvae succeed one another as different instars of the same life cycle. This kind of development is usually termed hypermetamorphosis (or hetero-morphosis by Chapman). Slight differences between larval instars are common in many beetles, and in species of Chrysomelidae, Bruchidae, Cerambycidae and Drilidae, etc., these differences may be more marked. However, the major changes which occur in hypermetamorphosis reflect major changes in the way of life of the larva in relation to both feeding and movement. So hypermetamorphosis is characteristic of those parasitic and semiparasitic beetles which transform the free-living first-stage larva into parasitic second-stage larva. They are found in the Meloidae, the Rhipiphoridae and the Stylopoidea.

This larval transformation was first discovered in the oil beetles. Up to the middle of the nineteenth century, the larvae of these widespread beetles were unknown. Only after the link between the first instar and the bee's nest was found could the life cycles be worked out. It was later discovered in America that blister beetles, whose larvae usually attack the egg masses of grasshoppers and locusts, undergo a similar series of larval changes. Meloids lay a large number of small eggs, usually in the soil but sometimes on flowers, and these hatch to each give small, active campodeiform larvae (fig. 24). This larva was known long before it was realised to be the first stage of an oil beetle. It was thought to be an adult insect, and as it was found on bees, Linnaeus called it *Pediculus apis*, the bee louse. Dufour later termed it *Triungulinus* after the three 'claws' (two bristles and a middle claw found at the end of each leg) in the species he examined; a first instar larva of this type is now known as a triungulin or triungulinid.

The triungulins of species of *Meloe* cannot develop further unless they can

81

enter the nest of a particular species of solitary bee. The tiny, active larvae have the urge to climb, and this means that they will frequently reach the flowerheads, where they wait. Their instinct is to cling to any hairy visiting insect, for if they are lucky it may be the right species of bee, and they will be carried back to its nest. The next major hazard which the triungulin encounters is the transfer from the bee to the bee larva's cell, which the beetle larva must enter. This transfer may be brought about by the accidental movements of the bee, or the triungulin may enter the cell when the bee lays her egg in it. The likelihood of any particular triungulin reaching a provisioned bee cell is very small, and it is apparent why a Meloid lays up to 5,000 eggs. Once the beetle larva has reached the bee cell most of its troubles

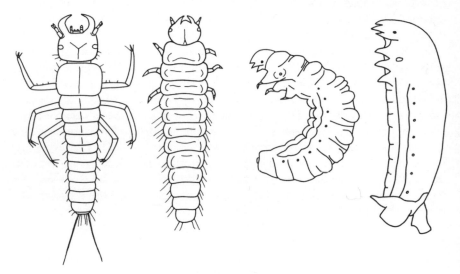

Figure 24. *Hypermetamorphosis*

Four larval stages from the life history of a Blister beetle (*Epicauta*, Meloidae). *Left:* first instar, triungulin larva from above; *second left:* second instar, 'caraboid' larva from above; *third left:* third or fourth instar, 'scarabaeoid' larva from side; *right:* fifth instar larva from side. (After Riley.)

are over. It first eats the bee's egg, thus removing its host, and then uses the food store of pollen and honey provided by the bee.

The triungulin usually moults immediately after eating the bee's egg, and becomes a second instar larva. This larva has smaller legs and mouthparts and a larger abdomen than in the first instar. Since it is curved ventrally, its boat-shaped body floats on the honey; it also has its spiracles shifted dorsally to be able to breathe. This second instar is sometimes called a 'caraboid' larva. The third stage is rather similar, but the fourth instar is grub-like;

and almost apodous. The fifth and sixth instars are even more embryonic in appearance; they have rudimentary legs and mouthparts and non-feeding stages. Blister beetles have a very similar larval succession, but the third and fourth instars differ from oil beetles in being scarabaeoid in appearance (fig. 24).

Both the Rhipiphoridae and the Stylopoidea have triungulin-type first stage larvae to search for the host. In Rhipiphorids, the triungulin penetrates its host body to become an internal parasite, although it re-emerges to form an external parasite in the second instar. In Stylopoidea, the triungulin enters the host (often a bee) and remains within it as an internal parasite for the succeeding instars. The second to seventh instars in many Stylopoids are apodous or nearly apodous, and in the second and third instars a row of fleshy dorsal processes are developed. The male pupates, and develops into an active, but short-lived, flying insect. In contrast, the female larva does not pupate (except in the most primitive, free-living species), but develops directly into a larviform adult. It remains an internal parasite, but protrudes its sclerotised cephalo-thorax through the body wall of its host to allow mating and egg laying to take place by means of a secondary female opening.

Some other beetles show a lesser degree of hypermetamorphosis. These are mainly Carabid and Staphylinid predator/parasites which will be discussed in Chapter 4. One further example of an unusual life history must be mentioned here, that of *Micromalthus debilis*, the only member of the Micromalthidae (Archostemata). The extraordinary life cycle of this odd-looking little beetle includes not only hypermetamorphosis, but also paedomorphosis (larvae producing larvae), viviparity ('born alive') and parthenogenesis (virgin birth). Other irregularities make this the most complex life cycle to be found in the Coleoptera.

5. How the Life Cycle is Controlled

We have seen that in the development of a beetle, a series of larval stages are succeeded by a pupa and then by an adult. These changes are produced in an insect by the concerted action of a number of hormones which seem to act in a similar way in many different insects. Much of the basic mechanism has been worked out in the last thirty years, particularly by Wigglesworth who studied the development of the blood-sucking bug, *Rhodnius*. Before an insect moults, it dissolves away the lower layers of the cuticle. The outer layer of skin, the epidermis, then secretes a new cuticle underneath the old one. The new instar emerges from the old skin by splitting it open along lines of weakness (ecdysial or cleavage lines). In beetle larvae, these pass down the middle of the back and usually form a Y-shaped pattern on the head.

The changes leading to moulting are started by the production of a secretion (brain hormone) by special brain cells (the neuro-secretory cells). The brain hormone is passed down long extensions of each cell, the axons, to a pair of glands (the corpora cardiaca) which lies near the brain. The glands also lie against the aorta, and they pass the brain hormone into the blood. In this way it reaches the prothoracic glands which are stimulated to produce the moulting hormone (ecdyson). This in turn affects the epidermis. During the growth of the immature stages, a second pair of glands which also lies near the brain, the corpora allata, secretes the juvenile hormone. This passes into the blood and also acts upon the epidermis. The combined effect of both moulting and juvenile hormones is to produce a moult giving another immature individual, i.e. a larva from a larva. When the production of juvenile hormone is greatly reduced, the next moult produces the pupa, and in the absence of juvenile hormone a final moult gives the adult. It is possible that one group of genes is responsible for producing the larval characters and is activated by the juvenile hormone, whereas when this is absent another group of genes which produces the adult characters is activated. Although the broad outlines of the control of development have been elucidated, many of the details still have to be worked out.

If something goes wrong with this hormone control system, the orderly pattern of development breaks down, and growth abnormalities may appear. This can occasionally happen in many species of beetles. It is most frequently noticed in populations of beetles which are kept in large numbers in laboratories, for instance, species of Tenebrionids such as the meal-worm, *Tenebrio molitor*, and the flour beetles, *Tribolium* spp. The growth abnormalities often appear as forms intermediate between the larval and pupal stages, or between the pupa and the adult. For instance, an apparent larva may develop rudimentary wings on its meso- and metathorax. The stimulus which upsets the hormonal mechanism may be an environmental one such as an abnormally low or high temperature, or the presence of certain chemicals, etc. Abnormal growth may also be caused by lack of food. Some beetle larvae are naturally slow-growing and have long life cycles. Root-feeding chafer larvae usually grow for two or three years, and root-feeding wire-worms for about five years. Timber and furniture beetles may live for longer as larvae, particularly if the food is dry and has a low food value. There was a record in 1890 of the case of an American Cerambycid larva which lived for over forty years in dry wood. Wigglesworth quoted an even stranger case. Larvae of *Trogoderma granarium* (a stored-products pest) 8 mm in length were kept without food for a period of five years. Surprisingly, they continued to moult, but at the end of this period they were reduced to 1 mm in length and $\frac{1}{600}$ of their original weight – the size of newly emerged first-instar larvae.

There are easier ways than this of withstanding food shortages or adverse climatic conditions, and the commonest way is for the beetle to lapse into a dormant condition. This is known as diapause, and when in this state all the body functions slow so that the insect's metabolism is just 'ticking over', and all growth is arrested. Any of the life history stages – egg, larva, pupa or adult can undergo diapause, but in a particular species it usually occurs at one particular stage. Although diapause may be necessary to survive either cold winters or hot, dry summers, it is not usually provoked by changes in the weather. It is usually triggered by a more reliable indication of the season such as day length (i.e. hours of daylight) or the gradual shortening of the day length, and these indicators affect development via the eyes, the brain and the hormone control system. Another important use of diapause in the larva or pupa is to synchronise the life cycles of individuals in a species in which the larval life may be at least six months or a year, so that all the adults emerge at the same time and are thus more likely to meet partners for mating. Diapause may also be used to 'gear' the iife cycle of a particular species to different regions of its geographical range which may have different climates. The importance of diapause in the ecology of beetles will be discussed later, in Chapter 6.

CHAPTER 4

Food and Feeding Habits

What kinds of food do beetles eat?

The answer is simple – not quite everything, but a very wide range of organic substances and a few inorganic ones. So the theme and variations here is that whilst almost all adult beetles have biting mouthparts, they deal with an immense variety of foods in many different ways.

Like ourselves, insects usually need proteins, fats, carbohydrates, mineral salts and traces of other substances (vitamins) in order to grow and lead active lives. Since beetles grow only in the larval stages, the adult may be able to maintain itself on less food than the larvae. Nevertheless, beetles often have a longer adult life than many insects, and the females need sufficient food to mature the eggs. A beetle's food requirements are easily met by a mixed diet, and this is also true of carnivores and scavengers with their 'pre-processed' food. Even specialised herbivores such as wood feeders find that the plant cells contain most types of foods. There are some beetles which can develop in artificially refined human foods, but they have solved the vitamin deficiency problem by carrying special micro-organisms internally.

The interrelationships between beetles and their particular foodstuffs can be summarised as follows:

BEETLES

PLANT FOOD   *ANIMAL FOOD*

```
LIVING PLANTS ──────────→ HERBIVORES
            ╲                PREDATORS ←──────── LIVING ANIMALS
             ↓  Leaf fall    PARASITES ←──────── Dung
             │  Litter and humus                   │
             ↓                ↓ SCAVENGERS ←──────── │
DEAD PLANTS ─────────────→ SCAVENGERS ←──────── DEAD ANIMALS
```

I shall consider each of these groups of beetles in turn.

In spite of the above division of beetles into herbivores and predators, many species eat both animal and vegetable food. For instance, some scavenging Carabids will eat a wide range of both types of foods, but some of the stricter predators will only resort to vegetable food if they are very hungry. Wire-worms are sometimes crop pests and are often thought of solely as root feeders; however, many species are also carnivores, and some may eat only animal food. Thus our feeding categories are often only a guide to the main foods of the beetles concerned.

1. Herbivores

Most beetles feed on plants or vegetable materials, and almost all sorts of plant are eaten by beetles. This includes a few of the lower plants. For instance, the small, burrowing Staphylinid *Bledius* eats simple algae, some Byrrhidae consume mosses, and horsetails and ferns such as bracken may be attacked by some weevils and chafers. With the exception of the fungi, however, the great majority of beetles are found on the conifers and flowering plants. With the conifers, we find that many species of beetles eat all parts of them, although their tough, narrow leaves attract fewer species than those of the broad-leaved trees. The latter, together with shrubs, herbs and grasses, are fed on by a host of beetle species. Almost all flowering plants are attacked by beetles. However, fewer species prefer monocotyledons such as grasses to dicotyledons since the leaves probably offer less shelter, and grasses are often tough and siliceous.

The specialisation of a beetle goes further than its merely selecting one or more species of plant to feed upon. It also chooses a particular part of the plant at a particular stage of its development. For instance, most of the third biggest family of beetles – the Chrysomelidae – have specialised on the softer parts of plants such as the leaves. The Scolytinae – the bark beetles – include a large number of small species which usually tunnel in the cambium layer just beneath the bark. Another large family – the Cerambycidae – has larvae which tunnel in the hard parts of trees, although the timber is often diseased and sometimes decaying. In fallen logs and timber in a more advanced state of decay we may find the huge larvae of Lucanidae, the stag beetles. Thus every part of a plant supports many species of beetles, and this wide feeding range is illustrated in fig. 25.

The most convenient way to deal with this great variety is to list the different parts of plants which are eaten, and to give a few examples of the different ways in which beetles feed on them. A number of beetles, for instance weevils and jewel beetles (the larvae of which are 'flat-headed borers'), could be fitted into several categories as they may eat bark, stems or roots, etc. Broadly, however, the catalogue of vegetarians can be divided as follows:

87

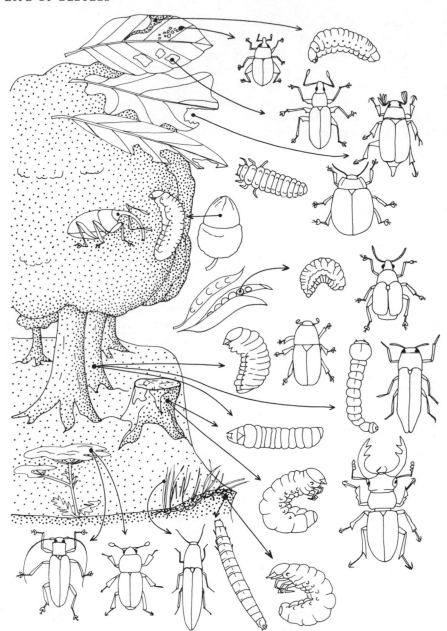

Figure 25. *Herbivores*
The diagram shows some of the many beetles, both adults and larvae, which feed on the different regions indicated of a variety of plants. The species illustrated (not to scale) are as follows:

A Foliage and flower feeders.
B Stem and bark feeders (mainly sub-surface borers).
C Timber beetles (mainly deep borers).
D Root feeders
E Seed, nut and fruit feeders.
F Fungus feeders.

A. FOLIAGE AND FLOWER FEEDERS

These have a soft and readily available food source; they include the majority of species in the huge families Curculionidae – weevils, and Chrysomelidae – leaf beetles.

There are several ways of dealing with leaves:

(a) *Cutting large holes in the margins:* Chrysomelidae, e.g. some larger poplar and willow beetles, *Melasoma populi* and *Galerucella lineola*; Short-snouted weevils, e.g. *Otiorrhynchus singularis* on conifer leaf margins; Scarabaeidae, e.g. the cockchafer, *Melolontha melolontha*. In Europe, this may defoliate large areas of broad-leaved woodland. In North America, another chafer – the Japanese beetle, *Popillia japonica* – is an even more serious pest.

(b) *Making small holes in leaves:* Many weevils; small leaf beetles such as flea beetles (Halticinae) and tortoise beetles (Cassidinae).

(c) *Eating the outer layers of leaves:* Chrysomelid larvae, e.g. the willow leaf beetles, *Phyllodecta vitellinae* and *P.vulgatissima*. These graze in 'herds' on the undersides of leaves and may skeletonise them.

(d) *Tunnelling or mining inside the leaf:* Larvae of some weevils, leaf beetles and jewel beetles, e.g. the weevil *Orchestes fagi*, the larva of which eats blotch shaped mines in beech leaves.

(e) *Rolling up leaves (by the adult) to protect the eggs and larvae:* Leaf rolling

---

Leaves: Orchestes fagi, adult and larva (Curculionidae); adult *Phyllobius argentatus* (Curculionidae) and *Melolontha melolontha* (Scarabaeidae); larva and adult *Melasoma populi* (Chrysomelidae); acorn weevil, *Curculio venosus* (Curculionidae), adult and larva; pea beetle, *Bruchus* sp. (Bruchidae), larva and adult.

Trunk: Scolytus sp. (Curculionidae), larva and adult; *Agrilus* sp. (Buprestidae), larva and adult; *Rhagium* sp. larva (Cerambycidae).

Stump: Rhagium sp. larva as above; *Lucanus cervus* larva (Lucanidae); male adult also shown.

Grass roots: wire-worm, *Athous* sp. larva (Elateridae); chafer larva, *Melolontha* sp. (Scarabaeidae).

Grass: click beetle, *Athous haemorrhoidalis* adult (Elateridae).

Flower head: Meligethes sp. adult, (Nitidulidae); timber beetle, *Rhagium* sp. (Cerambycidae).

weevils (Attelabidae), e.g. *Rhynchites populi* rolls the whole poplar leaf and *R.betuleti* deals similarly with hazel leaves. *Apoderus coryli* rolls only one side of a hazel leaf, whereas *Attelabus nitens* cuts both sides of an oak leaf to make an elongate roll in the midline.

(f) *Flowers:* Petals can be eaten like leaves by most leaf-eating beetles, e.g. the rose chafers, *Cetonia* spp. Pollen and nectar are used by many adult beetles, especially Cerambycidae, Lucanidae, Dascillidae, Melyridae, Oedemeridae, Mordellidae, Scraptiidae, Nitidulidae and Meloidae. Sugary sap flows may attract adult stag beetles, and some tropical Dynastines (Scarabaeidae) such as the elephant beetle, *Megasoma elephas*, may use horns or jaws to start sap flows. The most specialised nectar feeders are species of *Nemognatha* (Meloidae) in which the galeae on the maxillae are elongated to form a sucking tube (fig. 26) – a remarkable parallel to butterflies.

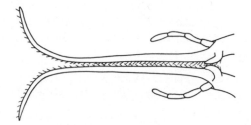

Figure 26. *Nemognatha tongue*
The maxillae of the Meloid genus *Nemognatha* showing the greatly elongated outer lobes, the galeae, which fit together to form a sucking tube. (Partly after Packard.)

B. STEM AND BARK FEEDERS

These include beetles that cut into young stems or bore under the bark of trees in order to reach the softer underlying tissues. This is a particularly succulent region of a tree and is a rich food source. If the end of a freshly cut trunk is examined (fig. 27), one can see a ring of soft tissue just inside the bark layer. This tissue includes the narrow layer of cambium – the rapidly dividing zone of cells which form the other tissues of the tree. Wood is produced inside the cambium, and bast and the underlayers of bark on the outside; the protective outer layer of tough bark encloses all these regions. The wood consists of vessels which carry water up the trunk, while the bast carries sugars and other carbohydrates. Thus the region of the trunk between the wood and the outer bark is rich in food materials, and this is taken advantage of by many beetles.

Adult Cerambycidae may act as 'twig-girdlers', but several weevils which bore into the growth zone are more serious pests. Adult pine weevils, *Hylobius abietis*, often feed on the young stems of forest and plantation conifers; its larvae feed in old stumps and logs. However, larvae of *Pissodes pini* bore feeding tunnels under the bark of young trees, although in this case, the adults do less damage by feeding on the plant surface.

The group of small insects which are generally known as bark beetles form the subfamilies Scolytinae, Ipinae and Platypodinae of the Curculionidae; they used to be grouped in the family Scolytidae. In these beetles, most of the life history, including the feeding and breeding of the adults, takes place under the bark. Species of bark beetles feed on almost all the parts of a plant, but their most characteristic activities are seen by stripping the bark

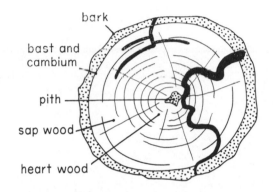

Figure 27. *Tree Trunk*

Some of the structures visible on a freshly cut tree trunk are shown. The narrow, branched tunnels of ambrosia beetles are shown above, whilst the unbranched tunnel of a single timber beetle larva is shown on the right. (After Chrystal.)

off fallen logs. Each species has a style of engraving which is due to the pattern of galleries cut under the bark (fig. 19).

The female cuts a short entrance tunnel through the bark to a pairing chamber, and after mating, the main tunnel or 'mother-gallery' is bored out from this. In the case of polygamous species where one male mates with several females, each female bores out her own mother-gallery from a central mating chamber. In the Ipinae, such as *Ips acuminatus* in pine, this gives rise to a star-shaped pattern, whereas in the monogamous *Scolytus* species of elm there is a single mother-gallery (fig. 19). The female cuts niches along the sides of this gallery to receive the eggs. When the legless larvae hatch (fig. 28), they start tunnelling at right angles to the main gallery and are at first parallel to one another; as they grow; so their tunnel width is increased. Each finally forms a pupal chamber at the end of its tunnel, from which the new adult will emerge via a short exit tunnel. Many bark beetles are economically important in that the adult feeding tunnels often damage the young shoots with their thinner bark, whilst the breeding tunnels may cause damage to standing trees. In most cases, except where the number of beetles is very large, bark beetles only attack weakened or sickly trees. If their numbers do reach plague proportions, however, population pressure may result in damage to healthy trees. The worst damage done is by infections such as Dutch elm disease which is transmitted by species of *Scolytus* (see Chapter 7).

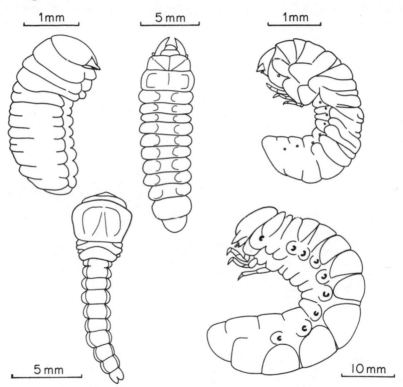

Figure 28. *Wood feeding larvae*
Top row, left: Curculionidae–Scolytinae (*Scolytus*) – view from the side of a bark beetle larva; *top row, centre:* Cerambycidae (*Rhagium*) – view from above of a timber beetle larva; *top row, right:* Anobiidae (*Stegobium*) – side view; *bottom row, left:* Buprestidae (*Chrysobothris*) – a 'flat-headed' borer viewed from above; *bottom row, right:* Lucanidae (*Lucanus*), a stag beetle larva seen in side view.

C. TIMBER BEETLES: DEEP BORERS

(a) *Pin-hole borers, or 'ambrosia beetles'*. These occur in both the Platypodinae and the Ipinae. They are small beetles which bore very narrow tunnels of about the diameter of a thick pin (fig. 27). After being drilled, the tunnels darken until they are almost black, and this is due to the spread of a fungus along the tunnel walls. This dark fungus was given the unlikely name of 'ambrosia' as it is actually introduced and cultivated by the beetles as food for themselves and their larvae. It may be brought into the tunnels in the form of fungal fruiting bodies stuck to the body hairs of the females, or it may be carried in the gut; the beetles may even have special pockets for the fungi. The Platypodinae are a numerous tropical group, although only a single oak borer occurs in Britain. Of the Ipinae, the two British species of *Xyleborus* each bore a common gallery for all stages of the beetle, and wall off part of this with boring debris to form a 'tomb' for dead beetles whose presence might otherwise interfere with the normal growth of the fungus in the main tunnel.

(b) *True timber beetles* (*Cerambycidae*). The Longicorns, or Longhorns, are a very large family which is particularly common in the tropics and sub-tropics, although they are amongst the commonest wood borers in Britain. It is only the larvae that tunnel; the adults are often found on flowers eating pollen, but they may feed on many other parts of plants. The eggs are laid in bark crevices, or in niches cut by the female. During the first part of its life history, the larva bores a tunnel which winds between the bark and the wood, and becomes filled with the resulting wood dust. Later, the older larva cuts down obliquely into the wood and tunnels in this region during the rest of its larval life (fig. 27). The pale, elongate larvae are often rather flattened and have a wide, heavily sclerotised head with powerful jaws (fig. 28). The legs are much reduced and are sometimes lost, as the larva pushes itself through its tunnel with the tough, partly sclerotised faces of its thoracic and abdominal segments.

In some species, the larva may remain in the richer sapwood, but in most it bores deeper into the heartwood and sometimes reaches the pith. Although the life cycle may be completed in a year, the larval life can be very much longer; this depends upon the larva's rate of growth, which is governed by the amount of food available. The larval food is not the indigestible wood (xylem) itself, but the food substances contained in the wood vessels. These are mainly the sorts of carbohydrates and proteins that might occur in our own diet, but they also include cellulose which we cannot digest, but which can be broken down by most Cerambycid larvae. Thus, they can live in the drier heartwood of a trunk. Its food value may be very low, however, and so the larva may take years to grow up; in fact, as many as forty-five years in the case of one North American beetle which lived in yellow pine.

In Britain, the inch-long, bright green Musk beetle, *Aromia moschata*, is occasionally found on willows, but the brownish *Rhagium mordax* and

93

R.bifasciatum, and some of the black and yellow species of *Strangalia* are much commoner. These British species are dwarfed by many beetles from the South American forests, for instance, *Titanus giganteus* and *Macrodontia cervicornis* vary between five and nearly eight inches in length (12–20 cm). The huge larvae of the latter species are considered a delicacy by some South American Indians who can easily dig them out of their tunnels in soft balsa wood.

(c) *Beetles attacking dying and dead timber.* Several families of small beetles are involved. Anobiidae are cylindrical species in which the prothorax conceals the head. The larvae, which do most of the boring, resemble small chafer grubs (fig. 28). The wood-worm, *Anobium punctatum*, attacks furniture and house timbers as well as a variety of deciduous trees out-of-doors. *Xestobium rufovillosum*, the death-watch beetle, attacks hardwood trees in woodlands and is a well-known pest of old oak woodwork in ancient buildings. *Ernobius mollis* is a common species found under the bark of conifers. Lyctidae, the powder post beetles (e.g. *Lyctus* spp.), have larvae which produce a very fine powdery dust rather than small pellets as in the Anobiidae. They mainly attack the softer sapwood. Very hard wood may be tunnelled by the larvae of *Lymexylon naviculare* and *Hylecoetus dermestoides* (Lymexylidae). The latter is another fungus feeder. The Bostrychidae and Brenthidae also include many species which bore in dead timber. One of the most unusual habitats is marine, waterlogged timber; the Oedemerid, *Narcerdes melanura*, has a larva which bores into piers and dockyard timbers.

(d) *Beetles boring in mainly rotten wood.* In their last stages of decay, tree trunks and stumps are tunnelled and often nearly disintegrated by the larvae of some of the largest beetles, members of the Lucanidae and Scarabaeidae. One of the largest British beetles is *Lucanus cervus*, the stag beetle, which is much rarer than the lesser stag beetle, *Dorcus parallelopipedus*. The third British Lucanid, *Sinodendron cylindricum*, may be found with its larva boring large holes in decaying wood. Lucanid larvae are soft, white C-shaped grubs (fig. 28). Some tropical Scarabaeids have similar larvae, but are even larger; for instance, the West African *Goliathus*, and Dynastinae such as *Strategus validus* which is found in decaying cane wood. The Passalidae (which were mentioned in Chapter 3) have aggregations of both adults and larvae living together in decaying logs. The oldest wood borings known were probably made over 250 million years ago by larvae of the Archostematan family Cupedidae. There is even a Caraboid family, the Rhysodidae, which is specialised to consume the bacterial-rich, rotten wood.

D. ROOT FEEDERS

It is mostly the larval stages of beetles that have specialised in root feeding.

The hidden position of roots in the soil is ideal for evading predators whilst getting on with the business of eating. Most of these larvae are either wire-worms (Elateridae), chafer grubs (Scarabaeidae) or weevils (Curculionidae), although many other families such as Buprestidae and Cerambycidae include some root feeders. Wire-worms are shiny, cylindrical larvae which are very tough-skinned and more active than most plant-feeding larvae found in the soil (fig. 21). Different species feed on a variety of roots, although some species are mainly carnivorous. Wire-worms are best known, however, as grass-root feeders. They may live for five years and can occur in grassland in densities of over one million per acre, and were thus a national problem in Britain during the last war when much marginal grassland was ploughed up for crops. Cereals were the most susceptible, but many other crops were attacked. The common wire-worms responsible were species of *Agriotes*, *Athous haemorrhoidalis*, and species of *Corymbites* in rougher hill country.

Chafer larvae are often found in the same situations as wire-worms but are a complete contrast in shape. They are fairly large, white C-shaped grubs with brown heads and long legs (fig. 22). The expanded end of the abdomen is curved under them and contains all the faecal material they have produced. They are able to wriggle violently, but are rarely able to escape once discovered. Chafer larvae often attack seedlings in nurseries, for instance, *Melolontha melolontha* and *Phyllopertha horticola*, the garden chafer. As before, the largest larvae are Dynastines, and a single, four-inch long larva of *Chalcosoma atlas* may kill the coffee tree or coconut palm it is feeding on.

Most of the root feeding weevil larvae in Britain are short-snouted weevils (Otiorrhynchinae) such as the green *Phyllobius* and the darker *Otiorrhynchus*, and their food may include both grass and tree roots. Some plants may produce a reaction to weevil feeding, for instance, marble-sized galls are induced on turnip or cabbage roots by *Ceuthorrhynchus pleurostigma* larvae.

E. SEED, NUT AND FRUIT FEEDERS

The seed eaters are probably the best hidden of all the beetles feeding on the aerial parts of plants. The flowering plants have well-protected seeds, and if a female beetle can oviposit in the flower or developing fruit, her offspring will inherit security and a rich food supply. Getting the egg to the right place inside a plant can be a tricky problem, for female beetles rarely have a well-developed ovipositor. In many cases the egg is laid on or near the surface, and the larva must burrow through to reach its food. In the weevils, the problem of no ovipositor has been partly solved by the development of a snout, with which the female can cut a hole into hard bark or wood if necessary, and then place her eggs right into their food supply.

95

The length of the rostrum varies considerably in weevils (fig. 29). Many of the short-snouted weevils have a root-feeding larva, so that it is only necessary for the egg to be laid just beneath the soil surface near the roots. In contrast, many of the weevils whose larvae live deep inside plants have long snouts. This is well seen in the nut weevils *Curculio* (= *Balaninus*); *C.venosus* bores into young acorns and *C.nucum* into hazel nuts. Other seed eating weevils include the gorse weevil, *Apion ulicis*, which is dispersed explosively with the seeds, and the grain weevils *Sitophilus* (= *Calandra*) *granarius* and *S.oryzae*, which are a major pest.

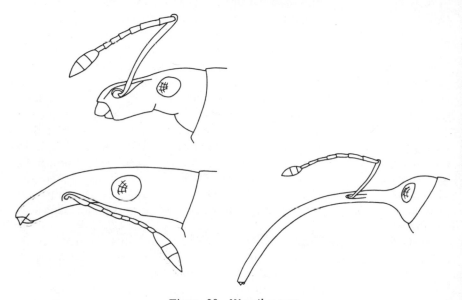

Figure 29. *Weevil snouts*
The heads of three weevils seen from their left sides. *Top left:* Short-snouted weevil, *Phyllobius* (Curculionidae – Otiorrhynchinae); *bottom left: Apion* (Apionidae); *right*: long snouted weevil, *Curculio* (Curculionidae).

The Bruchidae have specialised in feeding on the seeds of Leguminosae, the pea family, and include both pea and bean 'weevils' (they are more like leaf beetles than weevils). Several species are pests, for instance, the American bean 'weevil' *Acanthoscelides obtectus*, has been a pest for a very long time, as is known from Inca graves in Peru.

F. FUNGUS FEEDERS

Fungus is by far the most popular beetle food amongst the lower plants. Perhaps this is not surprising since it is easily digestible, and it is probable that fungus in decaying trees was the main food of the ancestral Polyphaga. Thus some of the 'lower' Staphylinoids such as the Anisotomidae include many fungus feeders. However, apart from the ambrosia beetles, most present-day fungus feeders are to be found especially in the Cucujoidea – the Clavicornia and Heteromera. Many families of these small beetles occur exclusively in fungi. These include the Mycetophagidae, Tetratomidae, Erotylidae, Cryptophagidae, Colydiidae, Lathridiidae and Cisidae. Some have specialised on fungi in the ground or soil such as puffballs, some (especially Cisidae) on the brackets of *Polyporus* found on trees, and many of the smallest Cryptophagids live on the fine strands of fungal mycelia that soon develop on all kinds of rotting organic matter. For instance, species of *Cryptophagus* and *Atomaria* can even live on damp blotting paper if it is left a few days to develop a thin silken covering of fungal threads.

WHY SPECIALISE?

A deceptively simple question is why does this beetle feed upon this plant? More precisely, why do asparagus beetles feed upon asparagus and colorado beetles feed upon potatoes? Why do they not eat grass or oak trees?

Most kinds of foliage would nourish most beetles because they all contain the main food substances – proteins, fats and carbohydrates. Fraenkel has pointed out that these primary substances are nearly tasteless, and the palatability, or unpalatability, of food is due to a wide range of secondary substances. It seems to be the 'tastiness' of the secondary substances that stimulate a beetle to start feeding on 'its' plant. In many cases, the evolutionary reason for the presence of these chemicals in the plant was just the reverse of being a feeding stimulant to a herbivore. Insects and modern plants have evolved together over the last hundred million years or so. During this time, many plants have evolved all sorts of insecticides or insect repellents. These include substances such as pyrethrin, and a variety of poisonous alkaloids. The more successful insects – those that survived – often countered this by ways of detoxifying their food, and so were actually able to use a formerly distasteful (or poisonous) substance as a feeding stimulant or attractant. Thus in order to feed successfully on plants, an insect must usually specialise on a particular species of plant in order to keep pace with the evolutionary 'tricks' of that plant. Just as some substances in the foliage of the food plant stimulate feeding in a specialist beetle, so substances in a 'foreign' plant tend to act as inhibitors and prevent feeding.

As well as chemical repellents and inhibitors, there are also straight-forward mechanical reasons in some cases for not feeding on particular plants. Some leaves such as holly are well protected by large spines. The effectiveness of these spines can be shown by cutting them off, when the edge of the leaf can be attacked by caterpillars and eaten. It has also been

97

shown that the veins on the leaves of some grasses are too close together for the mouthparts of the larvae of some grass feeding beetles to get between, and these grasses will therefore escape attention. Of course, not all herbivores are specialists; however, an ecological advantage of the chemical and mechanical specialisations of insects to plants (and vice versa) is to provide a great number of different niches with room for many species to co-exist.

2. Predators

A. FOOD

Predators obtain their food by killing and eating other animals. This is in contrast to scavenging beetles which consume dead animals or dung. These two categories intergrade, however, for some predators will feed on freshly killed small animals which they encounter, while some carcase-feeding beetles may eat fellow scavengers such as fly larvae. Predaceous beetles can be usually distinguished from herbivores by the size and sharpness of their mandibles, and by their greater speed and activity.

It is often very much more difficult to discover which animals predators feed on, but there are several ways of finding out.

1 The most obvious method is to watch the beetle feeding in its natural habitat, but this is more difficult than it might appear, and requires a great deal of patience and luck. Many predators only feed at irregular intervals, and following agile predators such as tiger beetles requires considerable agility on the part of the observer. Carabidae are usually found by turning over stones and logs in the daytime. Most of the beetles discovered are resting and are unlikely to be feeding. To see them hunting for food one must return at night and search for the active beetles with a torch. This will show that many common 'ground' beetles hunt and capture their prey up trees. The predators which are most easily studied in natural conditions are the slow-moving beetles such as Coccinellidae which are often surrounded by the sedentary aphids upon which they prey.

A less satisfactory alternative is to test the food preferences of a predator in captivity, where it may be possible to obtain a rough idea of which food is acceptable and which is rejected. The main difficulty is that conditions in captivity are always artificial, and the beetle may show an overwhelming desire for cream cake rather than its apparent natural prey. A compromise is to establish a large insectary for the predator; even this is bound to be partly artificial unless there is adequate knowledge of the beetle's natural habitat.

2 A quicker method of determining what type of food is eaten by an animal is to examine the contents of its fore-gut (before digestion has occurred)

or its faeces. In the arthropods, the examination of faeces is only practical where definite faecal pellets are formed, and most predaceous beetles do not appear to form these. The examination of gut contents is a more practical method in adult Adephaga where there is usually a crop to store the food before it passes through the gizzard. In predaceous adult Polyphaga, and in many larvae of both Polyphaga and Adephaga, the study of gut contents is rather frustrating since liquid and not solid remains are normally present. This reflects the method of feeding in such beetles as Staphylinidae where the more solid parts of the food are rejected and only fluid and small particles are ingested. Even in Carabidae, some species such as the mollusc feeding *Cychrus caraboides*, and often the large *Carabus* species, have fluid-filled fore-guts.

The study of crop contents has shown that not all Carabidae take animal food. The crops in species of *Harpalus*, *Bradycellus*, *Amara* and *Zabrus* usually contain plant materials such as seeds and parts of leaves and flowers. Even in the British Pterostichini, plant material is often present, and *Pterostichus melanarius* is known to have a liking for strawberries. However, such substances as pollen grains are often present as contaminants, and the plant material found may be from the gut of the prey. One question which is difficult to answer even when the insect's prey has been identified, is whether it was alive or dead when eaten. True predators are fastidious and must have their food in the freshest possible condition, but some beetles are less fussy and will eat a wide range of live or dead animals. Among the common British Carabidae, species of *Notiophilus*, *Nebria*, *Leistus* and *Loricera* seem to be rather strict predators which specialise on the mites, springtails, spiders and small flies which live at the surface of the soil.

3 One of the most ingenious methods used to link a supposed predator with a known prey is a serological one. The prey is crushed and an extract of it is made in saline solution (fig. 30). This is the antigen which is injected into a rabbit. The blood of the rabbit will react against this 'foreign' substance by producing anti-bodies, and after some days a small sample of the rabbit's blood can be extracted and stored. This is the antiserum. When this is tested against an extract of the prey species, a white precipitate is produced as the antigen and antibodies react together. Thus the antiserum is a substance which will react to minute quantities of the prey species, and the gut contents of the supposed predator can now be tested for the presence of the prey species. This is an elegant but rather complex method which requires elaborate techniques. It has been used in Canada by Fox & McLellan to study the predators of a wire-worm, and in Britain by Dempster to study predators of the broom beetle, *Phytodecta olivacea*. Since it identifies a prey species, it is obviously better suited to discovering the

various suspected predators of a prey species rather than to identifying the different food species of a single predator.

B. THE RANGE OF PREDATORS

There are just over two dozen families of beetles which are thought to be mainly predaceous, but many more families contain some predaceous species. Only the more important families will be mentioned here.

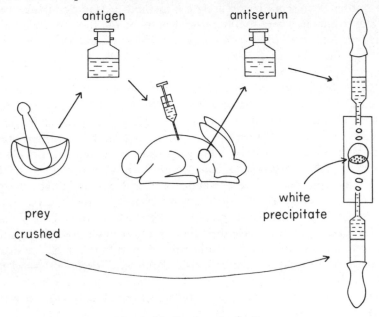

Figure 30. *Predaceous feeding*
A summary of the serological method of identifying the food of a predator (see text).

Caraboidea

Carabidae: The ground beetles are much the largest family in the Adephaga. Both adults and larvae are predators or scavengers, although a few groups (e.g. Harpalini and Amarini) are at least partly vegetarian. Ground beetles usually hunt for food in soil or leaf litter, and run rapidly over the ground, but they may climb flowers or trees to search for prey. Common nocturnal species usually hide by day in litter or under stones and logs.

Cicindelidae (or Carabidae–Cicindelinae): Tiger beetles could be described as 'super-Carabids' in which hunting adaptations have been taken to extremes (fig. 31). The adults run very swiftly and often fly, whereas their larvae lie in wait for prey in their tunnels (fig. 22).

Paussidae: mainly small, specialised beetles which live in ants' nests.

100

Dytiscidae: The largest family of carnivorous water beetles. It includes such 'water tigers' as the large and ferocious species of *Dytiscus* which will attack tadpoles and small fish. The larvae have long, sickle shaped jaws and are equally fierce. The most primitive water beetles are found in the little families Hygrobiidae and Amphizoidae.

Gyrinidae, the whirligig beetles, include the most highly modified aquatic Caraboids. They skate and spin very rapidly on the water surface by means of paddle-like middle and back legs. Their food consists of living or dead insects caught on the water surface.

Staphylinoidea

Staphylinidae: rove beetles. A very large family which contains many agile predator/scavengers. The largest species, such as the devil's coach-horse, *Staphylinus olens*, are fierce predators with huge jaws. Many species have similar habits and habitats to the Carabidae; however, the Staphylinidae probably includes more very small predators and scavengers.

Silphidae: many carrion beetles, which often feed on fly larvae, and several snail and slug eaters.

Some of the smaller beetles, particularly the Scydmaenidae and Pselaphidae, feed on minute animals such as mites.

Hydrophiloidea

Hydrophilidae: vegetarian water beetles. However, the larvae are usually predaceous. *Hydrophilus piceus* is probably the heaviest British beetle, and its larva feeds on common pond animals, especially water snails.

Histeroidea

Histeridae: both round, shiny black beetles associated with carrion (apparently maggot eaters), and bark beetle predators.

Cantharoidea

Most of the families in this group are probably predaceous. They have the 'malacoderm' appearance of a rather soft integument and loosely fitting wing cases. The Cantharidae includes the reddish soldier beetles (*Rhagonycha*) and the blue-black sailor beetles (*Cantharis*) which are often seen on flowers. Their predaceous larvae live in soil and litter.

The larvae of both the Lampyridae (glow-worms and fire-beetles) and Drilidae are also voracious predators, but they have specialised entirely on snails.

Cleroidea

This is also a group of families with predominantly carnivorous larvae. Cleridae are the 'chequered beetles' – mainly woodland species which are sometimes seen running on tree trunks. Adult Clerids often eat adult bark beetles whilst the larvae feed on immature bark beetles in their galleries. Clerid species are frequently specialised to hunt a particular prey species.

Cucujoidea

Coccinellidae: Because of their distinctive warning coloration, the ladybirds or ladybugs are the best known predaceous Cucujoids. Both adults and larvae feed upon aphids and scale insects (with the exception of a few herbivores such as *Epilachna*). Some of the common ladybirds may consume several hundred aphids during their lifetimes, but larvae of the biggest – such as the Chinese *Coria dilatata* – can eat up to 500 aphids each day.

Many other Cucujoid families have a number of predators, for instance, the Phalacridae and Nitidulidae with several scale and aphid eaters. Another set of families includes bark beetle predators, e.g. the Cucujidae, Passandridae and Colydiidae.

Other superfamilies

A few predators occur in families which are thought of as primarily herbivorous. For instance, many Elaterid larvae are carnivorous – particuularly those wire-worms that live in rotten wood. The Scarabaeoidea are almost exclusively herbivores or scavengers, but some species of *Trox* are know to eat locust eggs, and the Brazilian *Canthon virens* kills ants. There is also a South American weevil, *Ladovix fasciatus*, which eats locust eggs. One of the strangest examples of predation is that of the Cerambycid *Elytroleptus* which attacks distasteful Lycidae; this odd case will be discussed in Chapter 5.

C. DIFFERENT WAYS OF CAPTURING PREY

Like primitive man, predatory beetles either hunt or trap their prey. The Carabid is typically an active hunting beetle with long, thin legs, fairly large eyes and slender antennae. Similarly, many Staphylinids are agile hunters which are able to twist and turn rapidly through the leaf litter and soil in pursuit of prey. In both cases, the beetle may have to get very close to its prey in order to sense it. It may first react to a small moving object by rushing at it with open jaws when the animal makes a close approach. Its eyes probably convey little except that the object is small and moving – information on edibility has to wait until the outstretched antennae make contact. It then reacts by seizing the prey with its sharp, strong mandibles.

Tiger beetles are one of the best examples of active hunters. Species of the British *Cicindela* usually hunt over sandy ground, or bushy heath country with many open spaces. They use their huge eyes to hunt by sight, and the antennae are placed on the forehead rather than behind the jaws as in most Carabidae (fig. 31). The antennae may be of more importance in sensing the slipstream in flight than in sensing prey. To capture its prey the tiger

102

beetle often needs to make a dash across the last few inches, and can cover this sort of distance at speeds of up to 600 mm (2 feet) per second (approximately 1⅓ m.p.h.). Thus at top speed, a prey distance of 3 inches could be crossed in ⅛ second. Tiger beetles can probably run faster than all other land beetles, and are one of the fastest groups in the whole of the arthropoda. However, their speed can be matched on the water surface by the whirligig beetles which can move at up to 1000 mm (3⅓ feet) per second in very short bursts. Of course, running speeds of less than 2 m.p.h. seem small in human terms, but they must be judged against the small body size of these beetles. In these terms, a ½-inch long *Cicindela* moving at 2 feet per second is the equivalent of an 8-foot racehorse travelling at about 250 m.p.h.

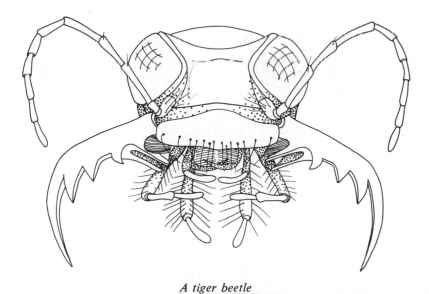

A tiger beetle

Figure 31. A 'prey's eye view' of the head of *Cicindela hybrida*.

Not all hunting beetles move rapidly, in fact many are quite slow moving, as their agility and speed often reflect those of their prey. (However, a beetle may have other good reasons for speed – escape reactions, for instance.) Silphids which feed upon fly larvae in carrion or upon snails and slugs do not need a rapid turn of speed to run down their prey. Ladybirds are slow-moving beetles because their prey consists of almost stationary aphids or sedentary scale insects, and they themselves are protected by distastefulness associated with their colour patterns.

The simplest form of hunting pattern would be a series of random movements on the part of the predator, which would thus encounter its prey by

103

chance. Laboratory experiments upon ladybird larvae have sometimes demonstrated this type of behaviour, but closer study has shown it to be more complex. The larva may make a series of random turns, but at each turn it swings from side to side before moving off in a new direction, thus increasing its search area. If aphids are encountered, the larva makes more turning movements, and this tends to keep it in a small area where there may be further prey. The larva of the ten-spot ladybird, *Adalia decempunctata*, has been shown by Dixon to move towards light and against gravity, i.e. upwards. Where the larva is feeding upon nettle aphids, its reactions send it up the nettle to the leaves, where it tends to follow the

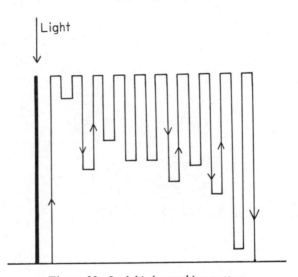

Figure 32. *Ladybird searching pattern*
The track of a fairly hungry, recently moulted fourth instar larva of a ten-spot ladybird (*Adalia decempunctata*) on a narrow, wooden pole. The latter is about the width of a plant stem (18 inches × ⅛ inch). (After Dixon.)

veins and the leaf edges. This behaviour automatically puts the larva into the places where it is most likely to encounter aphids. However, if there are no aphids on the nettle, this behaviour would trap it at the tip of the stem. In fact, on reaching the tip the larva makes short excursions down the stem and then up to the tip again. As it becomes more and more hungry, the length of these excursions increases until it eventually arrives at ground level again, where it may wander off to another nettle stem (fig. 32).

The special patterns of hunting have been studied in very few beetles, but the various times and places at which different species hunt are better known.

The most easily observed species are those that hunt by day in open places. We have noted that the British species of tiger beetles run and fly in open, sandy places; they are especially active on hot sunny days. Small Carabids, particularly species of *Elaphrus*, *Bembidion* and *Agonum*, can often be seen hunting in a rather similar way over the sandy or muddy banks of streams and rivers.

In woods, the big-eyed, bronze *Notiophilus biguttatus* is a common small Carabid which hunts over the litter for small arthropods. *Nebria brevicollis* eats much the same food, but hunts it at night rather than by day. Most Carabids seem to be nocturnal hunters, and many other species besides *Nebria* emerge at night to range the woods or meadows. A great variety of small animals fall prey to these hunters which do not only run over the surface of the ground, but may also dig their food out of the soil (e.g. moth pupae) or climb trees to find it. It has already been noted that some ground beetles such as *N.brevicollis*, and species of *Carabus*, can be found on tree trunks at night. *Calosoma inquisitor*, and the very rare *C.sycophanta* and the Silphid *Xylodrepa quadripunctata* climb into the foliage to hunt for caterpillars and other small animals. Many of the small Carabids with truncate elytra climb both trees and tall flowers and shrubs. These slender beetles include species of *Dromius* and *Demetrias* which probably eat aphids and other tiny arthropods. Perhaps the fastest and most agile of arboreal hunting beetles are tropical Cicindelids such as *Collyris* and *Tricondyla*. These beetles are much narrower than *Cicindela*, and they stand higher on their very long legs. Their ability to race up tree trunks makes their capture exceedingly difficult. In order to prevent the Madagascan *Pogonostoma* from being lost by its ascending into the foliage, Sharp described how two entomologists would converge rapidly upon the trunk from opposite directions and then join hands by flinging their arms around it.

Just as some Carabids accept a wide range of food, so too do some of the aquatic hunters such as the Dytiscidae. Most of the larger diving beetles seem to eat whatever small animals they can capture. Not all predators will accept such a wide range of food, for some have specialised on a particular group or even a single species of prey. It has been noted that Coccinellids have a diet more or less restricted to aphids or scale insects, and that many Clerids eat only bark beetles. Snail- or slug-feeding species often have narrow heads which can be pushed into the snail shells as the snail retracts. In Britain, this is seen in the Carabid *Cychrus caraboides* and the Silphid *Phosphuga atrata*, while in America a number of Carabinae have become modified in a similar way. Lampyrids and Drilids are also snail eaters, and the larva of the glow-worm, *Lampyris noctiluca*, often climbs onto the shell of a snail to attack it from above and behind.

Some beetles are found along the edge of the sea-shore where they catch

12¹

shore animals such as small crustaceans. *Eurynebria complanata* is a large, pale Carabid with black, chequered markings which may be found under balks of timber and stones near the strand line of the high tide. It preys on its fellow lodgers, the numerous sand-hoppers. A much smaller Carabid, *Bembidion laterale*, may also be found in these situations. Green noticed that it eats some of the same food as *Eurynebria*, and copes with the relatively large sand-hoppers by having elongated mandibles with which to grasp them (fig. 33). A few Carabids live even nearer the sea, down towards the mid-tide level where they are covered by the sea at high tide. They are *Aepus* and *Aepopsis*, tiny pale beetles which probably survive in air pockets in the cracks in rocks.

The most specialised predators have concentrated upon just one or two prey species. A good example is seen in the species of the Carabid *Dyschirius* which eats species of the Staphylinid genus *Bledius*. The latter are small algal-feeding beetles which dig burrows in wet sand in which they live with their larvae and pupae. The Carabids may also be found in these burrows where they sometimes attack *Bledius* species larger than themselves. As a rule, a particular species of *Dyschirius* is only found in the burrows of one or two species of *Bledius*. There are beetle predators which are even more specialised in that they feed upon only one species or even upon one individual of their prey, but these could best be considered as parasites, and will be discussed later.

Trapping is merely a variation upon the basic hunting theme, in which the predator waits until its prey comes to it, instead of vice versa. The larvae of some Dytiscids are good swimmers, but many wait until their prey comes within reach before seizing it in their needle-sharp jaws. The larva of a tiger beetle makes elaborate preparations to receive its prey. It excavates a tunnel or pit, usually in sandy soil, and waits at the entrance until a suitable insect comes within range. The prey is snatched by a rapid flick of the larva's head, and dragged into the burrow to be consumed. Although much of the beetle larva's body is rather soft, the shield-shaped head is very hard and blocks the entrance to its hole. A pair of hooks on the dorsal side of the abdomen help to hold the larva in its pit. The type of tunnel and its position varies from species to species. In *Cicindela campestris* it is a vertical pit, but in *C.hybrida* it is usually oblique and opens onto the face of a steep bank. In *C.purpurea*, the tunnel may be nearly horizontal, whilst in the oriental genus *Collyris* it is cut into the branch of a coffee tree. A most unusual beetle-trap has been attributed to the female 'lightning-bug', *Photuris* sp. Lloyd described how this American Lampyrid uses its luminescence as a lure in order that males of several other Lampyrids, species of *Photinus*, might be attracted and then eaten.

The act of prey capture is triggered when the hunting beetle senses that its

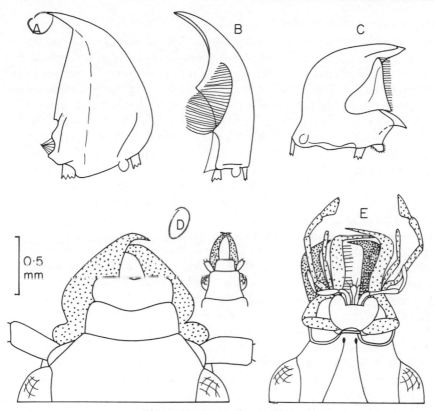

Figure 33. *Jaws of predators*
A: Left mandible of *Nebria brevicollis* (Carabidae) from below; B: Left mandible of *Philonthus decorus* (Staphylinidae) from below; C: Right mandible of *Coccinella septempunctata* (Coccinellidae) from below; D: Views from above of the anterior ends of two Carabid heads to show the mandibles (stippled); *left: Eurynebria complanata; right: Bembidion laterale*; E: Mouthparts of *Drypta dentata* seen from below. (Scale only applies to D, which is after Green.)

food is not only near, but close enough to be seized. In most cases, the senses involved are those of touch, and smell or taste. A nocturnal Carabid or a ladybird may have to 'blunder' into its prey before this is recognised. Sight is sometimes important, but in *Dytiscus* a chemical stimulus from the water around is also necessary. For instance, its hunting behaviour is evoked if a dilute extract of meat is added to the water. In both adults and larvae of *Cicindela* sight is of prime importance. The adult with its huge compound eyes can react to prey at a distance of five or six inches. Even the larva, which has complex ocelli, detects prey up to about two inches away, and is ready to seize it as it passes the entrance of its burrow.

107

D. DIFFERENT WAYS OF FEEDING

Mouthpart structure in predaceous beetles depends partly upon the way in which the prey is secured, and partly upon the way it is dismembered and swallowed. In almost all beetles, the prey is first seized by the incisor points of the mandibles. These points are long and sharp in many Carabidae and Staphylinidae (fig. 33) and may overlap at the tips. In tiger beetles, there are often three incisor points (fig. 31) and the enormous jaws have a large overlap. Large jaws are unnecessary in beetles such as aphid-eating ladybirds or mite-eating Scydmaenidae, as the prey is either soft or not very active. The jaws in these beetles are sharp but relatively small. Jaw size is often fairly closely related to the size of the prey. This was noticed earlier in comparing two sea-shore predators of sand-hoppers, the large *Eurynebria* and the small *Bembidion*; the larger beetle has normal jaws but the smaller beetle has very long jaws in order to grasp its relatively large prey (fig. 33). Beetles that hunt snails and slugs have food which is semi-liquid and difficult to scoop up. In both *Cychrus caraboides* and *Phosphuga atrata* the long mandibles are heavily fringed with hairs which help to brush in the fluid food.

The prey is not always seized by the mandibles, for in a few beetles either the maxillae or labium is used. In the small, slender Carabids of the genus *Drypta*, the maxillae are even longer than the long mandibles, and end in sharp, incurved hooks (fig. 33); this appears to be an adaptation for impaling prey. The small Staphylinid *Stenus* uses its huge eyes to stalk prey such as springtails. When close enough, the front of the labium is rapidly extended and the prey is grasped by the labial palps. This is a remarkably similar process to that used by the nymphs of dragonflies.

Once the food has been secured by the mouthparts, there are still three main ways of dealing with it. The most obvious way is to cut it up and swallow it, but an alternative method is to crush out the fluid and swallow this alone. Thirdly, the food can be converted to fluid by regurgitating midgut enzymes to digest it pre-orally. Some examples of these methods will be given.

1 *Prey dismembered and immediately swallowed.* E.g. many adult Carabidae and Dytiscidae. The food is cut into pieces by the scissor-like action of the mandibles and raked back into the mouth by the inner lobes (laciniae) of the maxillae, as in *Nebria brevicollis* (fig. 34).

2 *Prey crushed to extract fluid; partial external digestion by midgut juices.* E.g. a few adult Adephaga; probably many adult Staphylinidae and perhaps other Polyphaga. This method is clearly seen in the Staphylinid *Philonthus decorus* (fig. 34). Here, the mouthparts exclude solid food from the mouth. It emerges like a string of sausages through a notch in the labrum (fig. 35) before dropping forwards to be rechewed and recirculated. Fluids and the

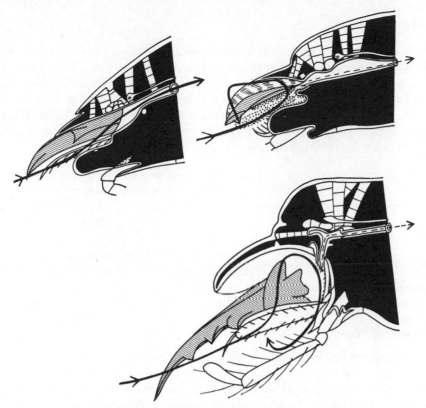

Figure 34. *Predatory feeding mechanisms*
Vertical sections through the heads of *Nebria brevicollis* (*top left*), *Philonthus decorus* (*top right*) and *Cicindela hybrida* (*bottom*) to show the paths by which food is swallowed. Solid lines (arrowed) show the pathways of solid food, and broken lines (arrowed) show the pathways of liquid food and very small particles. (From Evans, 1965.)

Figure 35. *Philonthus feeding method*
A side view of the head of *Philonthus decorus* to show the feeding method. (From Evans, 1964.)

finest particles are sucked out of the food mass, which becomes drier and drier until only a few crumbs remain. The adult tiger beetles have evolved a remarkable parallel to this. In *Cicindela hybrida* (fig. 34), the labrum has a smooth dome on its underside which helps to re-circulate the food mass whilst partly pre-digested food is sucked out. However, the rotation of the food in this crushing mill is backwards (along the labrum and down past the mouth), the opposite direction to that in *P.decorus*.

3 *Prey partly crushed, but external digestion of major importance*. E.g. many predaceous larvae, especially Carabidae, Dytiscidae, Staphylinidae and Cantharidae. These larvae usually have large mandibles to crush the prey but the other mouthparts are relatively reduced, and digestive juices are regurgitated. In *Dytiscus* and *Lampyris* larvae, even crushing is unnecessary for the sickle-shaped mandibles have channels linked to the mouth which inject midgut juices into the prey, and allow the pre-digested food to be pumped back into the gut.

3. Parasitic Beetles

A parasite is an animal that is given food and shelter by its host. It is usually the host's body that provides this, often to the detriment of the host. Fleas and flukes are typical parasites, and their existence at the expense of their hosts can be contrasted with commensalism, a relationship in which animals merely live together and 'feed at the same table'. A number of beetles show what seems to be the early stages of parasitism, where it is difficult to distinguish it from commensalism. In Britain, the little blind beetle *Leptinus testaceus* (Leptinidae) is an example of this. It has been found either on the fur or in the nests of mice and voles, and also in bumble bees' and ants' nests. It is likely that the beetle is a commensal which scavenges for food in the rodents' nest rather than an external parasite (ectoparasite). A similar tropical example is that of *Glaphyrocanthon* (Scarabaeidae), several species of which have been found in monkey fur near the anus. This is a dung beetle and its presence on the monkey is probably only occasional.

Leptinus might be regarded as a parasite if parasites of the home and food are included. Several beetles fit into this category. Some dung beetles steal the carefully prepared food of other dung beetles. *Aphodius procus* goes further. It enters the egg cavity of *Geotrupes stercorarius*, destroys the *Geotrupes* egg and then lays its own egg in the dung mass provided by *Geotrupes*. Similarly, the weevil *Lasiorrhynchites sericeus* takes over the leaf roll constructed by *Attelabus nitens*. Many Staphylinoid beetles live in ants' nests as welcome or unwelcome guests. Some are fed by the ants, others are tolerated but ignored, and some actually prey upon the ants or their larvae.

Although *Leptinus* and *Glaphyrocanthon* may be commensals, they both have relatives which could be considered as ectoparasites. In the Leptinidae, *Platypsyllus castoris* (fig. 36) is a parasite of the beaver which occurs in North America and Europe, and *Silphopsyllus desmanae* lives upon the desman of central Asia. *Platypsyllus* is better adapted to parasitism than *Leptinus*, and all stages of its life history may occur on the host. *Platypsyllus* and *Silphopsyllus* may be found over the entire bodies of their hosts, where they probably eat scraps of skin or hair, or even feed on other ectoparasites such as lice. About a dozen species of Staphylinidae are known to occur on South American rodents, where they are often found in the anal region. Some Scarabaeidae, like *Glaphyrocanthon*, are also found in that region of the host

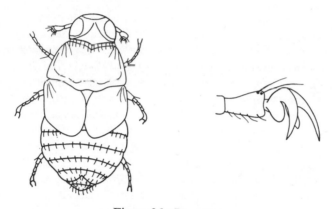

Figure 36. *Parasites*
Left: *Platypsyllus castoris* (Leptinidae), view from above. (After Jeannel in Grassé);
right: claw of *Macropocopris symbiotica* (Scarabaeidae). (After Paulian.)

body. For instance, *Trichillium bradyporum* is found there although *Uroxys gorgon* is usually found in the neck region. Several of these Scarabaeids are known from Australian mammals. Species of *Macropocopris*, which live on the kangaroo and bandicoot, have enlarged claws which are split to the base to enable them to cling tightly to the host's fur (fig. 36). The larvae of these ectoparasites are not parasitic, but live in normal Scarabaeid habitats such as dung or in the soil. The Scarabaeid *Zonocopris* (= *Plesiocanthon*) *gibbicollis* has an unusual habit; it lives in the shells of the large Brazilian snail *Bulimus*. These beetles are probably commensals as they appear to feed on mucus and faecal material. Up to a dozen beetles have been found on a single snail.

Whereas beetles parasitic on mammals have probably evolved from nest dwellers, beetles parasitic on other insects have presumably evolved from predators. This second group of parasites includes both ectoparasites and endoparasites, which develop inside other animals. An approach to this

111

second type of parasitism is shown by some specialised predators such as some species of beetle larvae which feed on scale insects. One of these is the Vedalia beetle *Rodolia cardinalis*, a ladybird which feeds on citrus scale insects. A single scale insect, or its egg mass, is sufficient food to allow for the growth and development of this beetle. The Anthribidae show a similar example in the case of *Brachytarsus* species in which the beetle's life cycle closely follows that of its prey (or host). After the female beetle has broken into the hard covering of the scale to feed, she lays her egg in the egg chamber of the scale insect, and then feeds upon its body contents. Even in large scale insects, only a single beetle develops. This type of feeding resembles that found in insect 'parasitoids' – such as parasitic wasps – which always kill their host before emerging.

In the more specialised of these predator/parasites (or parasitoids), the life cycle has been modified to include several different types of larva (hypermetamorphosis, see Chapter 3). The first instar is a very active, free-living triungulin which is succeeded by a sedentary, grub-like larva. This is normally a predator or an external parasite. Both the two largest families of predators, the Carabidae and Staphylinidae, have species which show this type of life cycle. In the Carabidae, species of *Lebia* and *Brachinus* are known to attack the pupae of some other beetles. The young larva of *L.scapularis* searches for the pupae of the elm leaf beetle, *Galerucella luteola*, in the soil. On finding one, the *Lebia* larva punctures the pupal skin and inserts its head to feed. The active young larva then moults and is succeeded by a grub-like larva which continues feeding on the pupa. The young larvae of the Staphylinid genus *Aleochara* and its relatives attack the pupae of flies (Diptera). These are also found in the soil, but they are enclosed in a hardened skin, the puparium, which the beetle larva must puncture to enter. Once in, however, the fly pupa is easily punctured and the beetle larva feeds on the exuding body fluids. As in *Lebia*, the second and third instars of *Aleochara* are grub-like larvae which feed externally upon their hosts. In the case of *Lebia*, the beetle is protected by its host's pupal cell, and in *Aleochara*, by the puparium. The *Aleochara* larva seals its entrance hole in the puparium with an anal secretion which not only prevents infection and desiccation, but also excludes other beetle larvae. Thus only one beetle develops in a puparium.

The largest beetle family with hypermetamorphic development is the Meloidae, including oil beetles and blister beetles. The adults are plant feeders, but the larvae attack two main groups of insects, locusts and solitary bees. In locusts, large batches of eggs are laid in an egg pod, which is buried in the soil, and the triungulins of *Epicauta* and *Zonabris* species take advantage of this. Their later grub-like larval stages (fig. 24) develop at the expense of the locust eggs, which provide the whole of the larval food supply. In the other group of Meloids, including *Meloe* and several other genera, the host egg or larva is an incidental food, merely an 'appetiser'. The triungulins of these beetles attack the nests of solitary bees such as species of *Andrena*. On entry to the nest, the beetle larva first consumes the bee's egg before moulting to form the sluggish second instar larva. This and later stages all subsist on the honey store provided by the bee. Thus *Meloe* larvae are firstly predators and then unwelcome guests, or nest parasites.

True endoparasites are found in the related family Rhipiphoridae, where as far as is known, all the species have larvae which spend at least part of their life inside the host's body. The British *Metoecus paradoxus* parasitises the larva of common wasps. The first stage larva of the beetle penetrates the skin of the wasp larva, and then enters it, where it becomes greatly swollen. The second instar larva is found as an external parasite encircling the neck

Figure 37. *Parasite*
Second instar larva of *Macrosaigon flabellatum* (Rhipiphoridae) in feeding position encircling host larva, *Rhynchium oculatum*. (After Grandi.)

of its host as in *Macrosaigon flabellatum* (fig. 37). *Macrosaigon cucullatum* is interesting because it parasitises a species of the Australian wasp *Campsomeris* which is itself an external parasite of larval Scarabaeidae. The wasp paralyses the soil-living Scarabaeid grub and lays her egg on it. If a triungulin arrives at this stage, it must wait upon the wasp's egg until its larva emerges and then wait until this has nearly finished its growth, for the beetle larva parasitises the mature wasp larva in its cocoon; it will probably not enter the wasp larva until it is at least partly grown. The most completely endoparasitic species are found in the genus *Rhipidius* which attacks cockroaches. The triungulin enters the body of either young or adult cockroaches, and then undergoes its whole development inside the host's body, although it emerges to pupate. In some species the adult female is also endoparasitic and the free male has reduced elytra.

113

This is a remarkable parallel to the most highly modified beetle parasites, the Stylopoidea (which used to be considered as a separate order, the Strepsiptera). This group contains two families of stylops (following Crowson's classification) which parasitise a range of insects, particularly leaf hoppers (Hemiptera–Homoptera) and bees and wasps. The eggs hatch to give triungulin-like larvae which enter their hosts to become endoparasitic larvae. Both the succeeding larval and pupal stages live inside the host's body. The parasite feeds upon the blood and fat body and does not usually kill its host, although the growth of some host organs may be affected by malnutrition. In a few primitive stylops both the adult males and females are free-living, but in most species the female is larva-like (fig. 38) and only protrudes her

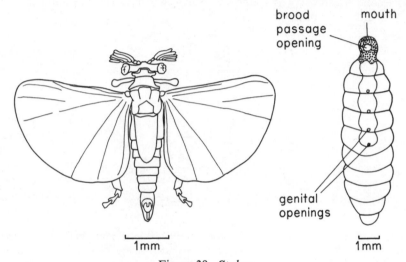

brood passage opening

mouth

genital openings

1mm

1mm

Figure 38. *Stylops*
Male (*left*) and female (*right*) stylops. The male is seen from above, and the female from below. (*Halictophagus* sp., after Ewin.)

front end through the body of the host. The free-living male has well developed sense organs and wings (fig. 38); its elytra are reduced to small club-like structures and the mouthparts are also poorly developed. Presumably, elytra and functional mouthparts are unnecessary for its very brief life span. The stylops does not usually kill its host, and is thus a true endoparasite rather than a parasitoid. However, various parts of the host body are altered in form, and the affected host is said to be 'stylopised'.

An interesting question arises at this point. Considering the huge number of beetles, why are so few species parasitic? This cannot be answered satisfactorily, but a partial explanation can be made in terms of beetle structure and evolution. The major groups of parasitic insects are the parasitic wasps and flies, which are far more agile and accomplished fliers than beetles. This has enabled them to find victims easily, and then to lay their eggs on or near their hosts. Secondly, female wasps and some flies usually have a highly specialised needle-shaped ovipositor which can inject eggs precisely into or on to the host. As beetles have a crude ovipositor, consisting of the extended back end of the abdomen, then when hard material needs to be pierced for egg-laying, this is usually cut by the jaws, as in many weevils. Thus beetle parasites, particularly the parasitoids, have to use the rather wasteful method of reaching the host by means of an especially active first stage larva.

Another kind of explanation can be derived from the evolutionary history of beetles. Beetles evolved 280 million years ago in the Permian period, and rapidly expanded in the succeeding Triassic and Jurassic periods. Both the higher Diptera (flies) and the parasitic wasps expanded much later than this, probably not before the beginning of the Tertiary epoch only 70 million years ago. Thus there may have been plenty of 'ordinary jobs' available for beetles during their most rapid expansion, and it would not have been necessary for many to have become specialised parasites in order to survive. In contrast, although the later flies and wasps had less choice of 'ordinary jobs, a wider range of hosts for potential parasites would have then been available. Of course, the lack of a specialised ovipositor in beetles may merely reflect their lesser involvement in parasitic ways of life.

Unfortunately, it is impossible to guess whether beetles would have ever developed such an ovipositor even if a wide range of potential hosts had been available to them at the crucial evolutionary stage. It may have been that from a structural viewpoint beetles had a long way to go to evolve a successful parasitic group. Those beetles which evolved along this pathway would become very highly modified and almost unrecognisable as beetles – like, for instance, the Stylopoidea.

4. Scavengers

Scavengers are animals that feed upon dead and decaying plant and animal materials. Since all living things die, there is obviously an abundant food source available for animals (and plants such as fungi) that are able to live on decomposing food. Ecologically, scavengers play a most important role in their communities since by consuming and breaking up decaying materials, they help to return organic substances more rapidly to the soil where they can be used again. There are a great many sources of rotting food in almost all habitats, but the carpet of shed leaves forming the leaf litter of woods is probably the greatest single source on land. This is gradually broken down into the soil by many small animals, mainly millipedes, woodlice, springtails, mites, fly larvae and earthworms. Most of the soil beetles are either predators, root feeders or fungus feeders, although there are a few herbivorous scavengers. These include the small, round beetles belonging to the Sphaeridiinae. The larvae of these beetles are predaceous, like their aquatic relatives in the Hydrophilinae. Adult Hydrophilids are sometimes called scavenging water beetles, for they mainly eat decaying vegetation in ponds and streams. The largest of these beetles in Britain is the great silver water beetle, *Hydrophilus piceus*, which at two inches long may not be the longest, but is probably the heaviest British beetle.

Other dead vegetation includes logs and tree-stumps, rotting fruit and nuts, fallen flowers and occasional accumulations such as flood rubbish and piles of grass cuttings. All these habitats have their own scavenging communities. The two main animal sources are dung and carrion. Most dung is in fact mainly vegetable in origin, since the largest accumulations of dung are from herbivorous mammals such as cows and horses. These large mammals eat huge quantities of grass, and some of this passes through the digestive system without being absorbed; in addition, there are bacteria and various digestive juices. Thus dung has a surprisingly high food value, and many beetles thrive on it. Many beetles also thrive on carrion, though the species present depend on the state of the carcase. A newly killed animal is almost fresh meat, but after a long period of decay, little except skin and bone will remain, and this will need specialist attention. Thus a carcase will be visited by a succession of different carrion feeders.

This process of decay applies to plants as well as animals, and can be seen in a dead log or a tree-stump. Wallace found that as a pine stump decays, its animal population changes. In fact, the species of animals present depend on many factors: the type of tree, its state of decay, whether it is in a wood or in the open, the amount of water in the soil, the climate and many other conditions. This continuous process of decay may be divided into three stages, based on the appearance of the stump, as follows:

1 Little different to living tree, firmly embedded in soil and cut surface light coloured.
2 Still firmly embedded, but wood starting to decay; cut surface dark, and bark starting to separate from wood.
3 Loosely embedded in ground, wood badly decayed and broken up; bark either absent or completely separated from stump.

The beetle inhabitants of the stump can also be grouped into these stages, although they tend to overlap:

1 Particularly weevils and bark beetles; some small predaceous beetles which enter the bark beetle's galleries, e.g. Staphylinids; some fungus feeders, especially Staphylinidae.

116

2 Cerambycidae and other soft-wood feeding larvae; some larger pre-daceous beetles; e.g. Staphylinidae; some fungus feeders.
3 Lucanidae larvae; some Cerambycidae larvae; many beetle predators, e.g. Carabidae, Staphylinidae, Elateridae larvae; many fungus feeding beetles.

The conditions governing the species to be found in a tree-stump also play a similar role with dung. Each patch of dung is an individual habitat with its own community of animals which depends on the age of the dung, the environmental conditions, and the time of year, etc. Landin has observed that the species of mammal forming the dung seems to be less important than the environmental conditions. For instance, *Aphodius zenkeri* prefers dung in shady places such as forests, and thus is found mainly in deer dung. *Typhaeus typhoeus*, however, digs its deep burrows in light soil, and so mainly uses sheep or rabbit droppings. The animal interrelationships are also similar to the tree-stump community. There are dung feeders, their predators and parasites, and fungus feeders to consume fungus growing on the dung.

A cowpat is a good example of a large accumulation of dung with its own specialised community. The easiest way to collect its inhabitants without sifting through the dung is to drop the cowpat into a bucket of water, stir, and out float the insects from its interior. Laurence calculated that each cowpat may contain one thousand inhabitants, and since a cow may produce over two thousand cowpats a year, its dung supports over two million insects a year. These are mainly dung-feeding fly larvae. The smell of fresh dung quickly attracts many species of flies which lay eggs on the dung. These soon produce maggots which have a rapid life cycle. Dung feeding beetles are also attracted to fresh dung (especially Sphaeridiinae and Aphodiinae); larval Aphodiinae are only found later on, and have a longer life cycle. After a day or so, the cowpat forms a crust which keeps its interior moist, and cuts off much of the smell. It then dries up rather slowly until it is a com-pletely dry 'chip'. In an intensive study of this succession, Mohr divided it into three stages as follows:

1 First 5 days: Adult *Sphaeridium* spp. and *Aphodius fimetarius* have arrived. Many dung feeding fly larvae present, which soon pupate. Beetle larvae present are predators, e.g. *Sphaeridium scarabaeoides* and various Staphylinidae. Inhabitants also attacked by parasitic wasps.
2 From 5 to 8 days: Maximum number of larvae present. Larva of a dung feeding soldier fly (Stratiomyidae) preyed on by larvae of *Sphaerid-ium bipustulatum*.
3 After 8 days: Dung feeding larvae of *Aphodius fimetarius* now present and preyed on by larvae of *Hister abbreviatus*.

117

Old dung often contains the larvae and adults of predaceous beetles (Staphylinidae, Histeridae and Carabidae) as they have a longer life cycle than the flies.

Although *Sphaeridium* larvae are predators the adults are dung feeders, as are several other species of Sphaeridiinae; for instance, many small species of *Cercyon* are common in dung. The larger dung beetles are all Scarabaeoids; in Britain, species of *Geotrupes* and *Aphodius* are particularly common. Some of the *Geotrupes* species reach about an inch in length ('dor beetles' or 'lousy watchmen' – so called because of their mites), whilst the largest species of *Aphodius* are only half this size. The larger beetles burrow through the dung regardless of the many other inhabitants. Besides consuming dung in the cowpat, species of *Geotrupes* tunnel down over a foot into the soil beneath the cowpat and take down large quantities of dung. These large dung beetles may remove so much dung overnight that the cowpat prematurely dries out.

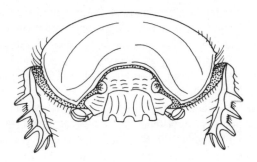

Figure 39. *Sacred beetle*
Scarabaeus sacer seen from the front.

In some dung beetles, the dung is removed in an ingenious way. In order to take as large a quantity of this desirable material as far and as quickly as possible, it is moulded into a ball and rolled away. Halffter & Matthews have shown that many of the species (especially Scarabaeini) which bury a dung ball construct a feeding burrow which is normally shallower and less elaborate than the nesting burrow for the brood ball. The best known exponent of this art is the sacred beetle of Egypt, *Scarabaeus sacer*, and the process has been amusingly described by the great French naturalist Fabre. On arriving at the fresh cowpat, the beetle plunges in by scooping and digging with its toothed head shield, and by sweeping dung aside with the toothed tibiae of its powerful front legs (fig. 39). Having made a space it now starts to collect dung and to construct a ball. Armfuls of dung are raked in by the front limbs and pulled underneath its body, between the middle and hind

118

legs. The pill thus formed beneath the abdomen is then held by the sharp claws of the long, slender hind legs and spun between them. In this way, fresh dung can be added all over the surface of the pill, which is quickly built into a ball. The surface is frequently patted down to smooth it by the front tibiae. This ball soon becomes walnut-sized and then apple-sized, indeed, it may reach the size of a man's fist. Fabre observed that this is no mean achievement for a 1½-inch-long beetle, especially when this ball will probably represent a single meal.

When the ball is completed, it is held between the back legs with the beetle head down, and only standing on its front legs. Movements of the hind legs now rotate the ball so that it moves away from the cowpat; thus the beetle, walking backwards on its front legs, trundles the ball away. If the ground is uneven, this may be a marathon journey, but although the ball

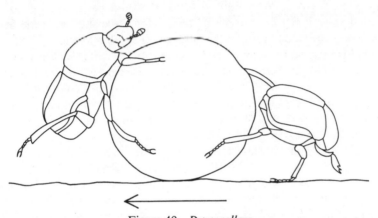

Figure 40. *Dung rollers*
Gymnopleurus geoffroyi (Scarabaeidae); male on the left, female on right. The direction of movement of the ball is shown. The female is pushing and the male clinging, although before this he had been pulling. (After Halffter & Matthews, from a photograph in Prasse.)

may often roll down hillocks, its own momentum dragging the beetle with it, ball and beetle are not usually separated for long. Quite often, a ball is found being manoeuvred by two beetles (as in the case of *Gymnopleurus* in fig. 40). Presumably the second beetle is attracted by the smell of the dung, and on arrival it helps the first beetle with its ball. One beetle, often the first, may stay in the head down position pushing the ball with its hind feet whilst the second beetle is head up and pulls the ball with its front feet. Occasionally, apparent differences of opinion may cause the ball to go round and round. The second beetle may give no assistance, but merely cling to the top of the ball and be rolled along with it. However, either

119

assisting or being taken for a ride, the true status of the self-invited 'partner' reveals itself if the first beetle loses the ball momentarily. The 'partner' then trundles the ball off on its own, leaving the first beetle to search for its meal.

The destination of the beetle and ball is a patch of shady ground or loose soil, where the beetle in possession parks the ball and digs a deep hole, which is large enough to take both itself and the ball. The entrance is closed once the beetle is inside, and it then starts to feed on its huge store. It usually goes on feeding until the whole ball has been eaten and passed through its alimentary canal, when the beetle emerges to search for more dung. While the dung lasts, feeding, digestion and defaecation are an almost continuous process. The faeces are discharged every minute, and form a long, unbroken cord. In one case, Fabre noted that after a twelve-hour meal, the faecal cord was well over three yards in length. That is, in twelve hours the beetle had digested nearly its own bulk in food. It would be interesting to know what food value is left in dung beetle faeces, for some species of the Staphylinid *Oxytelus* are said to feed on the dung of other dung beetles.

The pill-rolling Scarabaeidae belong to the Scarabaeinae and have a world-wide distribution. In Europe, the larger species belong to *Scarabaeus* and are found along the warm shores of the Mediterranean. The smallest European species are found in the genus *Sisyphus*, and are aptly named after the unfortunate founder of Corinth who was doomed continually to push a boulder up a mountain, only to have it roll down again on reaching the summit. In the United States, the dung rollers are called pill-beetles or tumble-bugs. Several large pill-rollers (over two inches long) are included in the genus *Heliocopris* which is found in both Africa and India. Some of its species are adept at dealing with the enormous piles of Elephant dung. Arrow recounts how, in India, the huge, clay-covered dung balls of *Heliocopris* (prepared for the larvae) were mistaken for old cannon balls when first dug up.

Mammals not only produce faecal material throughout their lives which provides food for flourishing insect communities, but after death their bodies provide food for another set of insects. Of course, not only mammal bodies, but all animal bodies may provide food for some insects. Predaceous beetles hunting over the surface of the soil for live prey will often take dead insects and other small arthropods. Although some Carabids nearly always take live prey, many Pterostichini and Agonini are basically scavengers and will feed on dead animals as often as live ones. This also applies to the Staphylinidae. Many of the smaller Staphylininae, Tachyporinae and Aleocharinae are as frequently scavengers as predators.

Obviously, the corpses of larger animals can support a larger and more specialised insect fauna although, as with dung, many of the beetles found in carrion are predators which feed on the fly maggots. The carrion-eating

120

beetles are mainly Silphidae and Staphylinidae which are attracted to the fresh corpse soon after the many species of flies have arrived. A fresh corpse starts to decay rapidly, and goes through a sequence of decomposition stages which each support a different insect fauna. For the first day or two, the body appears fresh but decomposition has already started. It is followed by a stage in which the flesh starts to putrify and the corpse becomes swollen with gases. It later collapses as the flesh starts turning black. After about a month the carcase is drying out although some flesh remains, and fermentation appears to be taking place. In the final stage, the carcase has almost dried out to skin and bone, and after about a year only the bones remain. In a study of carrion in Australia in which Bornemissza described these stages of decay, the beetles involved in each stage were as follows:

1 First stage: mainly bacteria, protozoa and roundworms; no beetles.
2 Putrefaction stage: the main carrion feeders eating the decaying flesh are blowfly and fleshfly maggots, mites and some Silphid beetles such as *Ptomaphila lachrymosa*. The predators of the maggots are adults and larvae of *Creophilus erythrocephalus* and *Aleochara* species (Staphylinidae), adults and larvae of the Histerid *Saprinus*, and the Silphid *P.lachrymosa*. Like many other Silphids, this species is probably both predator and carrion feeder. Little Ptiliid beetles were also found which probably fed on the mites.
3 The fermentation stage when the carcase is drying out: skin and ligament feeders predominate. They are mainly cheese fly maggots and the larvae of *Dermestes vulpinus* (Dermestidae) and *Necrobia rufipes* (Cleridae). If the carcase is still moist, larvae of *P.lachrymosa* are present. The predators of these are again Staphylinid and Histerid larvae.
4 In the last, very dry stage, the only carrion feeders left were a moth caterpillar feeding on the remains of the hair, and a large number of mites. The few small predators left were adult and larval Staphylinidae and adult Carabidae.

In Europe, the Silphid *P.lachrymosa* is replaced by the larger European Silphids, including species of *Necrophorus*. Again, in the last stages of decay, species of the carrion feeding Scarabaeoid *Trox* are often present (although it must be pointed out that *Trox* is also present in other habitats in Australia). In South America, Halffter & Matthews have observed that the Scarabaeinae replace the Silphidae as the main carrion feeding beetles. This is true of the tropical forest regions, where there are few large herbivores to leave dung. A number of Dermestidae are common in these final stages of decay. As well as *Dermestes*, the larvae of *Attagenus*, *Anthrenus* and many other genera feed on skin, tendons, hair and feathers. The last two genera are found especially in warehouses and other buildings where furs or skins are

121

stored. Museums are great storehouses of the dried out carcases of both vertebrates and insects, and Dermestids (especially species of *Anthrenus*) will attack many of these valuable specimens if allowed to do so.

Where *Necrophorus* species are present, the succession of species on the carcase may be halted due to its expropriation by these beetles. Burying beetles appear to feed on both the carrion and its maggot inhabitants (when they are present), but the whole carcase is buried and specially prepared by a pair of *Necrophorus* for their larvae. (The beginnings of parental care shown by *Necrophorus* have been described in Chapter 3.)

CHAPTER 5

Habits and Habitats

Any small animal must have some means of protection in order to carry out everyday activities such as looking for food or a mate.

How do beetles protect themselves from their enemies and from hostile environments?

All beetles are of the same basic physiological type, but they have an enormous variety of protective habits. These can be summarised as follows:

1 *Protection from enemies*
   A *By moving out of harm's way* – i.e. by actively escaping;
   B *By staying put and using protective habits*:
      (a) *Concealment* – by hiding, camouflage, etc;
      (b) *Defence* – with mechanical or chemical weapons, and by advertising
             these with warning coloration;
      (c) *Mimicry* – of the species with warning coloration.

2 *Protection from hostile environments*
   There are many examples which could be mentioned here, but *water* is particularly important, i.e;
   A *Too much water* – aquatic adaptations;
   B *Too little water* – how do desert beetles survive?

1. Protection from Enemies

A. MOVING OUT OF HARM'S WAY

Beetles differ a great deal in their ways of moving and the habitats in which they move. Locomotion is often the primary means of avoiding enemies or uncomfortable weather, as well as being necessary in the search for food or a mate. The Coleopterist is well aware of the effectiveness of rapid running for the beetle's escape when he is searching for them by turning over stones.

The Carabidae or Staphylinidae uncovered may first 'freeze' into immobility, but they soon make a run for it, and are often very difficult to catch. This is particularly obvious with tiger beetles running over sand dunes in the sun. They cannot out-run a reasonably active Coleopterist, but their erratic stops and starts, and changes of direction are very effective in evading him, and when capture is imminent, they merely open their wings and fly off. Flight is also a common method of escape in many plant beetles which are not otherwise very agile.

In beetles that are fast runners, the legs must be moved very rapidly, and they are usually long and slender to produce a long stride. This is most noticeable in tiger beetles and ground beetles, where the thorax is normally compact and the legs have a simple, fixed swing. The front coxa, occasionally the middle coxa, and the hind coxa (as in all beetles) have a lower (sternal) pivot as well as the upper (pleural) one, and this provides a strong articulation for the leg. In Staphylinidae, however, the rapid runners may have relatively shorter legs, and here agility in turning and twisting through cracks in the soil may be more important than sheer speed and obtrusively long legs. An unusual feature of these beetles is that the long front coxa of the larger species can swing about its single, dorsal pivot, and this may increase the stride of the leg and so increase speed. The basal leg muscles of fast-running beetles are attached very near the coxal pivot. This is clearly seen in species of *Cicindela*. It enables a small movement of the muscle to produce a large, rapid movement of the leg. This means that it operates at a low mechanical advantage, but a powerful movement is not necessary if only the beetle's own body weight is to be moved.

In burrowing and boring beetles, the opposite modification is found. Here, it is necessary for a large force to be applied rather slowly; this is seen in many Scarabaeoidea. In dung beetles such as *Geotrupes*, the muscles producing the powerful backstroke of the front leg are attached to the coxa some way from the pivot, and have a high mechanical advantage, and thus a considerable leverage, These large muscles are attached to much of the undersurface of the pronotum. The front coxa itself is also specialised in a way that seems to be correllated with digging efficiency. The coxal articulation has been moved far dorsally, until it has reached the underside of the pronotum. This has enabled a very strong pivot to be formed, and has also allowed a large, elongated coxa containing powerful leg muscles to be evolved without protruding so far downwards as to obstruct digging.

The method of excavation in many dung beetles with the compact build of *Geotrupes* and *Scarabaeus* is to push forwards with the hind legs and upwards with the front legs, and to sweep 'armfuls' of dung or soil backwards and sideways with a 'breast stroke' performed by the front legs. The tibiae do most of the sweeping, and they are flattened and toothed to give them a

124

larger surface area. The front tarsi have little to do and are often small compared to those of chafers, in fact, in *Scarabaeus* they have completely disappeared. The front legs are aided to some extent by the large jaws in Geotrupidae. In Scarabaeidae, where the specialised mandibles are flimsy and flattened, the front of the head is often toothed or scooped out dorsally, and is used as a shovel (fig. 39). Many of the smaller Scarabaeids such as *Aphodius* can bulldoze their way directly through dung and loose soil.

Similar, but less obvious modifications occur in many other burrowing beetles, and are found in a wide range of families. These beetles lack the Scarabaeoid type of front coxa, but often have broadened or strongly toothed front tibiae. The powerful burying beetles (*Necrophorus*) are good examples, as are many Tenebrionidae. In Britain, species with flattened tibiae such as *Melanimon tibiale* and *Phylan gibbus* are commonly found on heathlands or near sandy shores; many larger Tenebrionids with digging habits are found in deserts and arid regions. In the little mud-tunnelling species of *Heterocerus* the tibiae are clearly flattened and toothed, but many small burrowing beetles are not so obviously adapted. The Staphylinid genus *Bledius* has strongly toothed forelegs, but in *Oxytelus* the teeth are sometimes no more than small spines, although the beetles are efficient burrowers. Many larvae dig tunnels before pupation, and true soil inhabitants such as wire-worms spend their lives tunnelling through soil. Cicindelid larvae dig burrows in which to conceal themselves whilst awaiting their prey. Some adult Carabids also dig burrows for themselves, for instance, the many large species of *Scarites* do this in warmer parts of the world, whilst their relations in Britain are the two small species of *Clivina*, and the tiny species of *Dyschirius*. These genera are obviously 'waisted' and this presumably gives the body some flexibility within its tunnel.

Turning within a tunnel always presents difficulties, particularly if the medium is hard, like wood. This almost always requires the use of the jaws to bore the tunnel. Some beetles (e.g. *Sinodendron*) may make parts of the tunnel wide enough to turn in, but other beetles, particularly bark beetles, cannot turn within their tunnels. Larsen noted that *Ips* actually has a special muscle at the base of its hind legs to enable it to push backwards more easily in its borings.

Boring, which requires the use of the jaws, can be distinguished in most cases from burrowing, in which the legs are of major importance, although the two categories overlap to some extent. Many timber-boring larvae lack legs completely (see Chapter 4), but the best burrowers have them well developed. The most highly modified burrowing beetle is the South American Cerambycid *Hypocephalus armatus*, the 'mole beetle'. It bears little resemblence to a normal timber beetle, but looks remarkably like the mole-cricket, *Gryllotalpa* (which looks remarkably like a mole). The huge hind legs and

125

cylindrical prothorax enable it to tunnel efficiently in sandy soil and decayed wood; however, it is restricted to small areas in the south of Brazil.

Boring into wood or burrowing down into the soil are clearly very useful means of moving out of harm's way, but another way of escaping unwanted attention and of discovering food is to do just the opposite, and climb up-wards. Most of these climbing beetles are herbivorous, although a few predators also ascend in search of prey. For such beetles, i.e. beetles that can walk up vertical or nearly vertical surfaces, the important part of the leg is the tarsus, which has to hold the beetle onto its substratum. *Dascillus cervinus* may often be found on flower heads or the foliage of plants such as

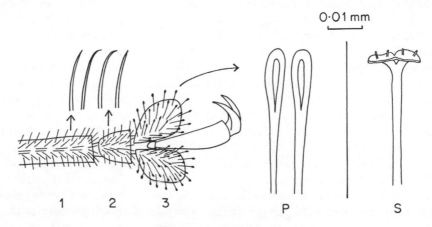

Figure 41. *Tarsal hairs*

On the left is a diagram of the hind tarsus of a weevil or a leaf beetle as seen from below. The approximate arrangement of the tarsal hairs is shown on the first three segments. On segments one and two, the hairs are sharply pointed. Segment three has a pair of hair pads which carry hairs with more specialised tips. Two examples of these are shown on the right at high magnification. P – *Phyllobius argentatus* (Curculionidae); S – *Sermyla halensis* (Chrysomelidae).)

bracken, and an examination of the underside of its tarsi shows a series of pads of hairs on each tarsal segment. The largest families of beetles that walk up and down leaves and stems are the Curculionidae, the Chrysomelidae and the Cerambycidae. All have apparently four-segmented tarsi (due to the greatly reduced fourth segment) which bear pads of hairs on their under-surfaces. The third segment is usually strongly bilobed, and carries large hair pads. If the tarsal hairs of a weevil or leaf beetle are examined micro-scopically, it can be seen that in some species the hairs are fine and pointed on all segments except the bilobed pads; here, the tips of the hairs are broadened and flattened, and specialised in various ways (fig. 41). It is possible that these hairs hold on to a surface in a similar way to the hairs on the foot of a house-fly or on the adhesive pads of the bug *Rhodnius*. Wigglesworth explained that on a flat surface, the lubricated hair tips can be slid forwards, but if pulled backwards the tips (which are cut across obliquely) are pulled into very close contact with the surface, and adhere. Wigglesworth thought that an oily secretion from the hair base was necessary; however, Edwards & Tarkanian have recently suggested that the *Rhodnius* hair pad works in the same way as the gekko's. If so, no secretion would be necessary, but fluid already present on the surface would add its meniscus force to the frictional force due to adhesion. Very smooth surfaces are uncommon in nature, however, and it is likely that the brushes of thin hairs on the tarsi will provide purchase against the minute irregularities found on the surfaces of leaves and stems, and in this way help the beetle to climb. Some strongly flying, herbivorous beetles such as chafers lack these hair pads on the tarsi. Chafers usually have long, strong tarsi with large claws which enable them to cling easily to the foliage to which they have flown.

Several groups of predaceous beetles climb up vegetation in search of prey and these include ladybirds and checkered beetles (Cleridae). It was noted in Chapter 4 that some night-active Carabids, which range the soil surface of woodlands in search of food, treat trees as an extension of the woodland floor, and may be found climbing tree-trunks. They include common ground beetles such as *Carabus violaceus* and *C.problematicus*, *Agonum assimile* and *Nebria brevicollis*. A few large Carabids such as *Calosoma inquisitor* spend much of their time in trees, but most of the 'arboreal' Carabids in Britain are small, slender species of *Dromius* and *Demetrius* which ascend both trees and herbage in search of small prey such as aphids. The larger Carabids show few obvious modifications for climbing, but in *Dromius* and *Demetrius* the tarsi are equipped with hair pads. (It should be remembered that almost all male Carabidae have tarsal hair pads on the front legs to help as claspers.) A few small Staphylindae such as *Stenus* and *Oligota* also prey on tiny animals in trees and on herbage.

Running or flying (where the wings must first be unpacked) are not as quick a means of escape as jumping. A jump may not move an insect as far as flight will, but it does accelerate it very rapidly away from an immediate danger, such as the jaws of a predator. The usual jumping mechanism is for the legs to apply a rapid push on the ground, and many animals from kangaroos to grasshoppers have evolved a well-muscled, elongated pair of legs for this purpose. Many leaping beetles have enlarged hind legs which produce the jump and, as with grasshoppers, the hind femora are expanded to take the big jump muscles, and the tibiae are correspondingly lengthened to lever the beetle into the air. This kind of adaptation is found in flea beetles (Chrysomelidae–Halticinae), weevils such as *Orchestes*, and

127

occasionally in members of other families such as *Scirtes* (Helodidae). A few beetles that have enlarged back legs apparently do not jump. In some Oedemeridae this is characteristic of the males. In *Sagra* (Chrysomelidae), huge back legs are present in both sexes, and Crowson has suggested that they may be correlated with the vertical position adopted on stems by the beetles, which thus squat on their hind legs and may require large leg muscles to maintain this posture.

Click beetles (Elateridae) are a large family of beetles which are able to jump without using their legs. If one tries to touch a click beetle sitting at the top of a grass stem, it will probably drop to the ground to evade capture, (this 'drop-off' reflex is very common in beetles living on vegetation). If the beetle lands the right way up it will quickly run off into the surrounding grass or soil, but if it lands upside down on a fairly smooth surface, it may produce a sudden 'click' and jump into the air. Some species will click in any position to evade capture, and the leap is not basically a righting mechanism but an escape reaction. In the half-inch long *Athous haemorrhoidalis*, which is common in early summer on grass in woodlands, the leap is quite spectacular, and anything up to a foot in height.

The unusual jumping mechanism depends on the loose fit of the prothorax on the mesothorax; in order to jump, the prothorax (and head) are arched dorsally upon the rest of the body in the inverted beetle, and then swung very rapidly through at least 45° (fig. 42). This very rapid movement raises the centre of gravity of the beetle fast enough to throw it into the air. The energy needed is produced by a pair of large muscles lying against the roof of the prothorax. These build up tension which is resisted in a similar way to the powerful spring of a 'breakback' mouse-trap which is held open by a peg. When the mouse, by taking the bait, knocks out the peg the upper arm of the trap accelerates rapidly down upon it. In the click beetle, the two parts of the body are likewise held apart by a peg which projects backwards from the middle of the prosternum. The peg has a roughened step which acts as a friction hold, and rests on the anterior lip of the mesosternum when the beetle is lying with its back arched. When the beetle wishes to jump, or when enough time has passed for sufficient tension to have built up, the friction hold suddenly gives, and the peg slides over the edge of the mesosternal lip; as the peg is swung very rapidly down into a deep pit in the mesosternum, its underside slides along a curved track which is extremely smooth, and so offers minimal resistance to the accelerating peg.

When the prothoracic movement is stopped it is by 'bumpers' on the prothorax which hit the rim of the mesothorax, and not due to the rather pointed tip of the peg hitting the bottom of the pit (with possible dire results to the beetle's insides). The reaction of the ground to the beetle's sudden change in position is transmitted via the elytra, which may hurl the beetle

128

into the air at a speed of over 8 feet per second (250 cm/sec) – the velocity necessary to project it vertically upwards to about a foot above the ground. The most remarkable feature of such a jump is that in order to build up sufficient speed over the short distance through which the beetle's centre of gravity is raised, the prothorax and its peg must be accelerated to several hundred times the 'force' of gravity (up to 700 g.) in about $\frac{1}{2000}$ of a second! The beetle is flung upwards, usually spinning end over end, and may somersault at least six times in half a second before it falls back to the ground. Whether it lands the right way up or returns upside down seems to be a matter of chance – it can always leap again if necessary.

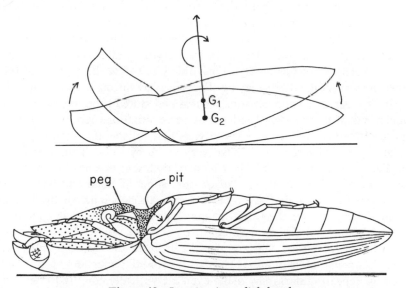

Figure 42. *Jumping in a click beetle*
Above: two profiles of the Elaterid *Athous haemorrhoidalis* are shown superimposed. They are taken from a high speed ciné film, and represent positions not more than 0·64 milliseconds apart. In the pre-jump position (the lower of the two profiles) the centre of gravity of the beetle is at G_2. It is raised to the G_1 position as the beetle jack-knifes, and in this position the beetle is actually just off the ground; *below:* side view of *Athous* in the pre-jump position. The prothoracic peg and the mesosternum are heavily stippled, whilst the underside of the prothorax is lightly stippled. The position of the pit (in the midline) is shown on the mesosternum. (After Evans, 1972.)

B. PROTECTIVE HABITS (Ways of staying put, and not having to run, jump, fly or swim for it).

So far, most of this chapter has been concerned with the ways in which beetles move, particularly as a means of evading a variety of hazards. The

129

alternative approach to the problem of danger from predators is to have some sort of protective device which makes flight unnecessary. The commonest protective habits in the animal kingdom are either for the prey to hide or be camouflaged. Alternatively, if a potential prey has an efficient means of defence it can face up to a predator; it is an advantage to a species protected in this way to draw attention to itself with warning signals. A third possibility is for an unprotected species to deceive its predators by mimicking a protected species; a slightly different form of mimicry is that where a number of pro-tected species all look alike.

(a) *Concealment.* A beetle that hides itself shows cryptic behaviour, and if it is camouflaged this is termed cryptic coloration. Cryptic behaviour is charac-teristic of the great majority of beetles, indeed, compared to the Lepidoptera or Diptera, the Coleoptera are basically a cryptic order. As I noted earlier, it is characteristic of beetles that they hide just below the surface of things rather than prominently displaying themselves by flitting about above. Thus soil and timber, dung and carrion, detritus and stored products all have their populations of unobtrusive beetles, but some situations require a degree of exposure. Herbivorous feeders on flowers and foliage are often exposed to predators such as birds which have very sharp eyesight. Thus many Chry-somelidae are green to match their background, and this also applies to leaf weevils such as *Phyllobius* and *Polydrosus*. Some of these leaf weevils limit their exposure by feeding at night, but even though inactive by day, they presumably benefit by their camouflage. Many Carabidae that hunt on the woodland floor at night are dark-coloured or black, and contrast with some of the day-active species that are metallic green or bronze. One difficulty of colour matching in camouflage is the shadowed underside of the beetle, which by appearing dark may make even a cryptically coloured insect stand out against its background. This effect can be eliminated either by counter-shading (obliterative shading), or by the insect's being flattened and having the margins of the body extended outwards to meet the surface. This latter modification is found in the tortoise beetles (Chrysomelidae–Cassidinae, fig. 43). A green species such as *Cassida viridis* not only closely matches the colour of the leaf, but has no revealing shadows, and is very easy to overlook unless it moves.

If the outline of the beetle cannot be concealed, an effective alternative is to break it up with a contrasting pattern, or an apparently random 'blotchi-ness'. This disruptive coloration makes it difficult to see some timber beetles when they are at rest on a tree trunk. Again, the attentions of predators may be escaped if a beetle is easy to see but resembles something other than food, such as an inanimate object. Good examples are the exposed pupae of lady-birds such as the common two-spot, *Adalia bipunctata*, which resemble bird

130

droppings on a leaf. This similarity to non-living things has been made use of in the cryptic behaviour of many species. Beetles living on the exposed foliage of plants often fold up their legs and drop to the ground when disturbed. Having fallen to the ground, they lie still with their legs and antennae retracted. This has been termed 'feigning death', but it is their lack of movement and their likeness to non-living objects such as pieces of soil that deceive the predator. Such cryptic behaviour is common in leaf beetles, weevils and click beetles. The latter often have grooves in the underside of the body to take the antennae and sometimes the legs. However, the best adapted species in this respect are the pill beetles (Byrrhidae). In the common pill beetle, *Byrrhus pilula*, grooves are present into which the legs and antennae

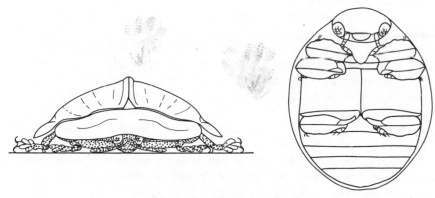

Figure 43. *Cryptic beetles*
Left: a tortoise beetle, *Cassida viridis* (Chrysomelidae) seen from in front; *right:* a pill beetle, *Byrrhus pilula* (Byrrhidae) with all its appendages folded away, seen from below.

exactly fit, thus giving the motionless beetle a completely rounded outline (fig. 43) – quite unlike that of an edible insect. The small British beetle *Georyssus crenulatus* (Hydrophilidae) may be found living in damp sand or mud near coasts or river banks. It is often covered with sand grains which are stuck to its cuticle, making it resemble a tiny pill of sand. Some of the best examples of 'stick-on' camouflage in beetles have been described by Gressitt from Papua. A number of weevils (and one Colydiid) which are found on the leaves of woody plants in the moss forest have a variety of algae, fungi and liverworts growing on their backs, and these even contain a characteristic fauna of minute animals. In the weevil *Gymnopholus*, the upper surface has special depressions with hairs, scales and a sticky secretion for maintaining its living camouflage. This kind of disguise is not uncommon in the sea on animals such as hermit-crabs, but it is remarkable to find it in a small, terrestrial animal.

131

(b) *Defence*. Beetles that have large jaws for capturing prey have an advantage over herbivores in that they can use their jaws to defend themselves. Large ground beetles, tiger beetles and carnivorous water beetles can often inflict a painful nip on one's fingers, and these predators are well able to protect themselves from similar sized animals. Of course, this may not be effective against much larger predators, although some of these beetles can appear to be quite dangerous to deal with when they adopt a threat posture with wide open jaws. This threat display is well shown by large Staphylinidae such as the devil's coach horse, *Staphylinus* (= *Ocypus*) *olens*. This is one of the largest British Staphylinidae, and when it stands erect with its large jaws gaping and its abdomen cocked forwards over its back, it is quite a formidable sight.

A number of beetles have evolved special devices and apparatus for defending themselves. The characteristically thick cuticle of most Coleoptera is in itself an efficient first line of defence, and many beetles have spines or thick hairs which may deter would-be predators. In some very spiny leaf beetles (Chrysomelidae–Hispinae), much of the adult life is spent among spiny fruits and seed-pods, and the spines have probably been evolved as camouflage. With the larvae of the Dermestidae, however, the spiky hairs seem to have the same function as the spines on a hedgehog or a porcupine. The hairs are easily shed and can penetrate vertebrate skins to act as irritants. Dermestid larvae may use these hairs to defend themselves actively. Nutting & Spangler noticed that the larva of *Trogoderma variable* would raise its abdomen and make striking movements in response to being touched, or even when exposed to a strong, chemical vapour. When it struck, masses of complex, spear-headed hairs were released (fig. 44). When attacked by ants or other beetles, these elaborate hairs interlocked, and the predator became entangled in them or was repelled. Larger insects could feed on the larvae, but their intestines soon became blocked with the hair masses. However, some vertebrates such as toads, lizards and small birds were apparently not affected or repelled. An ingenious device mentioned in Chapter 3 was the pupal 'gin-trap' which acted against small arthropods. Lewis has described a similar mechanism in the adult stage of the large African Buprestid, *Sternocerca castanea*. This can inflict a painful nip by pinching together the sharp edges of the back of the prothorax and the front border of the elytra.

Some beetles use chemical repellents instead of straight-forward mechanical devices such as spines. Chemical defence mechanisms use smelly, foul-tasting, corrosive or poisonous substances to deter enemies, and beetles have developed a great variety of such substances, many of which have been described by Roth & Eisner. The most readily available repellent substance is faecal material, and several Chrysomelidae have put this to good use. The larva is a particularly vulnerable stage, and the soft bodied larva of the asparagus beetle, *Criocerus asparagi*, literally smothers itself in liquid faeces. Eisner and his colleagues have described a more elaborate use of faecal material in the larva of the tortoise beetle, *Cassida rubiginosa*. This larva holds a dense mass of cast skins and faeces over its back by means of a fork sticking forwards from the end of the abdomen. This faecal shield (or 'stercoraceous parasol') can be rotated in any direction, and is effective against many of the larva's predators, especially ants. The shield is swung so that it confronts an attacking ant. Contact with the liquid faeces on the shield leads to a hasty retreat and cleaning reactions by the ant; this is a similar effect to that produced by some chemical repellents. The effectiveness of the shield was easily shown by removing it from a larva, when it became vulnerable to ant attack.

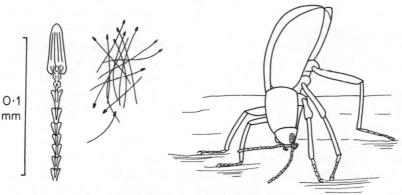

Figure 44. *Defence mechanisms*
Left: a magnified view of a barbed hair ('hastate seta') of *Trogoderma variabile* (Dermestidae). The barbs cause these hairs to interlock, and 'mat' together (after Nutting & Spangler); *right: Eleodes* sp. (Tenebrionidae) in head-down, spraying position.

Many Chrysomelid larvae have special glands which secrete repellent chemicals, particularly various foul-smelling aldehydes. For instance, the larva of *Melasoma lapponica* has eighteen glands which open upon two rows of tubercles along the back. The defence glands store their products in reservoirs which open at the tips of the tubercles and, when disturbed, the larva ejects a drop of fluid from the tip of each. These drops remain there for less than a second, when they are simultaneously sucked back in; this process is repeated five to six times in succession. In *Melasoma tremula*, the pupa 'inherits' this mechanism. It retains the last larval skin attached to the end of its abdomen, and this contains the reservoirs of the defence glands. If the pupa is disturbed, droplets appear on the ends of the tubercles on the larval skin. Those leaf beetle larvae that feed on willows may produce salicylaldehyde – a substance related to aspirin – from salicin present in the leaves.

133

Tenebrionidae and Carabidae have defence glands which often produce quinones – rather corrosive substances which have blistering effects upon vertebrate skins. Defence glands are present in many Adephaga. In most families, the glands are pygidial, and lie near the anus. Most common ground beetles leave an unpleasant smell if they are handled. Dytiscidae and Hygrobiidae are unusual in also having prothoracic defence glands. In *Dytiscus marginalis*, these produce a milky white substance (a steroid) which acts as a repellent in small quantities, but in concentrated form – especially if it enters the bloodstream directly – is toxic to fish or frogs. Ladybirds have a slightly different, but equally effective mechanism. The blood is distasteful, and it can be leaked through pores in the arthrodial membranes of joints. *Epilachna varivestris*, the Mexican bean beetle, shows this 'reflex bleeding' from the leg joints nearest to the unpleasant stimulus. Its larva also shows a similar localised response from hollow, brittle spines which break. This blood usually hardens on exposure to the air, and effectively 'gums up' an attacker such as an ant. The best known reflex bleeders in Britain are probably the bloody-nosed beetles, two species of *Timarcha* (Chrysomelidae). When *Timarcha* is handled, its blood is forced out at the arthrodial membranes, especially around the mouthparts. The blood is bright red and has caustic properties.

Where these defence secretions are caustic, they may be very effective against vertebrates with sensitive skins, but less so against arthropods with hard cuticles. Thus many of these secretions have special components to penetrate the epicuticle and allow the main poison to spread over the surface of the aggressor. This spreading is often aided by the cleaning reflexes of the attacker, especially if the secretion is sticky. If the substance is not sticky, it must be very poisonous, and must either be produced rapidly or efficiently stored. Obviously, there is a problem to be overcome by a beetle which stores a poisonous chemical. Roth & Eisner have observed that besides these points, it would be a great advantage to the defender if it could accurately aim its secretory discharge.

Some Tenebrionidae can do this very effectively. The North American *Eleodes* adopts a head down attitude with the tail end sticking up and pointed at the source of the unpleasant stimulus (fig. 44). *Blaps nitens* can spray its blistering quinones to a distance of over a foot. Some smaller beetles have equally useful chemical weapons operating over shorter ranges. Tiny Paussidae can produce an explosive discharge from the pygidial glands at their back ends. The group that do this in the most spectacular way are the bombardier beetles, for instance, Carabids of the genus *Brachinus* (fig. 45). These small beetles are found in many parts of the world, and include a species which is locally common in chalky districts of southern England. A detailed study has recently been made by Aneshansley and his colleagues of a

South American species. This is an expert marksman, and can swivel the end of its abdomen to spray its adversary with quinones. These issue explosively with an audible 'pop', and produce a burning sensation on the human skin. Besides vertebrates, the discharge is an efficient deterrent to arthropod predators such as ants or larger Carabids, and can be rapidly repeated several times in succession.

The problem of storing a noxious chemical has been solved by ejecting it immediately it is formed from its precursors, hydroquinones and hydrogen peroxide. These substances are secreted into a reservoir, and when needed

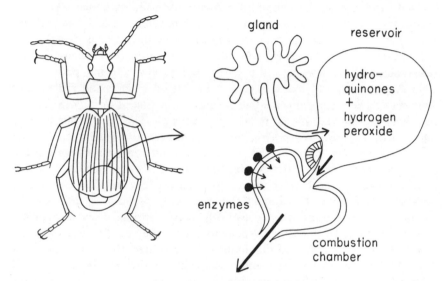

Figure 45. *A bombardier beetle*
Left: Brachinus crepitans (Carabidae); *right:* diagram of the 'bombarding' mechanism located in the hind end of the abdomen of a bombardier beetle. (After Aneshansley et al., copyright 1969 by the American Association for the Advancement of Science.)

they are passed into a 'combustion chamber' which opens at the back end of the abdomen. Enzymes are secreted into this 'combustion chamber', and they produce the reaction:

Hydroquinones + hydrogen peroxide $\rightarrow$ quinones + water + oxygen.

This reaction is almost instantaneous, and the oxygen formed blasts out the quinone spray under high pressure (fig. 45). The most interesting side effect of this reaction is that that it produces enough heat to vaporise one fifth of the spray and to raise the temperature of the rest to boiling point. So the discharge is not only smelly, but also boiling hot. (The experimenters

135

observed that the beetle can make itself felt thermally even when the chemical message cannot get through.)

A beetle that is poisonous or distasteful to a predator will obviously be better protected if it has a signal which proclaims this before it is eaten. For instance, bombardier beetles are often conspicuously coloured. Obvious colours and patterns are found in many animals that are known to be protected by a sting or a poisonous or distasteful chemical. This warning coloration is clearly shown by the black and yellow striped common wasp; the ease with which a black and yellow pattern can be distinguished by a vertebrate eye has led to its use by the Automobile Association for its notices. There are many other obvious colours or patterns which have been used by animals in a similar way to warn would-be predators that they should be avoided.

In beetles, we have noted that the ladybirds are distasteful because of their reflex bleeding. A few have the black and yellow warning pattern (e.g. *Thea 22-punctata*) and many have a variation of a black and red pattern. This may be very constant in some species, as in *Coccinella septempunctata*, or it may be very variable, as in *Adalia bipunctata*. The other reflex bleeders mentioned, *Timarcha tenebricosa* and *T.goettingenesis*, are large, or fairly large, slow-moving, black beetles which stand out against a background of green grass, or a sandy path. Again, their blood is bright red, and thus we have another red and black combination. Oil beetles (Meloidae) are a close parallel to *Timarcha*. Females of the oil beetle, *Meloe proscarabaeus*, are often very conspicuous when egg-laying in the spring. They also protect themselves by reflex bleeding. When disturbed, they exude distasteful, oily blood from their joints, and this habit has given them their common name. Most Meloids contain at least some cantharidin in their bodies, and in some species it is present in large quantities. When this is so, it renders the beetle not only distasteful, but quite poisonous. Cantharidin is a blistering agent which was at one time obtained for medical use from the elytra of the 'Spanish fly' (or blister beetle), *Lytta vesicatoria*. (Cantharidin was also used as an aphrodisiac because of its mildly irritant properties in very small doses). In Britain, *L.vesicatoria* is a rare species which is occasionally found in southern England; it is more characteristic of southern Europe. The elytra of this species are a bright, metallic green, and presumably serve as an easily recognisable warning.

Besides the Meloidae, warning coloration is also seen in Cantharidae and Lycidae, which have distasteful body fluids or obnoxious secretions. Both these families have many species in which the dominant colours are reds, yellows, browns, blues and black. The Lycidae are a mainly tropical group in which the elytra of many species are characteristically widened behind. Staphylinidae are normally sombrely coloured, but a few may have bright red or blue colours as well as black. These include species of the genus

Paederus, which contain another blistering agent – paederin. This chemical can cause necrotic sores on the skin, and has been responsible for cases of dermatitis. Some beetle poisons are particularly virulent if they enter the blood stream directly. For instance, species of Chrysomelidae have been used in the preparation of poisoned arrows. The South African bushmen of the Kalahari desert use pupae of the leaf beetle, *Diamphidia locusta*, to prepare a poison which, when injected into the blood stream, will paralyse a small mammal. The importance of these poisons to the beetles concerned is not that they kill predators, but that small quantities of the poison act either as a repellent, or are very distasteful, and the predator learns to associate this with an easily recognised colour or pattern.

(c) *Mimicry*. Some animals that lack protective secretions, or a sting, have managed to take advantage of the situation in which warning coloration proclaims a protected species. Such species are often quite palatable to predators, but by evolving close resemblances to warningly coloured species, they deceive their predators and are left undisturbed. This copying of a warningly coloured unpalatable model by a palatable mimic was first described by Bates, and has since been termed Batesian mimicry. Bates described this kind of mimicry amongst the butterflies of the Amazon region, but it can be seen in all parts of the world in many groups of animals, including many kinds of insects. Amongst British beetles, a good example is the Cerambycid, *Clytus arietis*, the wasp beetle. With its black and yellow stripes this species has a similar pattern to the social wasps, and is quite different in its coloration to other Cerambycidae. This also applies to its structure, for the antennae are shorter, and thus more wasp-like, than in other timber beetles. Even its behaviour is similar to that of a wasp, for it is often to be seen perched on old tree stumps which are also visited frequently by wasps. *Trichius fasciatus* is a very local British chafer which is also yellow and black. However, it resembles a bumble bee more closely than a wasp. Many Staphylinidae which live in ants' nests have markings which give them a similar appearance to their hosts'. The resemblance is not so obvious as with the wasp or bee beetles, and the significance of this 'ant mimicry' is still rather obscure.

It is clear that for a warning coloration based on colour and pattern to work, the predator must have good eyesight and be intelligent enough to learn fairly quickly and remember what it has learnt. Thus this kind of protection works particularly well against vertebrate predators – especially birds, which include many insect-eating species. For Batesian mimicry to be effective the predator must learn to recognise the mimic as distasteful, so for such a species to be successful it must be much rarer than its warningly coloured model. The signal displayed by the mimic is not restricted to colour and pattern, the whole behaviour of the mimic may be involved, as with the

137

wasp beetle. A rather similar case which is quoted by Wickler is that of the Tenebrionid *Megasida* which mimics the defensive posture of *Eleodes*, but has no defensive secretion.

Of course, we take particular note of colour and pattern in mimicry because our eyes are our most important sense organs. If our nose and ears were better developed we would probably notice many examples of olfactory and auditory mimicry. For instance, Rothschild & Lane suggested that the buzz or hum made by a grounded bumble bee when caught in the early morning before its temperature has risen high enough for flight is mimicked by *Necrophorus investigator*, which stridulates by rubbing its abdomen on its elytra. It also mimics the stinging reaction performed by the semi-comatose bee on its back. Sight is of major important to birds, and since these are probably the most important vertebrate predators of insects, most insect warning signals, and their mimicry, are probably by means of colours and patterns.

We have seen that Batesian mimicry paradoxically requires a successful mimic to be rare. However, there are many cases of apparent mimicry where the similar species are all common. Bates had noticed this, but it was first explained by Muller, also in relation to Brazilian butterflies. In Mullerian mimicry, a number of different species share the same pattern (or sound, as in *Necrophorus* and the bee) and all are distasteful. The advantage to all the species in such a grouping is that a predator has only to taste one individual of one species for all the species to gain protection from this experience. Thus a protection ring – termed a 'warning club' by Wickler – is set up. Such warning patterns may be shared between many species of quite unrelated insects, especially in the tropics, and they occur in a variety of beetle families such as the Lycidae, Cantharidae and Cerambycidae. Of course, such a ring may include Batesian as well as Mullerian mimics. Darlington described a complex ring of this sort involving a number of Cuban beetles. It included three species of Lycid, an Oedemerid, three Cantharids, two Elaterids and six Cerambycids. Of these, the Lycids and the Oedemerid seemed to be Mullerian mimics, but the status of the other species was less certain.

The relationship between Lycidae and Cerambycidae can be rather complex, as demonstrated by Eisner and his colleagues (and quoted by Wickler) with two Lycids and two Cerambycids in Arizona. The Lycidae were *Lycus loripes* and *L. fernandezi*, which are found in the same habitat as the Cerambycids *Elytroleptus ignitus* and *E. apicalis*. *L. loripes* and *E. ignitus* are light orange in colour and the other pair are rather similar to this, but have black tips to the elytra. In each case, the Lycids were about a hundred times more common than the Cerambycids. It was shown by feeding experiments that the Lycids were distasteful to both the vertebrate and invertebrate predators tested. However, wounds were noticed at the base of the elytra of some Lycids collected, and the predator responsible surprisingly turned out to be one or other of the *Elytroleptus* species. The latter, on meeting a *Lycus*, would climb onto its back to a position similar to that adopted in mating, and then proceed to gnaw through the Lycid cuticle and drink the blood from the wound produced. Occasionally, much more of the Lycid might be consumed. The Cerambycids were shown to be normally edible if the equivalent Lycid pattern had not been learnt by the predator, so this might seem to be straightforward Batesian mimicry. However, if the Cerambycid had just been feeding on Lycid blood, it was suggested that it would be unlikely for this distasteful substance to break down very rapidly, so the Cerambycid would itself become distasteful. In this case, the resemblance between the Cerambycid and the Lycid would be Mullerian mimicry, which would then revert to Batesian mimicry when the distasteful Lycid material had broken down. Wickler emphasised the unknown features of this complicated case.

Apart from this example, perhaps the oddest case of beetle mimicry was that of the female glow-worm *Photuris* which mimicked a *Photinus* female with its luminescence. Lloyd noticed that it attracted male *Photinus* to itself and then seized and ate them – a siren with a flashlight rather than a song!

2. Protection from Hostile Environments: Beetles and Water

In order to illustrate some of the relationships between beetles and water, I shall contrast two groups of beetles: aquatic beetles, and beetles adapted to very dry habitats such as deserts. Most beetles inhabit terrestrial environments where the moisture content lies between these two extremes, but the difference between these wet and dry habitats clearly illustrates the range of adaptability found in the Coleoptera.

A. WATER BEETLES

No truly marine beetles are known, although some sea-shore forms such as *Aepus* and *Aepopsis* (Carabidac) and some Staphylinidae, Hydraenidae and Dryopoidea can withstand temporary immersion in sea water. This is true of insects in general. The sea seems to have presented almost all of them with insoluble problems, and nearly all the 'marine' insects are found on the sea-shore between the high and low tidemarks. Fresh water presents fewer problems, however, and several different groups of beetles have independently evolved aquatic forms.

The largest group of water beetles is the aquatic Adephaga which has evolved from terrestrial Caraboid ancestors. Some aquatic species such as the North American *Amphizoa* (Amphizoidae) are very Carabid-like in appearance. The Dytiscidae and the Gyrinidae are the most successful

139

familes in this group. The Haliplidae show a number of major differences from these, and it is just possible that they may have evolved from a separate group of Caraboids. The Hydrophilidae are a Polyphagous family which parallel the Dytiscidae in showing a wide range of species in ponds, rivers and lakes. Their rather more primitive relatives are found in the Hydraenidae. In the Hydrophiloidea, the adults are better adapted to aquatic life than the larvae, and they form an interesting contrast to the Dryopoidea, where the larvae show more obvious aquatic adaptations than the adults. Crowson has suggested that these differences may reflect the different lengths of adult life in the two groups – long in the Hydrophiloids (with short larval lives) and short in the Dryopoids (with long larval lives).

Another quite independent invasion of the water is found in the Donaciinae (Chrysomelidae). The adults are often common on waterside plants but may descend below the water level, especially to lay eggs; these produce larvae which are adapted to live in water. An unusual form of locomotion is found in some Steninae (Staphylinidae) which are not truly aquatic, but can move rapidly across the surface film. They produce a secretion from glands near the anus which lowers the surface tension of the water immediately behind them. Since the surface tension immediately in front of the beetle is now greater than that behind, the beetle is drawn rapidly forwards over the surface in a similar manner to a toy camphor boat. These are the major groups of aquatic beetles. There are a few other species occurring sporadically throughout the Coleoptera in which aquatic adaptations are found. They include the larvae of Helodidae, which are unique amongst the larvae of beetles in having evolved many jointed antennae. There are also a number of aquatic weevils.

Several problems must be solved to allow a terrestrial insect to live successfully in water. If we exclude such physiological problems as the balance of salts and water in the body, the main physical problems are those of moving and breathing in water. Let us first consider the difficulties of moving in or on water. Slow-moving insects such as some beetle larvae which move around on the bottom or on plant surfaces need very few special locomotory adaptations. Ordinary slow walking enables them to crawl around almost as if they were on land. Faster-moving beetles actively swim through the water. Since water is denser than air, it needs a greater effort to push through it, and this has led to the streamlining of the body in many adult beetles. Although the body has more resistance to its movement than in air, the legs have less purchase than on solid ground, and this has led to their flattening to form oars or paddles. These paddles need a powerful musculature to move them through the water, and this, operating on flattened legs, forms an interesting parallel to the similar condition found in burrowing beetles. However, water also provides resistance to the return (forwards) stroke of the leg, and

140

feathering mechanisms for the oars are necessary if the beetle is to move forwards. The amount of support needed for the body varies. The body may be slightly denser than the water and thus sink slowly if it is not moving, but it is more likely to be positively buoyant because of its air store.

The whirligig beetles (Gyrinidae) have become specialised to live on the surface film, although they are true water beetles, and can dive and swim underwater. One big advantage of the surface film is that it supports the weight of a small animal, and has very little resistance to be overcome by a moving animal (provided it is not too small). Thus the limbs can be used

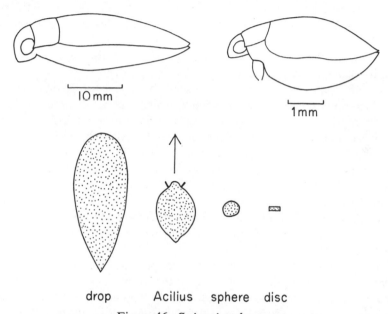

drop   Acilius   sphere   disc

Figure 46. *Swimming shapes*

Above, left: side view of the large Dytiscid *Acilius sulcatus; above, right:* side view of the small Dytiscid, *Hyphydrus ovatus; below:* the four different bodies shown all have the same resistance to movement through water in the indicated direction. (After Nachtigall, in Rockstein, copyright Academic Press.)

entirely for locomotion and feeding, and whirligigs are extremely fast and agile surface skaters.

Detailed studies of how water beetles swim have been made by Nachtigall and Hughes, and some of the most interesting points can be summarised here. In large Dytiscidae, resistance to movement is reduced by the oval shape of the smooth body (fig. 46); it is rather flattened and has sharp, wing-like margins. Large Hydrophilidae have a similar shape, although they tend to be rather more compact. In small Dytiscidae (e.g. *Hyphydrus*), the

141

sharp body margins are absent, and the beetle tends to the 'swimming-ball' shape. A body which would move through the water with the least possible resistance, and therefore the least expenditure of energy in propulsion, is an 'ideal streamlined body', and it would be drop-shaped. The body with the greatest resistance to movement – the 'ideal retarding body' – would be parachute-shaped. Measurements of the resistance of the large Dytiscid *Acilius sulcatus* which were made by Nachtigall have shown that it has about three times the resistance of the best streamlined body, but only one sixth of the resistance of the worst (fig. 46). Smaller water beetles may have about 50% more resistance than *Acilius*. The hydrodynamic quality of the body shape in *Acilius* is comparable to that of a fast racing car. However, why not have drop-shaped beetles?

The snag is that such a body shape is not very stable, and if it deviates from its straight line progression, its course is difficult to correct. If *Acilius* swings off course slightly, it automatically swings back again; the sharp elytral margins create some turbulence which has a 'damping' effect on oscillations (i.e. overswinging). The same principle – a rapid build-up of turbulence and therefore drag when the beetle deviates from its course – is used to facilitate rapid turning and braking. Thus the shape of large Dytiscids is a compromise. It has low resistance with very good stability and fairly good manoeuvrability. It is a contrast to the shape of Gyrinids which also has low resistance, and has very good manoeuvrability (on and under the surface) but which is unstable. Gyrinidae therefore require constant course corrections, and have a propulsive system which can provide this; in this respect they differ from Dytiscidae.

The legs of water beetles are used for both propulsion and steering (fig. 47). In large- and middle-sized Dytiscidae, the front legs are used for prey capture, the middle legs for both steering and propulsion, and the hind legs – which are most obviously flattened – for propulsion alone. In small Dytiscidae, Hydrophilidae and larval Dytiscidae and Hydrophilidae, all three pairs of legs are used for propulsion and steering. Gyrinidae are the most highly modified water beetles. Their first pair of legs is similar to that of Dytiscids and is used for prey capture, but the second and third pairs have been converted into very short, flattened paddles which are used for both steering and propulsion. One advantage bestowed by the Adephagid type of hind coxa (which is fused to the metasternum in most of the aquatic species) is that the trochanter swings in a constant relationship to the body, always giving the main thrust in the same relative direction. In comparison with terrestrial Carabidae, the swimming legs of Dytiscids are rather shorter, much flatter, and have the tarsal region expanded while the proximal part of the limb is relatively reduced in length. The swimming legs are fringed with long hairs which are even more important in providing thrust than the

142

limbs themselves. For instance, in *Acilius sulcatus*, the hairs on the hind limb contribute 68% of the thrust it generates, and the tarsal hairs alone provide 75% of this. In *Gyrinus*, the fringing 'hairs' are tiny blades which add considerable extra thrust to that of the solid paddle, but are not as important as in *Acilius*.

The great advantage of the hair fringes is that they allow feathering of the limb on the return (forwards) stroke, which is necessary if more thrust is to be provided by the back stroke. The hairs on the swimming legs of *Acilius*, and the little blades on those of *Gyrinus*, collapse on the forwards stroke, but

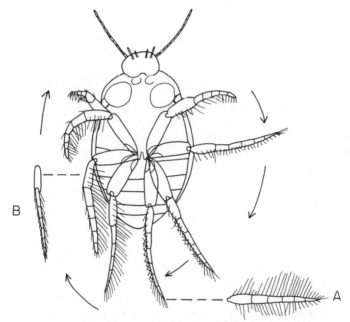

Figure 47. *Swimming in Dytiscidae*
View of the underside of *Acilius sulcatus* to show the swimming and recovery strokes of the hind legs. Four phases of the rowing stroke are shown on the right, and four phases of the recovery stroke on the left. During the rowing stroke the leg hairs are stiffly extended to give a large surface area pushing against the water. (A – side view of the limb at the end of the back-stroke.) During the recovery stroke, the limb is pulled forwards close to the body by bending it, and the tarsus is twisted to feather it. (B – side view of the limb half way through the recovery stroke.) (After Nachtigall, in Rockstein, copyright Academic Press.)

due to their basal articulations, they stand out stiffly on the back stroke and thus the oar blade is renewed at each stroke. In *Acilius* the tarsi are also feathered. On the backstroke their articulations with the tibiae hold them stiffly erect, but when the limbs are swung forwards the tarsi are free to move (fig. 47). They rotate on their longitudinal axes so that only their narrow edges are pulled forwards against the resistance of the water. An equally ingenious system is found in *Gyrinus* where the lower part of each paddle folds up like a fan on the forwards stroke.

In Dytiscidae, both the left and right hind legs swing together, and alternate with the left and right middle legs. This gives a fairly straight course through the water with little unwanted twisting. In Hydrophilidae the leg movements alternate rather as in walking insects, but unlike walking insects the right middle and left hind leg beat backwards simultaneously. Omitting the slight pause between the movements of the two limbs which occurs in a walking insect, this means that pairs of opposite legs beat together, and this has the same advantage as for the Dytiscidae in cutting down unwanted side to side turning movements. *Acilius sulcatus* beats its legs between three and ten times a second, and this can move it through the water at just over 1 foot per second (350 mm/sec). The top speed burst from an individual stroke, which can be produced when the beetle is pursued, is $1\frac{2}{3}$ feet per second (500 mm/sec). *Gyrinus* moves its paddles far more rapidly. The hind legs beat fifty to sixty times per second whilst the middle legs follow at half this frequency. The whirligig can move at the remarkable speed of $3\frac{1}{4}$ feet per second (1 metre/sec, or nearly 200 body lengths per second) in short bursts on the water surface, although it does not exceed one tenth of this speed below the surface.

The second major problem of aquatic life that I shall briefly consider is that of respiration. How do beetles which evolved from air breathing ancestors breathe under water? Three main ways have been devised to solve this problem. The most permanent solution, which is found in larvae, is to have gills. These are thin-walled projections of the body surface which extract oxygen from the air dissolved in water, and return carbon dioxide from the animal to the water. In most cases, the gill contains a network of tracheae from a closed tracheal system (i.e. no spiracles communicate with the air until the pupal or adult stages are reached). In a few cases, tracheae in the gills are absent, and these 'blood gills' only contain blood spaces. Gills are usually elongate filaments which occur on the abdominal segments. They are found on the underside of the abdomen of *Hygrobia hermanni* (Hygrobiidae) which spends its time in the bottom mud of ponds. They project from the side of the abdomen in some Haliplidae and in Gyrinidae, where a large pair of gills is borne by each of the abdominal segments. Where gills occur in larval Hydrophilidae, they vary from species to species. For instance, they are long in *Berosus* but short in *Hydrochara*. They lie at the end of the abdomen in Helodidae, and in Elmidae the retractable gills are enclosed in a terminal gill chamber which can be shut with a lid. Gills with a rather different structure were found by Hinton on the abdomen of the pupae of Psephenidae (Dryopoidea), and on the larvae and pupae of some Myxophaga.

144

These gills are slender, hollow tubes which extend from the spiracles. Parts of the walls are thickened to prevent collapse, and parts have minute perforations which exclude water but not air. These spiracular gills are air filled and can function in either water or air. They are an ingenious adaptation to an aquatic habitat which may dry up.

The second approach to the respiration problem is the one most often

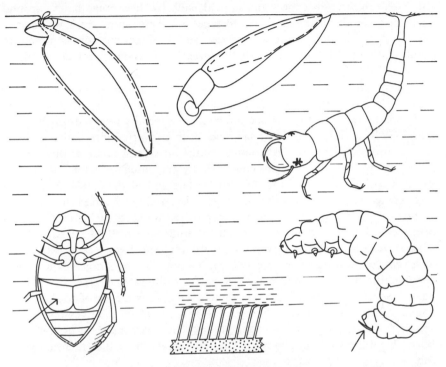

Figure 48. *Obtaining air*

The adult beetles shown all have air stores, which are shown by a broken line in the two upper beetles. *Top left: Hydrophilus* replenishing air at the surface; *top centre: Dytiscus* replenishing air at the surface; *top right: Dytiscus* larva replenishing air at the surface; *bottom left:* underside of *Haliplus* to show the expanded hind coxal plates; *bottom centre:* Plastron of *Elmis* highly magnified; *bottom right: Donacia* larva showing abdominal spine.

found, that which might be expected of groups with terrestrial ancestors. This is simply to rise to the surface of the water to breathe, and to hold an air store while swimming under water. The position of the air store and the way in which it is replenished differ in the various beetle families (fig. 48). Adult Dytiscidae and Gyrinidae hold an air store under the elytra. As a Dytiscid rises to replenish the store, the more buoyant abdominal region is

145

allowed to rise until the tip of the elytra and abdomen breaks the surface. Air is then taken into the sub-elytral cavity, and into the abdominal spiracles, particularly the enlarged last pair. The *Dytiscus* larva takes in air in a similar way. It also surfaces with the more buoyant tip of the abdomen, which in this case bears a pair of slender filaments which break and hold the surface film. The only two functional spiracles open at the tip of the abdomen, and these take in air whilst the water is held back by 'hydrofuge hairs', around them and on the filaments. The surfaces of these hairs repel water in a similar way to a waxy or greasy surface. An additional air store is present in adult *Haliplus*. This lies beneath the greatly expanded hind coxal plates characteristic of this beetle.

Hydrophilidae and Hydraenidae renew their air stores in quite a different way. A Hydrophilid rises to the surface head first, and tilting slightly to one side, breaks through the surface film with a specially adapted antenna. In many Hydrophiloids, the antennae have been converted into short, clubbed devices for establishing an air channel to the air stores. Some of the original antennal functions have been taken over by the elongate palpi – hence the old name of 'Palpicornia' for this group. The end of the club (the last 3, 4 or 5 segments) is covered with hydrofuge hairs, and this enables the antennae to break the surface film. Air is not only stored under the wing cases, but as a film held by a dense pile of hairs on the underside of the beetles, and this ventral store is replenished from the antennal channel via special hair tracts. The ventral air store of *Hydrophilus piceus* has the appearance of a bubble surrounding the beetle, and is the reason for calling it the 'great silver water beetle'. Some Chrysomelid larvae (Donaciinae) have made use of an alternative source of air. The grub-like larvae of *Donacia* and its relatives tap the air spaces found in the roots of water plants. The larva inserts a hollow spine borne on the tip of the abdomen, and this leads in to the tracheal system (fig. 48).

The third approach to the respiration problem has been made almost exclusively (in Coleoptera) by a variety of adult beetles. This method also involves an air store, but it makes use of this as a 'physical gill'. The bubble forming the air store of any water beetle can act to some extent as a gill if it is not used up too quickly. This is because as oxygen is used up from the bubble, fresh oxygen from air dissolved in the surrounding water diffuses in to replace it. Of course, this can happen only as long as the bubble lasts, i.e. as long as the other main gas in the air bubble – nitrogen – stays in the bubble. Since nitrogen diffuses out of the bubble more slowly than oxygen diffuses in, the bubble can act as a kind of 'gill' for at least a short period. The use of an ordinary air store as a physical gill only seems to be adequate in small insects, or in very inactive large ones (in hibernation, for instance). An active *Dytiscus* would apparently not gain much extra oxygen in this manner. However, if the bubble can be stabilised and prevented from collapsing, then the physical gill becomes much more effective. This is done by a dense layer of fine, short hairs on the body surface; if these are hydrofuge they will repel water and allow a thin layer of air to be held over the body.

Such a thin layer of air was called a 'plastron' by Thorpe; it acts as a physical gill and not as an air store, and is very resistant to collapse under pressure. *Elmis* is a small beetle which has a permanent plastron (fig. 48), and it can capture air bubbles to add to it. Hinton has observed that a plastron has been described in most Elmidae, many Dryopidae, and some Hydrophilidae, Hydraenidae, Donaciinae and Curculionidae. Besides these adult Polyphaga, he has recently described a plastron in some Myxophaga, many of which are aquatic. The Torridincolidae are remarkable in having a plastron in larval, pupal and adult stages. In *Hydrophilus*, the permanent plastron is overlaid by long hairs holding a temporary plastron which is used both as an air store and as a physical gill whilst it is present.

The different kinds of adaptations for breathing developed by water beetles clearly show how different groups of beetles have evolved along parallel lines to produce very similar devices, as for instance in adult Dytiscidae and Hydrophilidae. The presence of a terrestrial pupal stage in many water beetles shows that even within one group, the larvae and adults have probably evolved aquatic adaptations independently. We can ask at this point, why do most adult beetles and many larvae retain the old air breathing system which relies on a continually replenished air store, and not go in for gills as in most successful aquatic animals? A possible answer might be that aquatic beetles have evolved more recently than most terrestrial ones and have not got around to gills yet. However, Dytiscidae are known as fossils from over 100 million years ago – a period of time in which both the birds and mammals have evolved – and this ought to have been long enough. It is more likely that the air breathing system has been retained because of the flexibility it offers in being able to move from one habitat to another. Pond beetles must be able to search for other ponds if their own dries up, so the ability to fly (which requires air breathing) is extremely valuable. Thus almost all adult water beetles are flexible enough in both their respiratory and locomotory systems to get about both in the water and on land.

B. DESERT BEETLES

At the opposite end of the moisture spectrum to water beetles are those beetles which are adapted to live in very dry conditions. The Tenebrionidae are the largest group to have specialised in desert or arid habitats. Not all Tenebrionids are found in these places, however. Many are found in a wide range of soils in temperate regions, for instance sandy soils in Britain have several common species; others occur in fungi and dead trees, and a few are predators of bark beetles. Some species have become pests of stored flour and grain, particularly species of *Tenebrio* and *Tribolium*. *Tenebrio molitor*, the meal-worm, is spectacularly waterproof. If the beetle is kept in air with relative humidity of 95% (very moist, but not saturated) it blows up! It is so waterproof that its metabolic water (a by-product of the normal body processes) cannot escape. Many 'ordinary' insects which are less efficient at preventing water losses than *Tenebrio* nevertheless seem to be more water-proof than is necessary for water conservation. This paradox (which depends on the impermeable insect cuticle) was noted by Beament, who suggested that the explanation may involve insect adaptations for flight. Beament also observed that many other 'water conservation' adaptations could equally well be water-reducing modifications (i.e. weight-reducing modifications) and thus adaptations for flight.

In particular, the highly efficient respiratory system is air filled, and does not need an intermediary fluid transport system such as blood in vertebrates. However, the tracheoles are fluid-filled in the embryo, and again become filled at each moult. An immense amount of energy would be required to clear these capillary tubes of liquid directly, but the insect has a simple mechanism for doing just this. It uses a very thin layer of wax – one molecule thick – to coat the insides of the tracheae. Wax has hydrofuge properties, and the liquid is easily expelled and replaced by air. Beament has suggested that the excessive impermeability of the cuticle to water is a by-product of this process.

Whatever the explanation, the high impermeability of the Tenebrionid cuticle has enabled these beetles to become one of the commonest types of insect to be found in hot, dry deserts. Few other invertebrates can match them in this respect. For instance, Lawrence has observed that the invertebrate fauna of the very dry Namib desert of South West Africa consists almost entirely of spiders, a few other arachnids, and Tenebrionidae. An obvious characteristic of hot, dry deserts is the very high temperature reached by the surface of the sand in the sun. Shade makes a great deal of difference. If a beetle is out during the hot day, an ability to search for any shaded situation will take it out of the direct sun. Cloudsley-Thompson noted that when the normally nocturnal Tenebrionid *Pimelia grandis* was placed on the sand during the day, it ran towards large objects such as rocks and trees. It even followed a man about so that, given the opportunity, it could crawl into the shaded instep of his shoes.

Other characters of deserts are the great fluctuations of temperature on the surface over a period of twenty-four hours, and over the year. C. B. Williams took a number of temperature measurements in the Egyptian desert (fig. 49) which clearly show this, and they also show the 'buffering' effects of the sand. If the desert insect can be active at dawn and dusk, or during the night, it will miss the extreme mid-afternoon heat. Cloudsley-Thompson found that the beetles of the Tunisian desert could be arranged in a series which was to some extent correlated with their times of activity over a twenty-four-hour period. Those species with the highest rate of water loss in dry air were strictly nocturnal, whilst those with more impervious cuticles were twilight or daytime active. Whenever its main period of activity, if a beetle can burrow beneath the sand during the hottest part of the day it will miss the most extreme period of heat at the surface. Rhythmic patterns

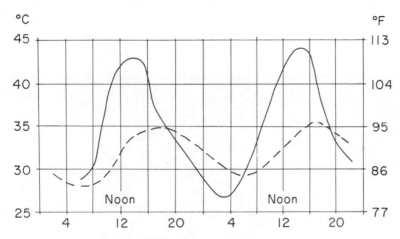

Figure 49. *Desert temperatures*
Hour by hour temperature changes during two days in the Egyptian desert near Cairo (4 and 5 August 1922). Solid line: sand surface in sun (antlion pit); broken line: hole under stone. (After C. B. Williams.)

of behaviour are shown by many desert beetles, and many Tenebrionids also have a well-developed ability to burrow.

The oddest Tenebrionids occur in the Namib desert, where some are apparently active by day and not nocturnal. One of these is *Sternocara phalangidium* (fig. 50) which has extremely long legs to carry it well above the blistering surface of the sand. Even with behavioural and structural devices for evading the highest temperatures, it would obviously be advantageous for desert beetles to be able to withstand fairly high temperatures. For instance, another Namib species, *Onymacris plana*, has been shown by Edney to have an upper lethal temperature of as much as 50°C (122°F) (half of a group could survive at this temperature for thirty minutes in saturated air). This species was active by day on open sand dunes. In contrast, *Trigonopus capicola*, which was found in light woodland, had an upper lethal temperature of 42·5°C (109°F). For desert beetles, high temperatures are usually linked to low humidities, and this must also be considered. Cloudsley-Thompson found that the lethal temperature for the Tenebrionid *Ocnera hispida* was 45°C. (113°F) (in this case for a twenty-four-hour exposure at a relative humidity of 10%.) This was lower than that of some arachnids, but higher than that for other insects tested. An important point is that pre-conditioning for twenty-four hours have a greater resistance to high temperatures for up to four hours. Thus acclimation ('acclimatisation') to these extreme temperatures is possible to some extent.

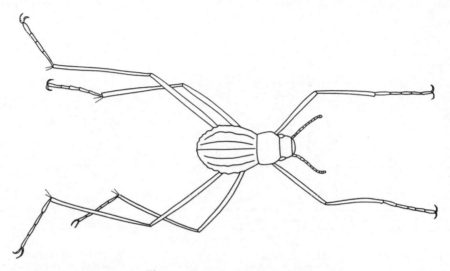

Figure 50. *A desert Tenebrionid*
Sternocara phalangidium as seen from above. (After Cloudsley-Thompson.)

A third major hazard of hot, dry deserts is the lack of food. Relatively few plants or animals occur in deserts, and much of the small amount of vegetable matter present is blown into them from less arid areas nearby. If it is not eaten immediately this vegetation may be buried and re-surface years later without having decomposed (due to the absence of the appropriate bacteria). It can then provide food for some Tenebrionid larvae. Other Tenebrionids feed on dung or carrion such as dead arthropods. However, a major adaptation to a desert life is the ability to go without food for long periods of time, and several Tenebrionids have been shown to survive prolonged starvation. A remarkable example is that of the *Blaps requieni* from Tunisia which lived in Cloudsley-Thompson's laboratory for over five years without taking food!

A feature common to many desert Tenebrionidae and Carabidae is a uniform dull black colour. Many suggestions have been made to explain this; they range from a heat-absorbing device to increase their activity and running speeds, to strong pigment to shield the beetles from dangerous exposure to ultra-violet rays. However, heat absorption during the desert day would seem to be unnecessary, indeed dangerous, and heat absorption during the night impossible. As for shielding, any insect cuticle, apart from the thinnest and most transparent, is an efficient screen for ultra-violet. The Tenebrionidae of the Namib desert (one of the oldest deserts in the world) break this general colour rule, for although there are black species, others are white, or black and white. Cloudsley-Thompson has suggested that the white species are cryptically coloured, i.e. camouflaged against the light-coloured sand. He also suggested that the black species are poisonous or distasteful, and are so coloured to make them obvious to potential predators. The common black coloration would thus be 'biological economy' whereby protected species mimicked one another, i.e. a case of Mullerian mimicry.

CHAPTER 6

Populations and Communities

The ecology of beetles – how do beetles fit into their environment?

An individual beetle is normally part of a population made up of many individuals of its particular species. In a particular habitat, populations of different species usually affect each other to such an extent that they can be thought of as composing a single community. Populations and communities can only be considered in relation to their particular habitats, and this study of the interrelationships between animals and their environments forms the branch of science known as ecology. The ecology of a species can be studied at the level of the individual, the population, or the way the population fits into its community. At a higher level, ecology may be concerned with the structures and interrelationships of communities. The range of ecology is enormous, and a comprehensive treatment of beetle ecology would fill several textbooks. Here, one can merely illustrate some of the ways in which several species of beetles react with their environments. Since communities usually contain many other species besides beetles, a study of any complete community would be outside the scope of this book. Nevertheless, one can examine the beetle segments of a community in order to point out some of the general principles involved.

The term 'environment' often seems rather nebulous. The environment of an animal is composed of both its inanimate physical surroundings and other living things. The physical environment includes the total effect a piece of countryside has upon a beetle inhabitant; it involves the habitat and the weather that the beetle experiences whilst living in it. Weather is dependent upon the particular climate of the region, and its extremes may be greatly modified by the beetle's habitat. Plants which are present may merely have the physical effect of providing shelter, but they are part of the living environment and so form a food source for herbivorous beetles. The latter provide a food source for predatory beetles; these in turn may be eaten by larger predators, and all may be attacked by parasites. Even other members of a population of a particular species are an important part of an individual beetle's environment, since they may compete with it for resources in short supply such as food, shelter or a mate.

These topics will be dealt with as follows:

1 *The physical environment;*
2 *The living environment:*
  A *Populations;*
    I. Interactions within the population of a species;
    II. Interactions between populations of different species:
      (a) In the laboratory;
      (b) In nature;
  B *Communities.*

1. The Physical Environment

An animal's physical surroundings – the shape and composition of its habitat – depend upon the geology and physical geography of its small part of the world. Vegetation is also part of this physical environment, and both this and the animals present are dependent upon a particular climate. The most important resource that the physical environment offers an animal is shelter, a place to live which provides some protection against the extremes of weather and the attentions of enemies. Such shelter may be permanent, as for soil-inhabiting beetles, or restricted to one or two life history stages as with the enclosed larvae and pupae of timber beetles. It may be available seasonally, as for deeply buried hibernating ground beetles, or it may be used daily as with ground beetles which hide under stones by day and hunt at night. For soil beetles and timber beetle larvae, food is available in their sheltered habitats, but many species must emerge from shelter to discover it. All beetles are exposed to some hazards for some time in their lives, and their special adaptations for survival depend upon which hazards they try to beat, and which they attempt to evade.

Shelter is also important to water beetles, but some of their requirements are rather different from those of their terrestrial relatives. For instance, since they live in the three dimensions of water rather than on the two dimensions of a land surface, a place to perch is important to many rather inactive aquatic predators; larval water beetles may find it easier to seize passing prey rather than swim in pursuit of it. For aquatic animals, the condition of the surrounding water is of vital concern. The amount of oxygen it contains is usually related to the turbulence or speed of flow of the water, being low in stagnant pools and high in fast-flowing streams. Oxygen concentrations also depend upon temperature, and many other factors, such as the presence of various salts, may have a profound effect upon the life of the animals present.

The climates of natural habitats present such a wide range of temperatures and humidities that many experiments have been carried out in the laboratory upon single species of beetles in controlled climates to try to simplify the interpretation of the beetle's behaviour. The beetles chosen for such experiments have usually been flour or grain beetles such as species of *Tenebrio*, *Tribolium*, *Rhizopertha*, *Oryzaephilus* and *Sitophilus*. The ease with which laboratory colonies of these beetles can be maintained makes them idea experimental animals, and in fact Chauvin has observed that the ecologist's *Tribolium* jar will end up by rivalling the geneticist's *Drosophila* jar. For instance, to determine the effects of heat and cold upon the development of a species of grain beetle, batches of eggs were incubated at different temperatures, each with a fixed amount of grain of a fixed moisture content. The proportion of larvae which hatched and lived gave the survival and death rates at a particular temperature, and the range of temperatures over which the beetle would develop was determined.

This sort of experiment has shown that there is an optimum temperature for a low death rate. If the experiment is repeated with a fixed temperature and a range of moisture contents, it can be shown that there is also an optimum humidity. This varies with the temperature, and this interaction between temperature and humidity was neatly demonstrated by Birch, who conducted a series of experiments on *Rhizopertha dominica*. In each test, he measured the proportion of larvae that failed to reach the end of the first instar. He found that at a particular temperature, the death rate depended upon the amount of moisture present in the grain, and that at a particular moisture content the death rate was related to the temperature. This is clearly illustrated by his three-dimensional graph (fig. 51) which shows the optimum climate (i.e. temperature and moisture content) for the grain beetle in these particular conditions. In nature, the situation is far more complex than in the laboratory, but the existence of a climatic optimum is true for many species.

Temperature is important because it affects both the activity of an adult beetle and the time needed for the young stages to complete their development. Its influence is most easily seen in those species which spread across a wide range of climates. For example, the seven-spot ladybird, *Coccinella septempunctata*, has an optimum temperature range best suited for its activity and development, but it has been forced to modify its life cycle in different ways in different places in order to adjust it to the local temperature range. Bodenheimer has quoted the life history variations in a series of localities from northern Europe to North Africa (fig. 52). The ladybird's optimum temperature range is between 15°C and 22°C. Its preferred humidity range

154

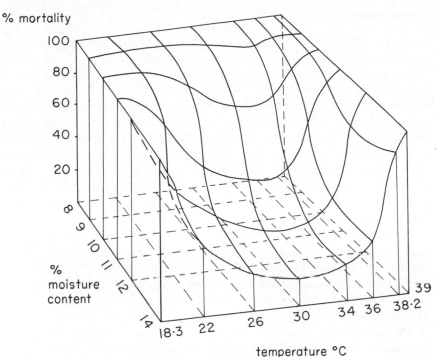

% mortality

% moisture content

temperature °C

Figure 51. *Climate and mortality*
Three-dimensional graph to show the relationships between temperature and moisture and the percentage of deaths of *Rhizopertha dominica* (Bostrychidae). (After Birch, in Browning.)

LOCALITY	J	F	M	A	M	J	J	A	S	O	N	D
London												
Berlin												
Paris												
Nice												
Naples												
Athens												
Ankara												
Tel Aviv												
Cairo												
Khartoum												

Figure 52. *Climate and life cycles*
Part of a world chart of life cycles of the ladybird *Coccinella septempunctata* in several different climates. Months are shown along the top of the table. Black shows the period of development, light stippling indicates hibernation, and close stippling indicates aestivation. (After Bodenheimer.)

is between 65% and 85% relative humidity, i.e. both very high and low humidities are unfavourable. When the average temperature falls below 15°C, its activity and development are greatly reduced or come to a halt in diapause (see Chapter 3). Thus in winter in northern Europe, the beetle hibernates. If the average monthly temperature rises above 23°C, activity and development again stop; this high-temperature period of inactivity is termed aestivation. In the northern part of their range, for instance in Britain, young adult beetles come out of hibernation in the spring when the temperature rises above their activity threshold. Mating is followed by egg-laying, and the larval development takes place in spring and early summer. The next generation of adults are active in late summer or autumn, but do not usually lay eggs until the following year.

The life history in the coastal plain of Israel (Tel Aviv) is a complete contrast. Many beetles hibernate, but they may become active and even oviposit at times during the mild winter. Most lay eggs in March, and these produce the first generation in April. A few of this generation lay eggs in May, but most of the April adults aestivate. They lay their eggs in the autumn and die. The larvae which emerge from these eggs are the second generation which emerge as adults in October. Again, a few individuals lay eggs immediately, but most hibernate and lay their eggs in the following March. Thus there are two generations plus two incomplete ones, compared with the single generation of northern Europe. However, the contrast could theoretically be even more marked, for Bodenheimer calculated that without the summer and winter checks on activity and development, there could be as many as nine generations a year. Figure 52 shows that there is no ideal climate anywhere within the beetle's range, but in spite of this the ladybird has become adapted to a wide range of climates over a very large area.

While the effect of temperature is usually upon the activity and rate of development of a beetle, the way in which beetles are affected by the moisture content of the air or soil may be less straightforward. Moisture is particularly important to the inhabitants of dry regions. *Aphodius howitti* is not a dung beetle, but a root feeder which spends all its life in the soil, except for the brief period of adult emergence, dispersal and egg-laying. It was studied in South Australia by Maelzer, who paid particular attention to the places in which the females laid their eggs. The pupae became adults in December, which is mid-summer and near the middle of the dry season. The beetles wait at the foot of their burrows until a thunder-storm in January or February wets the soil sufficiently to stimulate them to emerge. It is then necessary for the eggs to be laid in a burrow in the soil, and the beetles collect in large numbers in particular places. Maelzer carried out experiments to show that the selection of particular areas depended upon the moisture content of the soil. He also showed that it was not just the percentage of water in the soil

156

which was important, but the availability of this water to a soil inhabitant. Water is held in the spaces between the soil particles, and if these particles (and therefore the spaces) are very small, capillary effects make its extraction more difficult. Thus it is easier to suck water out of a sandy soil (composed of fairly large particles) than out of a clay soil (composed of very small particles) even when both soils contain the same percentage of water. The soil types were selected by the beetles on this more practical criterion of 'negative pressure' rather than on the percentage water content.

This reaction of an ovipositing female to moisture is not important for her own well-being, or for that of her eggs, but for the full grown larvae, pupae and emerging adults at the end of the next generation. This is the reason for the choice of particular soil areas which have been wetted by a short thunderstorm during the dry season. These areas have little vegetation and the soil is thus more easily wetted than the soil under areas of dense stubble, which keeps off the rain. In winter and spring, the barer areas form pastures in which the plants are not too closely packed, and the larval feeding activity makes the pasture even sparser. Thus not only is rain more likely to reach the soil, but there are fewer perennials likely to be present at the beginning of the dry season to compete for water with the dormant pupae and adults. What the adults' preference does, therefore, is to ensure that the dormant pupae and adults of the next generation will be living in relatively moist conditions at the period when there is the greatest danger of drying up.

The cases of *Coccinella septempunctata* and *Aphodius howitti* show two of the many ways in which climate affects the life cycle and distribution of beetles. However, the ladybird is unusual in having a very widespread distribution. Most beetles are more restricted geographically, and this can be seen even in the fauna of a relatively small area such as Britain where there are 'northern' and 'southern', or more usually north-western and south-eastern species. Some species are restricted to southern England, and quickly become rarer as one travels north. Our most spectacular species, the stag beetle *Lucanus cervus*, is not uncommon in the south-eastern counties from Kent to Hampshire, and it even occurs in south London. It is much less common north of the Thames, and only occurs sporadically as far north as Leicestershire and Lincolnshire. In contrast, a few species have a northern and western distribution: *Miscodera arctica* is a good example. This small, dark brassy Carabid, which has an obvious waist, is quite common under stones in mountainous areas and is occasionally found as far south as Shropshire.

Closely related species often have quite different geographical ranges. The five British tiger beetles are all found on sandy, heathy areas, or on sand dunes, but the green tiger beetle, *Cicindela campestris*, is the only one to be found in most parts of Britain. *C.hybrida* and *C.maritima* are very similar

157

species which are found in a few places on the coasts, particularly in the south and west. *C.hybrida* has reached as far north as Cumberland, but its habitats are all markedly 'southern' in their mild and sunny climates. *C.sylvatica* is an uncommon southern species which has occasionally been found as far north as the Midlands, and *C.germanica* is now restricted to one place in the Isle of Wight, although it has previously been found elsewhere in southern and western England. Most of these tiger beetles, which are rare even in southern England, are near the northern limits of their ranges in Britain. They are much commoner on the European mainland.

The British beetle fauna is considerably smaller than that of northern France, but it is composed of a mixture of species with very different climatic needs. To determine why Britain has this impoverished mixture, her recent geological past must be examined. The most profound event in our recent geological history was the series of ice ages and interglacial periods covering the last million years. However, it was as recently as about 10 000 BC that the ice sheets of the last glaciation made their final retreat from England. At this time, the English Channel and much of the North Sea were dry land since a great quantity of water was frozen in the ice sheets. The ice never reached southern England, but this area had a very cold climate with subarctic tundra present even in Cornwall. The only beetles present at this time were those species now characteristic of northern Scandinavia. Some of the species which arrived at this time from parts of northern Europe with a similar climate are now restricted to the higher and more mountainous parts of the country (e.g. *Nebria gyllenhali*). As the climate improved, the tundra zone followed the retreating ice northwards, and southern England acquired a grassland and scrub vegetation. The climate was probably still extreme but summers may have been quite warm. This climatic pattern is now found in central and eastern Europe, and species which are now found in these regions may have immigrated at this time. A possible example is *Nebria livida*, which is only found nowadays on some parts of the east coast.

Grassland in southern England was soon replaced by birch, pine, hazel and finally oak and other types of woodland. At this time, when the climate was similar to that of our own period, Britain probably acquired most of her present fauna. This was because the steadily rising seas separated Britain from the European mainland during this phase of deciduous woodland between 6 000 and 5 000 BC. Thus all our species, excluding later introductions by man, must have reached Britain between the retreat of the ice and the filling of the Channel. This relatively short time available for immigration is one reason for Britain's impoverished fauna. Just before the Channel was filled, southern England may have had a slightly better climate than the present one, and species now characteristic of the warmest and sunniest parts of Britain may have then entered. These would have extended their range within Britain during the climatic optimum which followed soon after the filling of the Channel. Our present slightly poorer climate might have been responsible for their present discontinuous distribution (e.g. *Cicindela hybrida*). It is likely that a few species have arrived with trade goods or ballast within historical times, and some have appeared within the last hundred years. The latter include such unwelcome visitors as the colorado beetle, and this species together with some other introductions will be discussed in Chapter 7.

Although the overall effect of climate is important in broad generalisations, it makes itself felt upon animals as changes in weather, and it is only the little bit of weather surrounding a small insect that directly influences it. This is the micro-climate, and within a sheltered habitat it may be much milder than the outer 'normal' climate. This was found to be so in the case of hot deserts (Chapter 5), but it applies to all types of habitats. The leaf-rolling weevils build themselves shelters which exclude most of the surrounding weather.

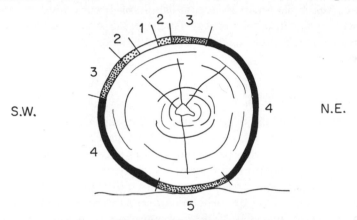

Figure 53. *Microclimates*
Cross-section of a log on the ground to show five different microclimates for the bark beetle, *Ips typographicus*. The favourable microclimatic regions (4) are shown in black. (After Geiger, in Chauvin.)

Fabre's dung beetles (*Scarabaeus sacer*) in southern France live in underground chambers beneath a soil surface which is baked by the hot summer sun. Soil beetles live in an environment which is always very humid and usually has mild, even temperatures. In contrast, a log lying on the surface of the ground may contain a wide range of microclimates. Geiger illustrated five of these (fig. 53), and found that they determined where the bark beetle *Ips typographicus* could live and breed. The bark of zone 1 faced the sun and was far too hot for the beetles even to lay eggs. Zones 2 and 3 were slightly cooler, but were still too hot for any larvae which hatched to survive.

159

Zone 5, under the log, was too damp for the larvae to live in, and only in zone 4 were the preferred temperatures and humidities present.

At certain times of the year, even conditions in the chosen microclimate may become unfavourable, and the activity of the beetle is temporarily halted. This can apply to any life history stage. In cool or temperate climates, overwintering (hibernation) is common. By burrowing down into the soil and becoming dormant, many beetles avoid the worst effects of the cold weather. Hot, dry seasons in warm climates are also unfavourable, and again many beetles have a dormant period (aestivation) in the summer. Even in Britain, some common species such as *Nebria brevicollis* have a summer activity pause. It was noted earlier that the seven-spot ladybird has periods of both hibernation and aestivation at the southern end of its range. Many ladybirds have the odd habit of congregating in huge numbers to hibernate or aestivate; as many as 70,000 beetles have been counted in some cases. It is not known why these associations are found, but they may serve some protective function. Such an accumulation of beetles must considerably alter the microclimate of their retreat. Thus even the presence of other members of the same species may affect the physical conditions of an individual's environment.

2. The Living Environment

One way to consider the living environment of an individual is to think of the contacts it makes with other individuals as occurring at two levels. The first level is within the species where there may be competition between individuals of a population for resources such as food or shelter. This would benefit the winners but penalise the losers either directly or in the next generation. Even if food or shelter is not in short supply, individuals may affect each other adversely if they become too numerous. Alternatively, there may be co-operation between individuals; male and female beetles sometimes work together, and larvae may gain from the presence of adults in the sub-social Passalidae (see Chapter 3). At the second level, individuals of one species contact those of other species, for in any normal habitat the population of a particular beetle lives within a community composed of many different species. The life of animal communities is the most complex aspect of the living environment, for its study may require a knowledge of feeding relationships, respiration rates, life cycles, migratory movements, activity periods, and many other details of the lives of the constituent species.

A. POPULATIONS

I. Interactions within the population of a species. The simplest possibility at the first level is to consider a single, isolated population of a species, in

160

particular a laboratory population. The 'Tribolium jar' provides a good example of the adverse effects of many individuals upon each other. One experiment by Birch, Park & Frank tested the effect of crowding upon the egg production of *Tribolium confusum*. Different numbers of beetles were kept for several weeks in tubes which each held eight grams of flour and yeast; the tubes were then stored under the same physical conditions. The flour was renewed each week, and the eggs present in the old flour were counted. One tube held a single male and single female beetle, one tube had eight pairs, one had forty pairs and the last had eighty pairs. Fifteen sets of these tubes were considered. The results showed that in terms of eggs per female, the single pair produced most eggs and the most crowded pairs least. This is partly due to cannibalism in the crowded tubes as eggs are eaten by the many beetles moving through the flour, and partly due to other effects such as the influence of crowding upon mating behaviour. There also appears to be a direct effect of crowding which reduces the numbers of eggs laid by females under these conditions, although it is not certain how this works. It may be due to a partial poisoning of the flour by accumulating excretory products which have a 'birth control' effect. (An excellent account of this type of work and its implications has been written by Chauvin, 1967.) The opposite condition, that of 'undercrowding' is fairly easy to imagine. If a single pair of beetles were put into a very large Tribolium jar, the male and female might never find one another to breed.

II. Interactions between populations of different species: in the laboratory. At the second level, a species comes into contact with other species. The latter may be predators, parasites or food. They may also be animals which do not make direct bodily contact, but which compete with the first species for limited resources. Again, the 'Tribolium jar' has been used to provide examples of this interspecific competition. Closely related species of *Tribolium*, such as *T.confusum* and *T.castaneum*, are adapted to live very similar ways of life. The 'jobs' each does for its living are very similar, and so one can say that each fills a very similar niche. If these species are put together into a tube of flour, they both try to occupy the same niche, and one of the two will win, and the other lose. Park and his colleagues demonstrated that in this sort of competition, climatic conditions (the temperature and humidity in the tube) were vitally important. They showed that although single species populations of either species could maintain themselves in any of six different sets of climatic conditions, when the two species competed one would eventually eliminate the other. These competitions were repeated twenty to thirty times in each 'climate'. In the cool-dry conditions, *T.confusum* eliminated *T.castaneum* in every case, but in the hot-wet conditions *T.castaneum* always won. Intermediate climates favoured either one or the other species

161

less obviously. Thus *T.confusum* won 69% of the contests in cool-wet conditions but *T.castaneum* won 86% of the trials in a warm-wet climate.

It is not yet understood how these two species are adapted to their preferred climates, but in some examples of competition between flour beetles the mechanism is clearer. Crombie found that when *Tribolium* and *Oryzaephilus* were kept together in the same culture, the latter beetles were eliminated by the *Tribolium*. The *Tribolium* larvae were larger than the *Oryzaephilus* larvae, and actually preyed upon their pupae. Crombie showed this to be the deciding factor by putting small tubes into the flour. This gave the smaller pupae a refuge, and enabled the two flour beetles to live together in the same culture. A single, extra factor thus drastically altered the outcome of the competition between the two species. This illustrates the artificial simplicity of the habitat in the Tribolium jar. In all the experiments described, different results would have been obtained had the beetles been able to leave their cultures, or if new additions to the population been able to immigrate from outside. Again, if the climatic conditions had fluctuated as in nature, the results of the experiments on competition between the two species of *Tribolium* would also have been very different. In fact, the outcome in each case would have been unpredictable, whereas Park could predict the outcome when the conditions were held constant and clearly defined. The importance of these experiments is not that they simulate nature, but that they provide simple models which can be used as starting points for attempted interpretations of small sectors of natural communities.

Interactions: in nature. One can look for examples of interspecific competition in nature, but it is often difficult to prove that competition is the factor limiting the overlap of specific niches. It could be shown experimentally by interfering with one of two closely related species at the edge of its niche, and waiting to see if the second species would take advantage of the situation. A few natural populations of animals have been studied in this way to demonstrate interspecific competition – for instance, barnacles, – but in most cases there is no such direct evidence. Such competition is often assumed where closely related species have clearly separate habitats.

Two very closely related Carabids are *Nebria brevicollis* and *N.salina* (= *N.degenerata* = *N.iberica*). The most obvious difference is the presence of minute hairs on the dorsal surface of the hind tarsi in *N.brevicollis*, and their absence in *N.salina*. *N.brevicollis* is a very common ground beetle inside woods, but it is usually less common outside them. In contrast, *N.salina* inhabits open areas such as sand dunes, and is apparently not found in woods. The two species appear to eat the same type of food – small arthropods – and are most active at the same periods in the year. One might suspect that the competition–exclusion principle was keeping their populations

162

separate. However, it has been shown by Fairhurst that *N.salina* is active in more extreme climatic conditions than is *N.brevicollis;* it can tolerate high and low temperatures and humidities better than the latter beetle. In other words, it is physiologically better adapted to its open habitat than is *N.brevicollis*, although the latter is well adapted to its milder woodland environment. This does not lose the competition–exclusion principle altogether; it merely moves it back to an earlier stage in the evolution of the two species. Suppose competition kept the species apart immediately after they had evolved from their common ancestor. The two species would become used to their different habitats, and these early habits would later have been reinforced by physiological changes to fit the beetles to the climates of their respective habitats. It is these later adaptations which now keep the species separate.

There are many closely related species which are geographically separated in this way. Besides the two species of *Nebria* mentioned above, there are two other British species which occupy other habitats. *N.gyllenhali* is fairly common in mountainous regions, whilst *N.livida* is restricted to sea-cliffs on parts of the east coast, particularly East Anglia and Yorkshire. This type of geographical separation often results in a gradient, with species being replaced in turn as one moves along it. Of course, closely related species may live together in the same habitat. In this case, one looks for other differences between the species such as different food supplies, or activity periods which occur at different seasons. This kind of species separation will be considered a little later. The point here is that populations of different species never completely overlap in all the details of their lives. Their 'jobs' are always different – that is, they occupy separate niches.

B. COMMUNITIES

Some of the reasons why related species may be spatially separated have been outlined, and I shall now consider a single habitat which may contain many unrelated species. Although species occupying similar niches may be separated by competition, many species occupy different niches which are complementary to one another. Thus 'jobs' are tied together in the form of predator–prey or parasite–host relationships. Both predators and parasites must ultimately depend upon herbivores, and these in turn rely upon either living or dead plant material. A single plant species may support a large community of herbivores and their predators and parasites. This is obvious if one thinks of a wood of oak trees, but it also applies to most other plants.

Many of the detailed relationships between the insects found on Scotch broom plants in the south of England have been worked out by Waloff, Dempster and Richards, and their colleagues. The broom was eaten in various ways by thirty five species of herbivorous insects, of which twenty-three species were studied in detail. The latter had seventy species of parasites and at least sixty common predators. The herbivores studied consisted of nine Lepidoptera, five Diptera, one Hymenoptera, thirteen Hemiptera and seven Coleoptera. The seven species of beetles ate most parts of the plant. Two species – the Bruchid *Bruchidius ater* and the weevil *Apion fuscirostre* – had larvae which lived on seeds in the broom pod. Both adults and larvae of the Chrysomelid *Phytodecta olivacea* ate the leaves, whilst adults of the weevil *Sitona regensteinensis* ate both leaves and stems. The larvae of this weevil lived in the soil and fed upon the bacteria-rich cells of the root nodules. Another weevil, *Apion immune*, had larvae which formed mines in the young twigs, whilst two species of bark beetles cut galleries in the woody stems. *Hylastinus obscurus* bored into living wood whilst *Phloeophthorus rhododactylus* only affected dead and dying wood. It is apparent that most of these beetles have clearly separate niches, and this feature is also characteristic of the rest of the community. In a stable community, one can expect interspecific competition to have been greatly reduced in this manner. However, at least two of the niches appear to overlap – those of the two seed beetles. These were studied by Parnell and their case is worth considering in more detail.

Although the larvae of both *Bruchidius ater* and *Apion fuscirostre* feed on broom seeds, the rest of the life histories of the two beetles are dissimilar. The adult beetles come out of hibernation and move on to the broom in spring. *Apion* hibernates in the broom litter, and emerges to start feeding on the young broom stems in March. *Bruchidius* overwinters away from the broom plants, and feeds upon gorse pollen after emerging. The beetles fly to the broom bushes as they come into flower. Both species move to the broom pods to lay their eggs. Those of *Bruchidius* are cemented to the outside of the pod, but the female *Apion* drills a hole through the pod wall, places its eggs beside the seeds and then plugs the bore-hole.

The exposed eggs of *Bruchidius* face many dangers and have a very high death rate (as much as 96% in one year on old broom bushes). The first stage larva which emerges from the egg also has a hazardous existence as it must travel through the pod wall and then find a seed to enter. Since only a single larva can develop in each seed, many larvae will die if large numbers of eggs have been laid on the pod, as happens if only a small number of pods are available. In contrast to this, the *Apion* larva emerges beside its seed, and can thus afford to be inactive. Many *Apion* larvae hatch earlier than *Bruchidius*, and these have the first choice of the seeds. However, they have a higher death rate due to parasitism than *Bruchidius*, and they stand less chance of survival if they have not completed their development when the ripe pod splits and ejects its seeds. *Apion* larvae are exposed if this happens, and have little chance of surviving. The *Bruchidius* larvae are better protected, as they can complete their development inside the ejected seeds if necessary. Thus the survival of each species from egg to adult depends on a rather different set of factors in each case, and the niches of the two beetles hardly overlap. However, there is one point in the life history where some overlapping occurs. Some of the *Apion* larvae are late in emerging, and they probably compete with the already overcrowded larvae of *Bruchidius*.

Both the seed beetles live in an enclosed habitat and although parasitism is an important factor in their lives, they are well protected from predators. Some of the other herbivorous broom beetles are much more exposed to predation, in particular the leaf beetle *Phytodecta olivacea*. *Phytodecta* lays its eggs on the leaves, and the larvae feed in an exposed position. It pupates in the litter beneath the broom bush, and after a short feeding period in the late summer and autumn, the adults return to the broom litter to hibernate. The biggest single cause of death in this species was insect predators feeding upon the eggs and larvae (particularly those of the early instars). This was effectively demonstrated by Dempster using the precipitin technique (see Chapter 4). The predators were mainly bugs of the families Miridae, Anthocoridae and Nabidae, but they also included the common earwig and a red mite. Much the same story was told for the weevil *Sitona regensteinensis*. Here, the eggs are laid on the soil surface and the vulnerable first stage larva must find its way to the root nodules to feed. Once inside the nodules they are fairly well protected from predators. The last instars however, are often too big for the nodules and must feed from the outside, where they are again vulnerable to predation. The predators include common ground beetles such as *Pterostichus madidus* and *Abax parallelopipedus*, and a variety of Staphylinidae. A different kind of predator was important in the case of the bark beetle *Phloeophthorus rhododactylus*. This was attacked by both parasites and insect predators such as the Cucujid *Laemophloeus ater*, but the most effective predators were birds. These were mainly blue-tits, which attacked the galleries during autumn and winter when their summer food supply of free-living insects had disappeared.

The most important aspect of the large number of studies made upon broom insects has been the analyses of the changes in numbers of the various populations. This has enabled 'life tables' to be drawn up for many species. These show what percentage of a population dies at each stage of its life history, and how many survive to form the population of the succeeding year. For instance, Danthanarayana found that in the spring of 1963, 6,799 adult *Sitona* produced 2,105,235 eggs. Of these, about 99·29% died at some stage before becoming adults. This left 15,001 adults to overwinter (plus another 1,413 survivors of the spring adults) and these reduced to 9,785 by the spring of 1964.

A number of different factors have been found to cause deaths at each life history stage of the species studied. They include parasites, various insect predators and vertebrate predators such as birds. Climate also has its effect, for in a hard winter more than usual of the overwintering stage will be killed. A hard frost in late spring may be even more drastic. For instance, in May 1961, sharp frosts killed two-thirds of the broom pods in one area, and both species of seed beetles died with the pods. If a factor is to regulate the size of a population, that is, to maintain the population at a fairly constant level, it must kill relatively more individuals when the population grows too large, and less when it becomes small. Such a factor would depend on the density of the population it affects. A parasite can work in this way by rapidly growing numerous when its host multiplies, and becoming rare as its host's numbers decline (because a rare host is more difficult to find). Insect predators may also fluctuate in this way, although many predators eat a wide range of food and can maintain their numbers by transferring to another prey species if their original prey declines. Vertebrate predators such as birds cannot multiply as fast as an insect prey species, but their searching pattern usually enables them to recognise and pick out relatively more of their prey when the latter becomes numerous.

Climate often acts as a limiting factor independent of density by affecting large or small populations equally, but it can also appear to act in a more density dependent manner; if a certain number of refuges from severe climatic conditions are available, a small percentage of a large population or a large percentage of a small population may equally survive. However, the effects of the 1961 frost was to crowd the surviving seed beetles into the remaining broom pods and thus increase competition between them. It seems that many different kinds of factors may help regulate the sizes of populations, and to these may be added 'self regulation' (as, for instance, in the *Tribolium* tubes where the larger the number of beetle pairs in a tube, the smaller was the number of progeny produced by each pair).

There is often one particular stage of the life history which is critical, and upon which the major regulating factor works. In the case of *Phytodecta*, this may have been the period of adult overwintering. The nature of the way or ways in which population regulation works is one of the central problems of animal ecology, and it has provoked several rival theories. These are beyond the scope of this small book, but they may be followed up in some of the excellent textbooks on animal ecology which are now available.

It will have been noticed that in the broom community, the base formed by the herbivorous insects supports a superstructure of predators and parasites. The broom bush has several species of carnivorous bugs which prey upon *Phytodecta*, and the broom litter under the bush has a number of Carabidae and Staphylinidae which prey upon the larvae and pupae of *Sitona*. All these predators may themselves fall prey to small insect-eating birds. These might

166

be tits or warblers in the case of the bugs, and ground feeding birds such as robins in the case of the litter beetles. It is just possible that an even larger predator, such as one of our few remaining sparrow-hawks, might prey upon one of the small birds. Thus starting from the weevil, there would be the sequence:

Sitona larva → Carabid → robin → sparrow-hawk.

Food chains of this sort can be constructed for all types of communities. The one given above is a daytime sequence, and it would be replaced by a different one at night. For instance:

Sitona larva → Carabid (nocturnal species) → Fox.

The herbivore at the beginning of the food chain depends upon a plant for its food, and this in turn is nourished by food built from simple raw materials by

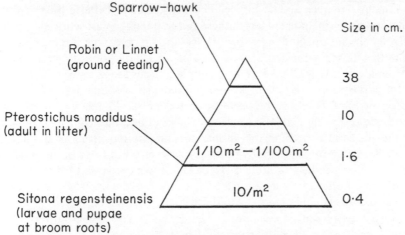

Figure 54. *A pyramid of numbers*
This is explained in the text. (Partly based upon data in Waloff.)

using the energy of sunlight. In the case of the *Sitona* larvae, the food is not only the broom root, but also the bacteria of the root nodules.

An obvious feature of most food chains is that the herbivores are smaller and more numerous than their predators. Similarly the primary predators are smaller and more numerous than the secondary predators – and so on. If, instead of arranging this sequence in a chain, the links are stacked on top of one another, a pyramid of different consumer levels is formed. This is a pyramid of numbers, but it could also be built for mass or energy. A possible pyramid of numbers based upon *Sitona regensteinensis* is shown in fig. 54. As with food chains, pyramids which show simple relationships between the various consumer levels can be constructed for all types of communities. As more is learnt about a particular community, so more food chains, often with alternative links, are worked out. The picture which emerges has been called a 'food web'; it gives a rough idea of the ways in which materials and energy are moved through a community. A deciduous British woodland is a good example of a complex community, and a simplified version of a food web it might contain is shown in fig. 55.

A woodland community contains a large number of animals, many of which are beetles. This is true even if one section of a woodland is considered, for instance, the woodland floor. The surface of the ground in a deciduous wood is usually covered with the partially rotted leaves of last year's leaf fall. As these decay into the soil, a rich layer of humus is formed which lies immediately above the top soil, and is often mixed into it. All these layers are inhabited by small litter and humus feeders such as millipedes, springtails, mites, small woodlice and fly larvae. These layers also shelter a host of small predators which include spiders, mites, harvestmen, pseudoscorpions, centipedes, fly larvae, ants and many beetles and their larvae. One can estimate the size of this 'host' by picking a small area of woodland floor and counting all the animals in it. I shall take as an example a thousand square metres of the soil of a fairly open patch of sycamore and ash woodland which has an undergrowth of bracken, bluebells and soft-grass. Estimates of numbers were made by taking regular samples of the litter and humus layers throughout the year and extracting the animal inhabitants by means of a Tullgren funnel. This apparatus gradually dries out a sieve-full of litter or humus from above, so that the insects are slowly driven downwards and eventually fall through the bottom of the sieve into a collecting bottle. Since the sample represents a particular area of woodland floor, the numbers of each animal per square metre can be calculated. Using this method, fluctuations in the population densities of many species of beetles can be followed throughout the year. A crude measure of the relative proportions of individual species has been made by averaging out the numbers of each species over the whole year. If the commonest species are arranged in order of increasing rarity, the results can be shown diagrammatically as in fig. 56, where the numbers of individuals are expressed per square metre of woodland floor.

Altogether, between seventy and eighty species of beetles were present, but the great majority of them were rare; it can be seen from fig. 56 that only a few were at all common. In fact, of all the individual beetles present, one third belonged to just one species, *Athous haemorrhoidalis*, whilst one half consisted of only five species. These included two wire-worms (*Athous* and *Agriotes pallidulus*), a small Staphylinid (*Sipalia circellaris*), a Hydrophilid (*Anacaena globulus*) and a member of the Pselaphidae (*Bryaxis puncticollis*), a family of beetles which are often considered to be uncommon. This

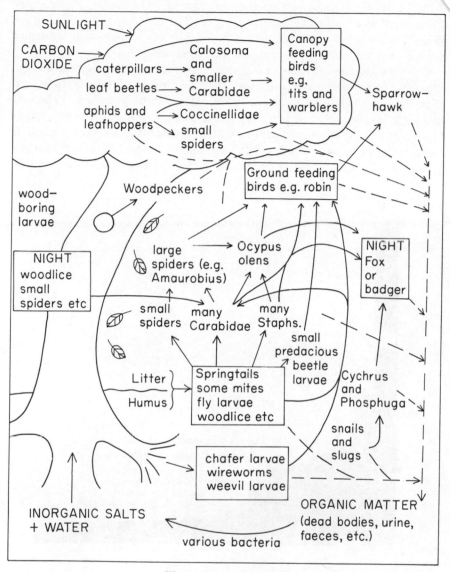

Figure 55. *A food web*

Part of the food web in a British deciduous wood. Arrows show the directions in which food and organic materials move.

distribution of common and uncommon species is typical of a particular community at a particular time and place. The actual species composition varies from one habitat to another, but the type of distribution remains the same with a few common species and many rare ones.

One big advantage of living in soil and litter is the shelter which the habitat provides. High humidities and 'buffered' (less extreme) temperatures are characteristic of the soil, and to a lesser extent of the litter layer. The soil and litter provide a hiding place for many animals, and some protection is even given against sharp-eyed predators such as insectivorous birds. Although some of the predaceous beetles in the soil spend all their time there, for instance small Staphylinidae, Pselaphidae and Scydmaenidae, others merely

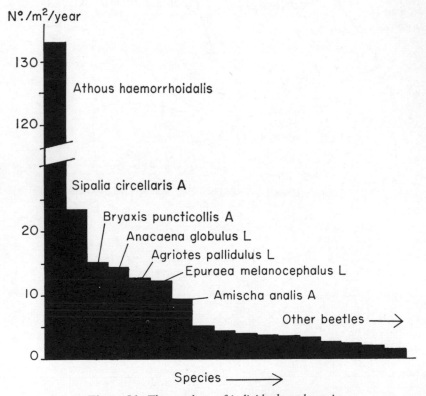

Figure 56. *The numbers of individuals and species*
The diagram shows the average number of individuals for each of the commonest species of beetles found in the litter and humus of a British deciduous wood. The species named are *Athous haemorrhoidalis* and *Agriotes pallidulus* larvae (Elateridae); *Sipalia circellaris* and *Amischa analis* adults (Staphylinidae); *Bryaxis puncticollis* adults (Pselaphidae); *Anacaena globulus* larvae (Hydrophilidae), and *Epuraea melanocephala* larvae (Nitidulidae).

170

shelter in the litter and soil during an inactive period. Some rest at night and come out to feed during the day, but in a woodland, many species rest during the day and emerge to hunt for food or mates at night. These surface-running hunters are mainly Carabidae and Staphylinidae, and a great deal of information has been gathered about them in the last few years. In Britain, studies of the Carabidae have been carried out by Gilbert, Briggs, Williams, Greenslade, Penney and many others.

Most of the studies have used pitfall trapping techniques. This involves pitfall traps, such as jam jars, being sunk into the ground until their openings are flush with the soil surface; thus beetles running on the surface can blunder into them. Once inside the container, the smooth walls prevent escapes and the beetles can be collected daily or weekly. Of course, there are drawbacks to this technique. Some beetles (especially Staphylinidae) may fly out, whilst others (e.g. *Nebria brevicollis*) may hang onto the rim of a jam jar with their back legs and so evade capture. Again, some species with good eyesight which are active by day (e.g. *Notiophilus* spp.) may see the trap soon enough to take avoiding action. There are other criticisms of pitfalling which relate to its use as a sampling method, but on the whole, it is a good, practical way of getting information about the activity (but not necessarily the numbers) of the surface runners.

The most interesting aspect of the work on surface running beetles is the way in which it has been shown how the many species of a community are separated up into their various niches. This separation is particularly clear in relation to different habitats, foods and periods of activity.

1 Habitats. A few surface runners have a fairly widespread distribution. For instance, *Carabus violaceus* and the three large species of *Pterostichus* (*P. madidus*, *P.melanarius* and *P.niger*) are commonly found both inside and outside woods. However, most species are more restricted in their habitats. In woodlands, the characteristic species of Carabidae include *Carabus problematicus*, *Cychrus caraboides*, *Notiophilus biguttatus*, *Nebria brevicollis* and *Calathus piceus*. The Staphylinidae *Philonthus decorus* and *Tachinus rufipes* are also extremely common, although – like some of the Carabids – not completely restricted to woods. Woodlands are by no means uniform habitats, and two extreme woodland conditions are the densely shaded, litter-covered zones deep inside woods, and the open grassy and scrubby edges of woods. *C.piceus* is probably most typical of the former region and *C.problematicus* is a common species of the 'edge' habitat. Many of these woodland Carabidae are dark coloured, and this seems to be connected with their nocturnal habits. The day-active beetles, such as species of *Notiophilus*, often have light metallic colours.

These colour and activity differences are also found in the Carabids of open

171

habitats such as fields, grasslands and heaths. Many species are metallic bronze, brassy or green in colour; these include species of *Harpalus*, *Amara* and *Agonum*, and *Pterostichus cupreus* and *Bembidion lampros*. All these are mainly day active. Like their woodland relatives, the noctural Carabids such as *Harpalus rufipes* are black. *Pterostichus madidus* is unusual in its more plastic behaviour. It may be found in both woods and open country, but although it is nocturnal in woods it switches to both nocturnal and daytime activity in more open habitats. Of course, 'open' habitats are a collection of very different regions, each of which have characteristic species. For instance, *Harpalus rufipes* is commonest on arable land, *Amara communis* is found particularly on grasslands, whilst *Calathus mollis* is a beetle of sand dunes and sandy heaths. In fields, Pollard found that the nocturnal species are most active in summer when the crops provide cover. At other seasons they are replaced by day-active Carabids and they return to the adjacent hedgerows, where they also overwinter.

Grass tussocks are like hedges in providing refuges for beetles. In summer, Luff discovered that their Carabid inhabitants have left their shelter and are mainly active in between the tussocks. Habitat differences occur not only between species and species, they may also occur between different populations of a single species in different parts of its range. In England, *Carabus nemoralis* occurs in both grasslands and woods, but in Russia it is characteristic of forests. It is also nocturnal in both northern and eastern Europe, but it becomes a day-active species in southern Europe.

2 Foods. There are very few detailed analyses of the natural feeding habits of most of the surface runners; although one can watch beetles feeding in captivity, it does not follow that their preferred food is eaten in the wild (Chapter 4). Most of the available information is based on stomach contents, and unfortunately the stomach contents of many beetles are always liquid. A few of the larger species are specialised predators such as the mollusc-feeding *Cychrus caraboides*, but most are general predators, predator-scavengers or mainly scavengers of dead insects and other small animals. These include several *Carabus* species and the larger Pterostichini; however, a 'general' predator may sometimes eat a fair amount of plant material. For instance, *Pterostichus melanarius* may eat seeds, and it is very partial to strawberries. Other Carabidae, notably species of *Harpalus*, *Amara* and *Zabrus*, have a diet which includes a great deal of plant material but they are in a minority which is particularly characteristic of arable land and other open country.

In woods, most of the Carabidae and Staphylinidae are predators and scavengers. The smaller species include many beetles which are mainly predatory on the small animals of the litter and soil. *Nebria brevicollis* was studied in some detail by Penney who found that the beetle caught prey up to about

4 mm in length, and that over 90% of this consisted of small flies, fly larvae, springtails and mites. *Notiophilus biguttatus* and *Loricera pilicornis* seem to have a rather similar diet. Two particularly common Staphylinidae, *Philonthus decorus* and *Tachinus rufipes*, are also general predators which feed on many kinds of small animals. In addition, *P.decorus* has been shown to feed extensively on the chrysalids of winter moths in oak woodland. It is difficult to determine Staphylinid diets because many species never have hard parts in their guts. This is due to their special feeding method, which was explained in Chapter 4.

It is possible to be more precise about food if one asks which species of predators are feeding on a single prey species. The precipitin technique was used by Coaker & Williams to show that the surface hunters feeding on young stages of the cabbage root-fly in cabbage plots included thirteen species of Carabidae and nine species of Staphylinidae. Other tests were used to establish how many root-fly eggs were eaten in a three-day period. Using this information, it was possible to work out what effect (in terms of the death rate) each predaceous species had upon the fly population. The two most effective Carabids were *Trechus obtusus* and *Bembidion lampros*. Much of the immature fly's death rate was due to beetle predation; of the total deaths, 24% were due to predation by Carabidae and 34% were due to Staphylinidae.

3 Periods of Activity. The difference between the day-active and night-active Carabidae has meant that in many habitats a shift system is worked, and the twenty-four hour period is split into day and night shifts. This has enabled species that are active at the same time of year to avoid direct competition. The alternative would be to spread the peak activity periods of the surface community over the year, and this situation is also found in most habitats. In any particular community the peak populations of the common species usually succeed one another throughout the year, although there may be considerable overlaps. There may also be species such as *Abax parallelopipedus* which are active for most of the summer, and others such as *Nebria brevicollis* which have both a spring and autumn peak period.

The Carabid life cycle usually takes a year to complete. In *Notiophilus biguttatus*, the adults become active early in the year, and breed in spring or early summer. Eggs laid at the beginning of summer produce larvae which feed and grow during the summer months. The new adult generation emerges in September or October, and these adults overwinter. This life cycle pattern of spring breeding and adult overwintering is also shown by *Carabus nemoralis*, *Loricera pilicornis* and *Pterostichus strenuus*. An alternative and more common life cycle pattern is seen in *N.brevicollis*. Here, the autumn period of peak activity is reproductive; breeding is followed by egg laying, and it is the larvae which eventually overwinter. They develop into adults in the following

173

spring, when the other yearly activity peak occurs. *C.violaceus, C.proble-maticus, Abax* and the larger species of *Pterostichus* all have this autumn breeding and larval overwintering type of life cycle. The type of life history and the beetle's habitat may be closely related. Murdoch showed that species such as *Pterostichus minor*, and some species of *Agonum* and *Bembidion* which lived in marshy areas were spring breeders and adult overwinterers. The advantage of overwintering as an adult was that flooding during the winter would be less likely to affect them; they would be more vulnerable if they overwintered as larvae.

The amount of adult activity varies from place to place and year to year, and it seems to be strongly affected by the weather. Nevertheless, it is essential for the members of a particular species population to become mature and active at about the same time. Some sort of synchronisation is necessary to achieve this, and diapause is one of the usual mechanisms. In *Pterostichus melanarius*, egg-laying takes place during much of the summer. The larvae diapause when they get to the second instar in either autumn or winter. Thus when they start growing again in spring they are all at the same stage. Other species may have a period of inactivity in the summer, particularly during July or August. In *N.brevicollis* the summer diapause allows the reproductive organs to mature, and when the beetles emerge from diapause in late summer they are all ready to breed.

By examining as many as possible of the different facets of the life of a species, one can gain some idea of how it fits into its community. In a highly evolved and stable community such as that of a woodland, competition between the species is present, but it has been cut to a minimum and the community's resources have been 'shared out' among a great many species. In less highly evolved communities which live in simpler and more homogeneous habitats, there are fewer species and there is often more interspecific competition. The artificial conditions of the Tribolium jar are an extreme example of this type of system.

CHAPTER 7

Beetles
and Man

What impact have beetles had upon man?

There seems to have been an indirect effect upon his imagination, and a more direct effect upon his bodily well-being and his food resources. In the past, beetles appeared in many myths and folktales, but modern man is most conscious that beetles are pests of his food supplies.

The interrelations between beetles and man can be listed as follows:

1 *Beetles in folklore and mythology;*
2 *Beetles in medicine;*
3 *Beetles as pests:*
   A Some economically important pest species;
   B Methods of controlling pests;
4 *Beneficial beetles.*

1. Beetles in Folklore and Mythology

We can only guess at the impact beetles had upon pre-civilised man. It was probably very small, since beetles are of little medical importance, and most lead hidden lives. They probably only entered the lives of early man as an occasional food source. Even today, many tropical peoples will extract large longhorn and weevil larvae from their hiding places and consume them with relish. Some of the earliest civilisations certainly had some entomological knowledge. The inhabitants of the neolithic town of Catal Huyuk in central Turkey had a considerable knowledge of the life cycle of the hive bee, and this was in the seventh millennium BC.

The greatest effect a beetle has had upon the culture and mythology of a civilisation was over 3,000 years later in ancient Egypt. The beetle concerned was *Scarabaeus sacer*, the sacred beetle. Its activities were seen by the Egyptians as a reflection, in miniature, of the world around them. They knew

175

that the sacred beetle rolled along a ball of dung and buried it, and that every year more beetles would appear suddenly by just crawling out of the ground. The ancient sun god Khepri was seen as a great scarab rolling the sun across the heavens, and every day the sun would be reborn. Thus the scarab became a symbol of rebirth in the same form after death. Scarabs, i.e. sculptured likenesses of the beetle – were put into the tombs of the earliest dynasties to ensure the soul's immortality. Scarabs are often found in funerary art, and a scarab heiroglyph (fig. 57) was used to write its name. The Egyptian name for the beetle is based upon a stem which meant 'become', which was also written with the scarab hieroglyph. Eventually, scarabs were worn as amulets by many people, and their original appeal as a means of ensuring rebirth after death became altered to that of a general good luck charm. So scarabs

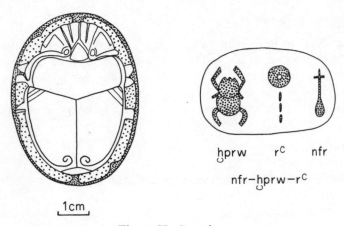

hprw   r^c   nfr

nfr–hprw–r^c

1cm

Figure 57. *Scarabs*
Left: copy of a large (heart) scarab of Tuthmosis III (18th Dynasty), seen from above; *right:* hieroglyphs composing the name of the pharaoh nfr – hprw – r^c, later known as Akhenaten. The three symbols roughly mean (in their order in the cartouche): becoming – sun – beautiful. (Courtesy of the Manchester Museum.)

were produced in huge quantities, and over 3,000 years after they first appeared, Roman soldiers had enough faith in their protective powers to wear them into battle. Even today, some people still see in the emblem of the scarab the symbol of good fortune.

Beetles also have an important place in many American Indian legends. For instance, in the mythology of one South American tribe, a huge beetle is the creator of the world, and from the grains of earth he had left over, he created men and women. (This certainly put humanity into its place *vis-à-vis* beetles.) In medieval Europe, several common beetles were incorporated into folklore, and Ewald Reitter has described how some of these myths have been handed down to the present day. Beetles appear as instruments of both good and bad fortune, and it is interesting that the dor beetle *Geotrupes stercorarius*, which is a relation of the sacred beetle, should usually be associated with bad luck. In parts of Austria, Germany and Sweden it is known as a witch beetle and was believed to be a familiar of the devil. Because of this it had supernatural powers. It could curse, or it could conjure up treasure. It was also known in Central Europe as the devil's steed. Killing a dor beetle would bring on a storm, but if a farmer rescued a dor beetle lying helpless on its back, he could save himself and his home and crops from the elements. Reitter explained this as the original association of the beetle with a storm god, and in Britain the beetle has sometimes been used for weather forecasting and fortune telling. The devil's coach horse (*Staphylinus olens*) is involved in a similar way in Irish mythology. In some stories it was supposed to have the power of killing by a look, or of cursing by raising its tail. Its supposed connection with the devil was in the form that eats the body of the sinner; indeed, it was apparently the symbol of corruption. If one had dealings with the devil, and accepted money, a devil's coach horse would appear in the hand.

The stag beetle, *Lucanus cervus*, is another beetle with a bad reputation, one of fire raising (by flying to a roof holding a glowing coal in its jaws) and of attracting lightning. Reitter again attributed this legend to an association of the beetle with a thunder god, and the fact that the larvae often inhabit isolated oak trees which are likely to be struck by lightening. The head and jaws were often kept as a lucky charm, or to ward off the evil eye, and they are apparently still sold in Istanbul as amulets. In Britain, the soldier beetle, *Rhagonycha fulva*, has acquired a bad reputation with many people, and children used to call these beetles 'bloodsuckers' when they suddenly appeared in large numbers in the summer. This name presumably reflects the colour of the beetle. This colour must also have given to it the more widespread name of 'soldier' beetle, for it is only in this century that soldiers have shed their red coats for more cryptic clothing. A similar colour association may also apply to the blue-black *Cantharis* species which are sometimes called sailor beetles.

In contrast to stag beetles and dor beetles, ladybirds always seem to have been regarded as bringers of good fortune, particularly to a person they alighted upon. Their associations are with God or Our Lady (the Virgin Mary) rather than the devil. Ladybirds have many names in different countries – for instance, ladybug, ladycow, Lady's beasts and God's beetles; most of these names refer to the widespread seven-spot ladybird. Such names are probably very old, and similarities occur even where different religions are involved. Reitter quoted an Italian name – the Lord's herdsman – which is remarkably similar to an Indian name – Indra's herdsman. These names probably refer to the association between ladybirds and aphids. When aphids are abundant on a particular plant, ladybirds may also be very numerous and easily noticeable. It has been suggested that the English nursery rhyme:

Ladybird, ladybird, fly away home,
Your house is on fire, your children will burn

arose from the custom of burning the hops after harvest, when many ladybirds and their larvae would still be present. However, similar rhymes are found in many other European countries, so it probably has a very ancient origin and perhaps a deeper significance. An ingenious German theory

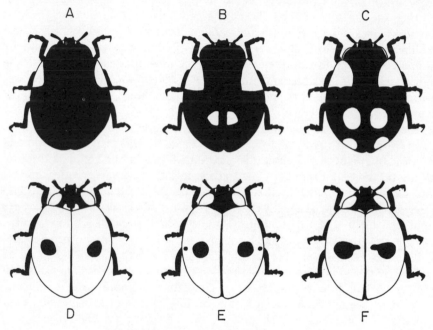

Figure 58. *Industrial melanism in ladybirds*
Six forms, three black and three red, of the ladybird *Adalia bipunctata* (the two-spot). The varieties are: A. *sublunata*; B. *quadrimaculata*; C. *sexpustulata*; D. typical; E. *stephensi*: F. *rubiginosa*. (After Creed.)

suggested that the rhyme originated as a charm to speed the sun across the dangers of the sunset, the burning red sky being symbolised by the house on fire. This association with the sun could be one of several features which may link the ladybird with the scarab and its associated beliefs.

Moving from folklore to fact, ladybirds have been affected by one of the most recent effects of man on his environment – that of industrial pollution.

Several species of animals have adapted to the blackening of their environment by showing an increase in the numbers of their dark coloured or black forms, and this is known as industrial melanism. This phenomenon is shown by species which exist in two or more distinct forms or colour varieties. The best known example is the peppered moth. The dark forms of this normally pale insect are favoured in blackened industrial areas and their surrounding blackened countryside because insect-eating birds overlook them and eat more of the conspicuous pale forms. It is obviously advantageous for the moth to match its background as closely as possible. This is not the case with ladybirds because they are usually warningly coloured and stand out from their backgrounds, yet the two-spot, *Adalia bipunctata*, has both red and black forms and shows industrial melanism.

The commonest varieties are the typical form which has two black spots on red elytra (plus a number of slight variations on this basic pattern), and two black forms, one with four and the other with six red spots (fig. 58). Creed showed that in England's industrial Midlands, in south Lancashire/ north Cheshire and in Yorkshire, populations of *A.bipunctata* had high proportions of melanic forms. It was 60 to 70% in Birmingham but as high as 90% in the Manchester and Liverpool areas. The red-spotted black forms are apparently as conspicuous as the black-spotted red forms, so camouflage is not a factor. Rather, the black forms seem to have some sort of physiological advantage over the red beetles. However, melanic forms are uncommon in both the London area and South Wales, so there is also a geographic factor involved (e.g. annual hours of sunshine), and the full story of ladybirds, men and their common environment is not yet complete.

2. Beetles in Medicine

Beetles and many other animals have an ancient use in folk medicine. Recipes for remedies to cure all sorts of ailments include parts of the more spectacular beetles such as stag beetle's elytra. Most of these physics were fairly harmless (if one had a strong stomach), but some were drastic and dangerous. This applied particularly to Meloid ingredients. Small doses of extract of Spanish fly elytra (*Lytta vesicatoria*, see Chapter 5) were used in many countries of Europe in aphrodisiac potions. In larger quantities, this extract – cantharidin – is a corrosive poison. It was well known to the ancient Greeks, and their word for 'beetle' was 'cantharos'. Accidental cantharidin poisoning (canthariasis) sometimes happens today, and those beetles in which the poison is present are probably the most important from a medical point of view. Paederin is another medically important blistering agent which occurs in some Staphylinidae (e.g. *Paederus* spp.) Merely handling these beetles has been known to produce a form of dermatitis with necrotic sores on the skin.

179

There have been occasional cases from both South America and North Africa. Some beetle poisons are extremely virulent if injected, for instance, the arrow poison mentioned in Chapter 5.

A few other beetles have attracted a little medical attention because of their bizarre feeding habits. Wigglesworth investigated one such case in Northern Nigeria. The 'Furau' had a bad reputation in one area for causing injuries to the bare feet of inhabitants. The insects proved to be tiger beetle larvae which had burrows beside well-trodden paths. Although they were effective enough against small insects, their man-biting activities were found to be illusory. More authentic cases of illness caused by beetles have been reported from India, Ceylon and Burma. Species of the small dung beetles *Onthophagus* have been found to cause diarrhoea by invading the rectum of sleeping children. This unusual behaviour has presumably arisen by the beetles following their food supply back to its source.

3. Beetles as Pests

The biggest economic impact which beetles make upon man today is as plant pests. A pest is an animal which competes with man for resources which he regards as his own. Insect pests often arise as a result of the mono-culture of plants by man, as for instance, with huge, unmixed acreages of wheat or conifer plantations. An enormous increase in an insect's food supply may allow it to outstrip its natural predators and parasites, and this is particularly true of introduced species and invaders. In these cirumstances, an enormous population of a herbivorous beetle may build up, and the damage it then does to its food plant puts it into the 'pest' category. Of course, this is not the only reason for the occurrence of pest species. Vagaries of climate and changes in the distribution of plants may also produce pests, and man may actually select a natural product with a built-in pest species. For instance, a tree grown for timber may have a 'normal' sized population of timber beetles which is quite sufficient to spoil an economically important percentage of the timber. The wide range of beetle feeding habits was discussed in Chapter 4, and this suggests that almost any natural product used by man can also be eaten by beetles. A list of economically important beetles will make this clearer, and it is convenient to consider these pests under four main headings: crop pests, forestry pests, pests of stored products and pests of houses and the structural timbers of buildings.

A. SOME ECONOMICALLY IMPORTANT PEST SPECIES

1 Crop pests

Elateridae: Wire-worms (larvae) attack cereals (wheat, barley, oats, rye, maize and rice) and root crops (sugar beet, mangolds and potatoes);

e.g. in northern Europe: *Agriotes*, *Athous* and *Corymbites* spp.; North America: *Ctenicera aeripennis*, the Prairie grain wire-worm; Queensland: *Lacon variabilis* – attacks sugar cane.

Scarabaeidae: Root-feeding chafer larvae attack cereals and root crops; adult chafers are leaf feeders; e.g. Europe: *Melolontha melolontha*, *Phyllopertha horticola* and *Amphimallus solstitialis*; North America: *Phyllophaga* spp., *Popillia japonica*, the Japanese beetle; Australia: *Aphodius howetti* (see Chapter 6); New Zealand: *Costelytra zealandica*; East Africa, South East Asia and South Pacific: *Oryctes rhinoceros* – adults attack coconut palms.

Chrysomelidae: Leaf feeders, e.g. *Criocerus asparagi*, the asparagus beetle; *Leptinotarsa decemlineata*, colorado or potato beetle; *Diabrotica* spp., cucumber beetles of North America which carry the diseases of bacterial wilt and cucumber mosaic (a virus).

Bruchidae: *Bruchus* spp. in Britain – pea and bean beetles; *Acanthoscelides obtectus*, North American bean beetle.

Curculionoidea: *Ceuthorrhynchus* spp. attack turnips (e.g. turnip gall weevil), cabbages and swedes; *Sitona* spp. – pea and bean weevils; *Apion* spp. – clover seed weevils; *Hypera* (= *Phytonomus*) spp. – clover leaf weevils; *Otiorrhynchus sulcatus* – a garden weevil, the vine weevil of Europe; *Anthonomus pomorum*, the apple blossom weevil; *Anthonomus grandis*, the cotton boll weevil.

Coccinellidae: *Epilachna varivestis*, the Mexican bean beetle of USA.

Carabidae: *Zabrus tenebrioides* – attacks wheat in south east Europe; *Harpalus rufipes* and *Pterostichus melanarius* occasionally attack soft fruit such as strawberries, etc.

2 Forestry pests

These include leaf beetles, but most are wood borers.

Cerambycidae: e.g. *Saperda* spp. in Europe and North America attack poplar, willow and apple trees, etc. The larvae are 'round-headed borers'.

Buprestidae: e.g. in North America, *Chrysobothris* spp. attack apple and other trees, and *Agrilus anxius* birches. The larvae are 'flat-headed borers'. There are many tropical species. The American *Scobicia declivis* is normally an oak borer, but may penetrate the lead sheathing of aerial telephone cables, and in California it is a serious pest.

Curculionoidea: *Pissodes* spp. and *Hylobius abietis* are conifer pests in Europe and North America. *Rhynchophorus* spp. attack cocount and oil palms; Bark beetles: In conifers – spp. of *Ips* in Europe and *Dendroctonus* in North America; In deciduous trees – *Scolytus* spp. in elms in Europe and North America; in tropical countries, *Xyleborus* spp. attack tea, coffee and cocoa plants.

3 Stored products pests

Anobiidae: *Lasioderma serricorne* – the cigarette beetle, often eats tobaccos; *Stegobium paniceum* – the drug-store beetle, will attack almost any plant or animal derivative.

Dermestidae: *Dermestes lardarius*, the bacon beetle, eats dried meats and other foods; *Attagenus* and *Anthrenus* spp., carpet beetles, attack fabrics, skins, furs, etc.

Ptinidae: *Ptinus* and *Niptus* spp. – spider beetles, eat many stored products.

Cleridae: *Necrobia rufipes*, a pest of smoked meats.

The following are pests of grain and flour, the most important stored foods.

Curculionidae: *Sitophilus* (= *Calandra*) *granarius*, the grain weevil; *S.oryzae*, the rice weevil; both species attack a variety of grain and flour.

Tenebrionidae: Meal-worms (the larvae) – *Tenebrio molitor* and *T.obscurus; Tribolium confusum* and *T.castaneum*, flour beetles.

Trogositidae: *Tenebroides mauritanicus*, the cadelle – eats flour and grain.

Dermestidae: *Trogoderma granarium*, the khapra beetle, mainly found in the tropics and sub-tropics.

Cucujidae: *Oryzaephilus suranimensis*, the saw-toothed grain beetle; *Cryptolestes ferrugineus*, a grain beetle.

4 Household pests

Dermestidae: *Dermestes lardarius*, the bacon beetle; *Anthrenus verbasci*, a carpet beetle common in Britain.

Anobiidae: *Anobium punctatum*, the wood-worm or furniture beetle; *Xestobium rufovillosum*, the death-watch beetle.

Ptinidae: *Ptinus* and *Niptus* – stored food pests.

Cerambycidae: *Hylotrupes bajalus*, the house longhorn – a pest of coniferous timbers in houses.

Curculionoidea: *Euophryum confine*, the 'New Zealand' weevil – attacks wet timbers such as badly drained foundations. Both this species and *H.bajalus* are introduced species which are gradually spreading through Britain. *Xyleborus perforans*, 'tippling Tommy', is an ambrosia beetle common in the tropics which bores into wine and beer casks.

Lyctidae: *Lyctus* spp., powder post beetles, or shot-hole borers, are an important timber pest in North America.

Many of the beetles in this list are of great economic importance, and a few of the best known species will be discussed further to illustrate the problem that they represent.

The major beetle pests of cereals are probably wire-worms, which include root feeding larvae with long lives. They cause damage particularly to wheat, maize and root crops such as sugar beet, mangolds and potatoes. The larvae eat seeds, tunnel into roots and stems just below the soil surface, and may even bite through the base of the stems. Wire-worms normally inhabit grassland, and may become a pest when this is ploughed up and planted with cereals. This was particularly important in Britain during the last war when great efforts were made to increase food production. Larval populations can be as much as 8 million to the acre (about 1,500 to the square metre). Potatoes suffer most severely, and even populations as low as 100,000 per acre will produce considerable losses.

The best known and most destructive of the leaf pests of major food crops is the colorado or potato beetle, *Leptinotarsa decemlineata*. Both the black and yellow striped adult and the red larva are very conspicuous, and the history of this beetle as a potato pest is well known. It originally fed on the weed buffalo burr which is found on the eastern slopes of the Rocky Mountains in the USA. Its food plant was a member of the genus *Solanum*, as is the potato, and when the region was settled in the mid-nineteenth century, the pioneers introduced the beetle to its new food plant. The beetle spread eastwards from one potato field to another, and often wiped out the whole crop. It reached the Atlantic coast in 1874, and had been introduced into Germany by 1877. It took some years to spread, but by 1922 it had reached France and Spain. In recent years, control has been fairly effective, but during the last war it spread unchecked through much of France. Occasional small invasions of southern Britain have occurred, but so far it has not become established and strict control methods are likely to exclude it indefinitely.

The most important weevil crop pest belongs to the same genus as the apple blossom weevil. It is *Anthonomus grandis*, the cotton boll weevil. The adult attacks the young blossom buds and eats cavities in them. The eggs are laid in these cavities early in the season, but later, eggs are laid in the cotton bolls. In both cases, the larva feeds in the hollowed out cavity. After a short pupal period, the adult cuts its way out; when mature, the adults may fly fairly large distances in a series of short stretches. The average time for a generation is only about twenty-five days, and up to ten generations may be produced in one year. The effect the weevils have upon a plant either kills the developing flower bud, or so damages it that when seeds are produced they contain very little fibre. It has been estimated that in the USA the annual cotton losses caused by the boll weevil are over 200 million dollars. The weevil is not a North American insect. It originated in Mexico or Central America and was first recorded from the southern tip of Texas in 1892. Its ability to fly enabled it to spread north and east across the southern states at a rate of about sixty miles a year (fig. 59). The weevil now occupies most of the American cotton growing belts (except California and Arizona) and extends as far as Costa Rica in the south and Cuba in the east.

Bark beetles and ambrosia beetles tunnel into many species of trees, but they are primarily important as the most destructive group of insects which

183

attack conifers, which are the major source of timber and wood pulp. In the United States it has been estimated that they destroy up to $4\frac{1}{2}$ thousand million 'board feet' of standing timber in a year, and this represents hundreds of millions of dollars. The most important American pests belong to the genus *Dendroctonus*, and of these the western pine beetle, *D.brevicomis*, is probably the most damaging. It only attacks Ponderosa and Coulter pines, but like other members of its genus, it can destroy mature trees. In contrast, species of *Ips*, the pine engravers, damage mainly young trees and the top shoots of older ones. *Ips* is one of the most destructive of the European bark beetles, for instance, *I.typographus* has often caused extensive damage to

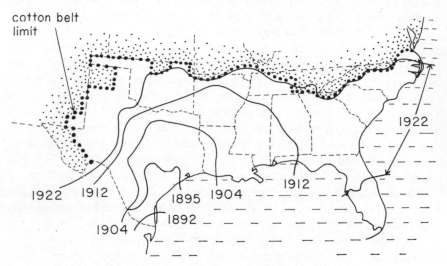

Figure 59. *The spread of the cotton boll weevil*
Map of the south-east U.S.A. to show the spread of the cotton boll weevil from 1892–1922. (Based on U.S.D.A. from *Destructive and Useful Insects* by Metcalfe, Flint and Metcalfe. Copyright 1962, McGraw-Hill. Used with permission of McGraw-Hill Book Company.)

spruce trees in mainland Europe, especially in Scandinavia. In Britain, the pine shoot beetle *Blastophagus* (= *Myelophilus*) *piniperda* is perhaps the commonest pest. It prefers Scots pine, but it will also attack spruce, larch and Douglas fir.

Many deciduous trees are affected by bark beetles, but their attacks are often not heavy enough to be economically important. However, bark beetles can cause serious losses to fruit trees and to some important timber trees. For instance, the hickory bark beetle of the central USA causes losses of about 15 million dollars a year. The worst-affected tree is probably the elm, which is attacked in Europe by the large elm bark beetle, *Scolytus scolytus*, and the small elm bark beetle, *S.multistriatus*. The latter beetle has been introduced into America, where there is also a native elm bark beetle. Most of the damage produced by the beetles is due to Dutch elm disease, a fungus which can kill an elm in a single season, and is almost impossible to eradicate. The rapid effect of the disease is due to the production of poisons which kill the plant tissues and cause swellings which block the wood vessels, and so deprive the tree of water. Either the crown of the tree or individual branches may be affected, but in severe attacks the whole tree is killed. The bark beetles carry the spores on their bodies and the fungus then spreads through their galleries under the bark. The disease first entered Britain in 1927 and then spread rapidly for the next ten years. In this time, 20% of the elms in southern England were killed before the disease died down. Unfortunately, another epidemic flared up in Britain in 1967, and by 1971 $3\frac{3}{4}$ million trees in southern England were affected. Of the 18 million elms in England south of Birmingham, nearly three-quarters of a million were dead and dying, the worst affected counties being Essex, Gloucestershire, Worcestershire, Kent and Hampshire. To try to prevent any further spread of the disease, a special order was approved by the Minister of Agriculture to enable the Forestry Commission to give local authorities powers to inspect infected trees, and to lop or fell them at the owner's expense if necessary. It was estimated that the total cost of this operation might be between £10 million and £20 millions.

Annoying household pests are often the same species as stored-products pests and the wood borers. The Dermestidae include carpet beetles, and in Britain attacks by *Anthrenus verbasci* have recently received some publicity. The hairy larvae are known as 'woolly bears', and attack stored clothing, soft furnishing, pipe laggings, and even bird's nests in roof spaces. Unlike clothes moth larvae, they do not merely attack soiled fibres, but will eat through any fibre fabric in their way, and this includes telephone wire insulation and even clean nylon garments. Until recently, in Britain, the species only had a wide distribution in the south of England, but recent improvements in British house design – mainly the widespread introduction of central heating – have greatly benefited both beetles and people. Thus one or two plagues of these beetles have been noticeable recently; for instance, in Autumn 1969 they invaded a council estate in Hereford, which until then had been to the north of their normal range (i.e. where they were sometimes common).

The most destructive household beetles are those which burrow in structural timbers, and the worst of these in houses is the wood-worm or furniture beetle, *Anobium punctatum*. It is commoner than many people realise, for a recent Rentokil survey of over 140,000 buildings (quoted by Hickin) estimated that three-quarters of British buildings are being attacked by this pest. The adult lays its eggs in surface cracks of woodwork, including furniture, and the larvae bore irregular tunnels throughout the wood. Their activities may reduce a piece of timber to a shell containing crumbling wood or powder. The larvae can live in old and well-seasoned heartwood, and the presence of 'worm holes' in furniture has sometimes been used as evidence of antiquity. It has been alleged that some furniture has been artificially aged by the addition of wormholes, and Imms reported (in 1947) that a sound of firing, as from a shotgun, was stated to have emanated on more than one occasion from a certain factory addicted to producing faked antiques. Since the war, however, there has been a great increase in the British population of the beetle, and its attentions have moved from furniture to building timbers including softwoods. Hickin pointed out that since the number of post-war buildings attacked is small, the proportion of pre-1939 buildings infested is actually over 85%.

The death-watch beetle, *Xestobium rufovillosum*, is another Anobiid which is occasionally found in old houses, but is commoner in the old timbers of churches, cathedrals and stately homes. It has caused extensive damage to many such buildings because of its preference for old oak, which was the commonest building timber. Many churches and cathedrals have current restoration appeals for money to replace unsound woodwork, particularly roofing timbers which have been attacked by death-watch beetles. The beetles usually came into the building with the timber when it was originally installed. It is unlikely that there are many new infestations; the beetles responsible may have left the timbers hundreds of years ago, for the damage is not always obvious, and may need careful investigation. The boring dust produced by the active larvae of both death-watch and wood-worm is the best indication of current feeding. The name 'death-watch' is supposed to refer to the superstition that the ticking sound made by the beetles was a herald of approaching death in the house. Such a sound might only have been heard by those nursing or sitting up all night with the seriously ill, and a death in such circumstances would not have been an unlikely event. In fact, the ticking noise is produced by the adult beetles banging their heads on the floors of their tunnels, and it is thought to be a mating call.

It is easier to appreciate the enormous damage done by beetle pests if this can be estimated in financial terms. The best-documented cases are from the USA. The invasion of the cotton belt by the boll weevil in the 1890s was a disaster not only for the cotton farmers, but for the merchants and even some banks, which failed. The overall losses increased rapidly, until in the worst year they reached over 1,000 million dollars. More recently, partial control of the weevil has cut down these losses, but in bad years the weevil still accounts for half the American cotton crop. Metcalf, Flint & Metcalf have given a table of the insects of the United States in account with the American people – debit – which quotes the estimated losses due to insects in 1957. Losses of forest trees and forest products, which were mainly due to beetles, were about 250 million dollars. The estimated damage to stored grain, which was due mainly to Coleoptera and Lepidoptera, was about 500 million dollars. The total amount of damage by all insects in this year to crops, forests, stored products and livestock amounted to about 3,500 million dollars. When one multiplies this figure several times when considering the losses on a world scale, it becomes obvious why extensive efforts have been made to control the numbers of insect pests.

B. METHODS OF CONTROLLING PESTS

There are three main ways of controlling insects: cultural methods, poisons (insecticides) of various sorts, and biological control methods. The first of these methods, cultural control, is basically common sense. It involves such things as crop rotation, so that if grain is particularly afflicted one year, it is replaced with another type of crop the next year. A change in sowing time may also be effective. In Europe, early sown Cruciferae may escape damage by flea beetles, whilst in America the early planting of cotton reduces boll weevil damage. Late sowing may be similarly used. Crop 'sanitation' is another important factor, for instance, burning the residual stalks of maize or sugar cane may destroy pests pupating in the stems. Weed control is another method of eliminating pests such as flea beetles which can breed in many types of cruciferous weeds. In forests, the removal of sickly trees and felled logs limits the breeding grounds of bark beetles and pine weevils. Stripping the bark from recently felled trees helps them to dry out rapidly and makes them less suitable for bark beetles. Again, pure stands of trees tend to have insect populations which show violent fluctuations whereas mixed woodlands have more stable populations.

Cultural methods are very useful restraints on pest numbers but more direct means of killing pests, either chemically or biologically, are usually necessary. Chemical methods usually involve poisons, which can be administered in several different ways. The surfaces of vegetation can be treated with sprays or dusts, whilst dense vegetation and pastures can be treated with absorbent clay granules containing insecticides. These normally act either as stomach or contact poisons. In enclosed spaces such as greenhouses, warehouses or ship's holds, fumigation is a very effective method. In this case, highly poisonous gases or vapours are used, for instance, hydrogen cyanide, carbon disulphide or methyl bromide. Simple inorganic compounds such as arsenicals were the first types of pesticides, but most of these have now been replaced by a variety of organic compounds. Some of these occur naturally, for instance, nicotine, pyrethrum and derris, but the majority of insecticides are synthetic. Although they are of many different chemical types,

187

two main groups of compounds have proved to be extremely effective – the organochlorines and the organophosphorus compounds.

The organochlorines include the best known modern insecticides, DDT and BHC. The insecticidal properties of DDT were first discovered in 1939, although the compound had been synthesised long before. It is a persistent poison which is highly toxic to insects, but much less so to birds and mammals. Unfortunately, as it is fat soluble as well as persistent, it accumulates in the fatty tissues of vertebrates. DDT has been used to control many species of insect. It was spectacularly successful against the apple blossom weevil which was a serious pest before the war, but which is now only an occasional nuisance. It has also been used effectively with BHC against the colorado beetle. Gamma BHC is the major constituent of products such as Lindane. It kills insects more quickly than DDT, but although it is less persistent it is more poisonous to mammals. It has been particularly effective against wireworms when used as a seed dressing on wheat, and it has been used successfully against the cotton boll weevil.

Chlordane and Heptachlor are both contact and stomach poisons which have a fumigant action. Chlordane is less toxic to mammals than DDT and has been used against household insects, whilst Heptachlor has been used as seed dressing. The Aldrin, Dieldrin, Endrin group were until recently widely applied insecticides, but their high toxicity to vertebrates has led to a considerable decrease in their use. In Britain, for instance, spring grain dressed with Aldrin, Dieldrin and Heptachlor caused the deaths of many birds. Most of the organophosphorus compounds are highly poisonous to all forms of animal life, and some, such as Parathion, have caused a number of human deaths. Malathion is much less toxic to human beings although it is a cumulative poison. Many of the organophosphorus group act as systemtic insecticides. They are taken into the plants treated and make their sap poisonous to attacking insects, thus they are particularly useful against sap suckers such as greenfly. It often means, however, that they cannot be used in food plants although they are particularly useful for crops such as cotton.

The control of insects by insecticides has had many spectacular successes, but the harm caused by side effects has become more and more apparent in recent years. The protection of employees who used insecticides is strictly regulated by law, although in Britain these laws do not apply to the general public. For the public, the main side effect has been the widespread contamination of foods and other materials by small amounts of insecticides or their derivatives. It has now been established that residues of persistent pesticides, especially organochlorines, can accumulate until they reach harmful concentrations in living tissues. The most drastic effects have been upon wild life, both vertebrate and invertebrate. Birds such as hawks, which are at the apex of the pyramid of numbers, have been particularly badly affected. Natural predators of insect pests have also been killed, sometimes producing the opposite result to that intended. For instance, in a test by Wright, in which DDT, BHC or Aldrin were applied to the soil of cabbage plots, the plants suffered more damage from cabbage root fly larvae than they did on untreated plots. This was because the Carabid predators (*Bembidion lampros* and *Trechus obtusus*) were more sensitive to the pesticides than were their prey. A final point is that many pests have evolved strains resistant to particular insecticides such as DDT, and either the concentrations of the chemical must be greatly increased or other compounds used.

All this suggests another approach to the control of pests; the method which attempts to use the natural enemies of a pest to combat it, known as biological control. This method of using an insect's enemies has been recognised for many years, and preceded the widespread use of synthetic pesticides. However, it is a much slower method to test, for all the potential predators and parasites of a pest must first be carefully screened to check both their effectiveness and their possible danger to non-pest species. Once in operation, unexpected factors such as weather or disease may limit its usefulness, but where it works it can prove an effective and – more important – a permanent method of control.

A common reason for an insect becoming a pest is its introduction to a new food source, or an old food source in a new area. Many of the most important pests such as the cotton boll weevil and the colorado beetle were invaders which were introduced without their natural enemies. In some of these cases, biological control has proved particularly useful, for it has been possible to introduce predators or parasites from the pest's original homeland. The first case of the effective use of biological control is a good example of this. The cottony cushion scale, *Icerya purchasi*, was accidentally introduced into California in about 1868. It had a disastrous effect upon citrus trees, and by the late 1880s it was threatening the orange-growing industry in the whole of California. The scale was discovered to have come from Australia, but it was not a pest in its homeland. Consequently, in 1888 an entomologist, Albert Koebele, went to search for its natural enemies in Australia. One of them was a ladybird, *Rodolia cardinalis*, the Vedalia beetle. Koebele sent back a total of 514 beetles to California. They soon became established throughout the citrus growing areas, and within two years their predation had completely checked the expansion of the scale, and brought it under control. They have since nearly eliminated the scale as a serious pest in California, although the widespread use of DDT and other organochlorine insecticides in the 1940s killed many beetles and allowed the pest to reappear in large numbers. Some areas had to be recolonised with the Vedalia beetle after the insecticide residues had disappeared from the foliage.

189

Koebele also introduced another Coccinellid – *Cryptolaemus montrouzieri* – from Australia to control another pest, the citrus mealybug. Although it did well at first, the beetle did not become properly established, so in 1917 it was one of the first control insects to be bred on a large scale. It was found that the citrus mealybug would live on sprouted potatoes, and large numbers of ladybirds were reared on these mealy bugs; for many years, over 40 million beetles were released annually into the citrus groves of California. Another beetle predator used as a control agent in America was the Carabid, *Calosoma sycophanta*. This was imported from Europe to combat a pest also introduced from Europe, the gypsy moth. Caterpillars of this moth had become a major pest of both evergreen and deciduous trees in New England. Several thousand beetles were introduced and many thousands more were reared, and released in the infected areas. Each beetle may eat hundreds of caterpillars during its lifetime, and as the species is now well established and has spread beyond New England, it is thought to be one of the most important checks on the gypsy moth populations. A good example from applied medicine is the use made of mollusc predators, particularly Lampyrids, Drilids and some Carabids, to control populations of snails which act as intermediate hosts for human parasites. The beetles have also been used to control populations of the giant African land snail.

Perhaps the most famous example of biological control was the opening up of huge areas of Australia which had been covered with an introduced cactus, the prickly pear. This was accomplished by the successful spread of a small moth, *Cactoblastis cactorum*, the caterpillars of which reduced the cactus to a pulp. An example of a beetle used in a similar way as a weed control agent comes from both Australia and New Zealand. St John's wort is a European flower which has thrived to such an extent in some parts of the southern hemisphere that it now covers a great deal of valuable land. The leaf beetle *Chrysolina quadrigemina* has been found to effectively reduce it in Australia, New Zealand, California and Chile. A British example is the recent introduction of the leaf beetle, *Haltica carduorum*, by Claridge and his colleagues in an attempt to control the creeping thistle, an important weed found in pastures and meadows.

Biological control has also been used against several important beetle pests, and there are some good examples of 'bacteriological warfare'. In Western Samoa the rhinoceros beetle has been killed in large numbers by a virus, and in the United States, the Japanese beetle (introduced from Japan) has been killed on a large scale by a bacterium. The latter produces the 'milky disease' of Japanese beetles and other chafers. The bacterium works well because it can persist for a long time in the soil in the form of infective spores. In the case of the eucalyptus weevil of Australia (*Gonipterus scutellatus*) which has been introduced into several countries with its host tree, a

190

Hymenopterous egg parasite, also from Australia, was found to act as a control.

Both chemical and biological control methods have obvious disadvantages. The use of chemicals is a short-term method which may poison not only the pest but also its natural enemies and its environment. Insecticides are rarely very selective, but while biological control methods are often quite specific and safe to use, they may be slow to act, and can rarely be used with immediate effect. A system which tries to use the best points of each method has been called integrated control. It attempts to combine the long-term control of a pest by biological means with a limited use of chemical control methods to hit population peaks of the pest. Thus, insecticidal sprays with short-term effects may be used on a crop or orchard pest during the period when its natural enemies are elsewhere or in resistant stages. Such a system requires a detailed knowledge of the ecology and life history of a pest and its predators and parasites, and so far it has not been widely used. However, the idea is slowly spreading, and Legner & Olton have described how it has been applied to housefly and stablefly control in California. The young stages of the flies live in dung and organic garbage near houses. If insecticides are applied to the larval sites all the natural enemies of the flies are killed, but if these predator and parasite populations are present they will kill over 95% of the immature flies. The predators include many species of beetles, particularly Staphylinidae, Histeridae, Scarabaeidae and Tenebrionidae, whilst the parasites include species of the Staphylinid *Aleochara*. Since it takes a long time to re-establish the predator and parasite communities, it is more economical to allow them to control naturally the young stages of the flies whilst the peak adult emergences are killed by insecticides applied to their resting sites. This has the added advantage that the flies build up resistance to the insecticide more slowly if the adults are attacked rather than the larvae.

Recently, a number of ingenious chemical weapons against pests have been added to the armoury of poisons. These are usually minute amounts of substances which have a biological action upon a pest. Insect repellents are now in fairly widespread use against mosquitoes and midges, but attractants have also been used to trap pests. In America, a bark beetle pheromone (see Chapter 3) has been used to lure bark beetles to their deaths. Some compounds have been sprayed onto crops to act as anti-feeding agents. They have the effect of putting herbivorous pests off their food to such an extent that they starve to death. Yet other chemicals have been used to sterilise male insects on a very large scale, so that they may be released to spread sterile sperm in a population. Sterility may also be induced radioactively, and this technique has been used successfully against screw-worm flies in Curaçao and in the south-east United States.

191

A final type of control might be termed legislative control, when a pest problem becomes so important that it is tackled at a governmental level. Many imported foodstuffs are inspected and a number of animals must be quarantined, but a good example of action directed against a particular pest is the case of the colorado beetle in Britain. The exclusion of this destructive insect from Britain is to a large extent due to legislation against both the beetles and their food plant. The importation of potatoes from infected areas is prohibited; this excludes potatoes from North America and several parts of Europe. Secondly, anyone finding a beetle in Britain is legally obliged to report it – there can be few other insects illustrated on posters in police stations. One is not even allowed to destroy the pest privately, it must be reported and officially sprayed. Legislation against insect pests is not a modern device, for in the Middle Ages plagues and pest epidemics were tried and usually cursed by ecclesiastical courts. Reitter has described this procedure and has quoted the case of an epidemic of cockchafer larvae in 1478. The Bishop of Lausanne instituted proceedings against these white grubs, and they were summoned before the Bishop's throne, where they were provided with learned council. The verdict excommunicated the larvae, and after it was announced from the pulpit, the congregation was asked to give its support by saying three Ave Marias and three paternosters.

4. Beneficial Beetles

This chapter has particularly emphasised the activities of beetles harmful to the human economy. This probably over-emphasises the role of beetles as pests, for while it is easy to catalogue the latter, it is more difficult to list all the beetle activities which benefit man. The importance of Coccinellids and Carabids in biological pest control has been mentioned, but the natural control exerted by the many beetle predators upon herbivorous insect populations is far more important. Perhaps the fundamental importance of beetles (and insects generally) to man is the part they play in providing the (relatively) stable environment in which we live. However, one particular beneficial activity of beetles is often overlooked and will be described briefly here; it is the role of dung beetles as scavengers. The habits of several types of dung beetles were described in Chapters 3 and 4. Although dung-feeding fly larvae are often more numerous than beetles in dung, the importance of several of the beetle species lies in their removal and subsequent burial of dung as food, either for themselves or for their next generation. Some years ago in 'A Naturalist in Hindustan', Major Hingston estimated that in active seasons of the year, two-thirds of the animal and human dung of India was buried by dung beetles. He thought that in May and June, as much as forty or fifty thousand tons of human excrement was carried into the soil each day. This figure would have been doubled or trebled if animal dung had been included. An enormous number of dung beetles must be involved in this activity, and as Hingston observed, if it were not for them 'Man assuredly would annihilate himself in the emanations from his own filth'.

Bearing this in mind, one can visualise the plight of a country which lacks dung beetles. In Australia, large numbers of cattle have been introduced, but there is no native dung beetle present to remove their particular dung. In Britain, a cow-pat only lasts for a few weeks in the warmer seasons of the year, and under ideal conditions in parts of Africa it may disappear in twenty minutes. However, in Australia, a cow-pat can last undisturbed for up to five years. The average cow produces ten to twelve pats a day, and this dung may cover an area of one-twentieth of an acre in a year. The cow-pat also stimulates a growth of rank grasses around it which are not eaten, and if the area of these is included each cow decreases its pasture by about a fifth of an acre every year. The total amount of pasture land lost in Australia by 1966 was about 300,000 acres, and this represents an annual loss of £2½ million in dairy products. A side effect of the accumulation of dung is the breeding ground it provides for harmful parasitic worms and flies. To deal with this situation, Bornemissza & Norris of the CSIRO at Canberra have started a project on the biological control of cattle dung. Large numbers of African and Mexican dung beetles have been released in northern Queensland in the hope that they will multiply. The 30,000 beetles released included not only four species of dung beetles but also three predators to deal with the fly larvae (including harmful species). By 1972, one of the dung beetles was well established in the Townsville area, and dung was being removed more rapidly during the wet summer season. It will be interesting to see if other species will establish themselves in the next few years.

Beetles have been put to several other unusual uses in the last few years, and I will mention three especially odd ones. In South America, some women have used beetles as ornaments. The use of the highly coloured elytra of jewel and diamond beetles is not particularly unusual but, recently, living ornaments have been worn with little silver chains to attach them to their owners. In Canada, the flour beetle, *Tribolium confusum*, has acquired a new role as a 'good food guide'. The beetles have been used to test the nutritional qualities of new strains of cereals. By measuring the length of time the larvae take to develop when feeding on a particular variety, it has been possible to check the nutritional value of a hybrid at a very early stage in its development. Thus unlikely varieties can be quickly dropped. Finally, an ingenious medical use has been discovered by the NASA Goddard Space Flight Centre for a reaction characteristic of some beetles – that used by fire-flies to emit light. The chemicals involved – luciferin and the enzyme luciferase – have been used to test for bacterial infections of the urinary tract (which can lead

193

to severe kidney infections). If living bacteria are present, they contain an energy rich compound called ATP, and in the presence of luciferin and luciferase this causes the reaction which produces a spark of light. When the amount of light emitted is measured by a sensitive detector, the level of bacterial activity can be deduced.

This chapter has been concerned with the ways in which beetles have affected both man's imaginative life – his mythology, and his practical life – his economy. However, I doubt if either the mythological or the economic implications of beetles explain why most Coleopterists are interested in Coleoptera, although they do serve as good rationalisations to explain this obsession to other people. When I first started collecting insects at school, the beetles stood out as a well-defined group of mail-coated, rather mechanical looking little animals. They had an air of beautifully finished, precision engineering to a greater extent than any other insects, and they showed an apparently endless series of variations on what was obviously the same theme. Perhaps it is this sort of impression that starts people collecting beetles in the same way as they might collect model cars or stamps. Of course, collections can be made to represent any particular facet of one's interest at any level of sophistication. The assembly of a small collection is probably the best way of commencing a study of beetles, and the huge reference collections of museums provide the essential foundations upon which all beetle studies build. But beetles are live animals, and dead beetles in collections look what they are – dead. After having determined the identity of a dead beetle, the next step is to find out what the live beetle does for a living (although one often finds a live beetle doing something interesting, and then has to kill it to find out what it is). This book has not attempted to catalogue the multitude of beetles, but has tried to give some examples of their habits and adaptations – in fact, their natural history. Perhaps surprisingly, one finds that the message of earlier naturalists still holds true for much of the important work needed on beetles today: one does not need a detailed technical background, but interest, patience and record-keeping are essential. Although we live in an age of beetles, the life cycles and habits of the majority of them are still unknown.

CHAPTER 8

Conclusion: An Evolutionary Viewpoint

The previous chapters have tried to present a survey of beetle activities. To conclude, let us speculate about the place of beetles in the natural order of things. What makes the beetles stand out against the immensely diverse background of animal evolution? What is the recipe for beetle success?

An initial advantage is membership of the great group of higher insects (Endopterygota). The latter have a life history in which the young stage is not merely a simplified adult, but an insect with its own specialities – a larva that gets on with eating and growing, whilst the adult is usually more mobile and mainly concerned with reproduction. The ancestors of beetles and other higher insects probably evolved about 300 million years ago (Upper Carboniferous/Lower Permian periods). The immediate beetle ancestor must have diverged soon after this. It was probably a rather delicate insect with unprotected wings, a tough but not particularly thick exoskeleton, and biting mouthparts. Its closest modern relatives are probably rather soft, weakly flying insects such as alder flies (Megaloptera) and lacewings (Neuroptera) However, beetles as a group are less aerial than these, or indeed than most higher insects. Although some beetles are strong fliers, most are less at home in the air than are flies, butterflies, bees, or wasps. Beetles are more closely associated with the ground or with vegetation; they are essentially surface or sub-surface dwellers. Sub-surface habitats are the obvious places for any unprotected insect to hide. The farther it could penetrate below the surface, the better protected it would be; so any increase in mechanical strength would have been a big advantage. In fact, it is probable that the adoption by the beetle ancestor of a sub-surface existence led to both the development of the particularly strong cuticle, and the retention and improvement of the biting mouthparts. These are perhaps the two most characteristic features of beetles.

The beetle cuticle has some remarkable resemblances to the structure of the composite materials that men have just started making. Its fibreglass or plywood-like properties and 'monocoque' construction make it an ideal material to withstand without breaking both the rapidly recurring small distortions due to flight, and the large distortions which accompany crushing. With the evolution of interlocking wing-cases, an armour that was strongly resistant to crushing forces completely enclosed the beetle body. Such an exoskeleton would enable a primitive beetle to move about under bark or logs without damaging itself, whilst most winged insects would merely find a temporary hiding place. To facilitate such activity, the most ancient beetles – the Archostemata – had a very thick, rugged cuticle; the Adephaga evolved a wedge-shaped body with special pushing hind legs, and the original Polyphaga were probably very small so that a greater range of sub-surface spaces were accessible.

The second major feature of beetles – the biting mouthparts – is usually considered to be more primitive than the specialised sucking or piercing mouthparts found in most other higher insects. However, biting mouthparts are more suited to the sorts of foods to be found under the ground or wood surface; for instance, decaying animal or vegetable materials, fungus, and small animals of various sorts all need chewing. Biting mouthparts also had the great advantage that when beetles moved into other habitats with other foods, these mouthparts were not too specialised to deal with them. Thus adaptations which were evolved for sub-surface life were very effective in allowing beetles to live on the surface of the ground or vegetation. The advantage of surface living is that a surface has a very large area with an abundance of niches, i.e. different jobs for different species. Thus the large number of species of beetles partly reflects the abundance of surface and sub-surface niches available to an insect group. It is the immense diversification of the original beetle stock – its 'adaptive radiation' – that is the measure of the success of modern beetles.

One can be more precise than merely saying 'beetles are a successful order', because the success of the beetles is the success of the few largest beetle families. For instance, there are five families which each contain 20,000 or more species (following Britton): the Curculionidae, Chrysomelidae, Cerambycidae, Staphylinidae and Carabidae. Together, these five families contain about 150,000 species – at least half of all the known beetles. The first three families are closely related surface dwellers as adults, although many species have sub-surface larvae. They cover the whole range of vegetable foods. The last two families are primarily sub-surface dwellers which are not closely related, but which both include a majority of predators. What are the strong points of these 'superbeetles'?

1 Skeleton. In many of the beetles we are considering, the skeleton is very strong and has precisely fitted sclerites which give the insect its characteristic air of 'beetleness'. This is particularly true of ground beetles and weevils. Weevils usually have a skeleton that is almost circular in cross-section, and is so strong and well integrated that they are very difficult insects to crush. However, there is a wide range of variation in leaf beetles and timber beetles, for some species have a fairly soft cuticle with an ill-fitted armour of sclerites. In many higher Staphylinidae, rigid armour has been sacrified to allow for greater mobility.

2 Movement. Carabidae and Staphylinidae are particularly rapid runners, as one might expect in carnivorous groups. Whilst Carabids in general have developed pushing power and a hard, wedge-shaped body to force their way beneath surfaces, Staphylinids have evolved flexibility and agility to twist and turn through spaces in the soil and litter; yet some Carabids are soft-bodied and not wedge-shaped, and some Staphylinids have tough and fairly rigid bodies. The plant feeders are well adapted to holding on to plant surfaces by their tarsal pads of specially hooked or flattened hairs. Whilst the weevils are often agile climbers, the timber beetles include many strong fliers. One of the largest groups of leaf beetles consists of small, jumping species, the flea beetles, and some weevils also jump in a similar way.

3 Mouthparts. Although the biting mouthparts of beetles have the capacity to deal with a wide range of foods, they also show a considerable range of variation. Amongst the plant feeders, some leaf beetles have small mandibles for soft leaves, but timber beetle larvae in wood have large, very hard jaws. Some weevils and bark beetles can bore through the hardest of woods, and here the mandibles are very small and hard, and form part of a drill-like tube. There is as much variation in the mouthparts of the predators. Both Carabids and Staphylinids often have long, pointed jaws for capturing prey, but in some ground beetles solid food is raked into the mouth, in others the food is mainly liquid, whilst in higher Staphylinidae there is a pre-oral mill for extracting liquid food. However, one group of Carabids – tiger beetles – has also evolved a pre-oral mill.

4 Water conservation. This is a most important requirement for small, terrestrial animals. All the five families have an efficient, waterproof cuticle, but the plant beetles also use their Malpighian tubules to retain water that might be lost from the hind gut. This device is lacking in Carabidae and Staphylinidae, perhaps because it is not so important for soil and litter insects to conserve water as it is for aerial, surface insects. However, many ground beetles use another device – rectal pads – to withdraw water from the hindgut.

5 Protective features. The methods used to protect beetles in these families from their predators are probably more diverse than any other set of characters. They include tough cuticles, large jaws, rapid running, flying, jumping, burrowing, good camouflage, cryptic habits, and a great variety of chemical weapons ranging from faecal shields to hot, corrosive sprays.

6 Life Histories. Carabid and Staphylinid larvae usually share the habitat and food preferences of their adults. However, they often show greater sub-surface behaviour, and this activity greatly reduces their need to conserve water. Leaf beetle larvae are also frequently found in the same places as the adult beetles – usually leaf surfaces. In contrast, weevil and timber beetle larvae lead hidden lives inside leaves, fruits, roots and timber or in the soil.

It is clear from this short summary that the five families have no single formula for success. Their particular successes are due to a multiplicity of reasons. Nevertheless, this does help us to understand – in general terms – how the beetles evolved. There seems to have been two important phases:

Firstly, the entry of the beetle ancestor into a sub-surface habitat – an obvious place to hide from predators. This led to the evolution of beetle characters, which allowed for a much more extensive use of the habitat.

Secondly, an extension into other sub-surface regions and an re-invasion of the surface habitats by insects which already possessed characters to make successful use of the many new niches now available (i.e. adaptive radiation).

But why should the Coleoptera and not another similar group of insects have had this success? Perhaps merely because the beetle ancestor was in the right place at the right time. Beetles were one of the earliest groups of higher insects to evolve, and so the primitive beetles would have been able to take advantage of the new ways of life before their higher insect relatives could compete.

Throughout this book, I have assumed that one criterion of the success of a group is the number of species which it contains. Obviously, there are other criteria for both groups and single species. One might choose the total number of individual animals, or their total body weight (biomass), or the amount of energy they use or pass through their bodies. Or one might not choose any of these superlatives, but consider success to be measured by the degree of integration a species or group has achieved to a particular way of life, and its ease of adjustment to change. Again, how does one compare the success of a species which is abundant in a particular restricted area (such as a water beetle in ponds) with one which is abundant over a much larger area (such as a small crustacean in the sea)? Such a comparison tries to equate quite different niches, and so must be biologically meaningless (but it is still an interesting question to ask).

One of the basic reasons for asserting that the number of species in a group is a reflection of its success is this: a multiplicity of species promotes prolonged success because it ensures that there is always a range of 'alternate species' to fit into the new niches of a continually changing environment. Since the surface of the earth and its vegetation often change rapidly – in geological terms – a group of animals must show continual evolution merely to stay in the same place. This is what the beetles have done, and are still doing. The reason why beetles are so successful at this makes them a fascinating group not only to evolutionary biologists, but to all those who are interested in the lives of animals, and the whys and wherefores of their existence.

TAILPIECE

Darwin and Beetles

It is not generally realised that the habit of beetle collecting was responsible for our modern ideas of evolution, for it helped to deflect Charles Darwin from his clerical studies to the study of science. William Irvine has recounted how 'Beetle collecting, begun without the slightest intellectual curiosity, developed observation and practical knowledge. Eventually, it led to constant attendance on J. S. Henslow, professor of botany at Cambridge; so that Darwin became known among the dons as "the man who walks with Henslow". And thus, entering science by the genial path of friendship, he absorbed a casual knowledge of zoology, botany and geology.'

(William Irvine, *Apes, Angels and Victorians*, London: Readers Union, Weidenfeld and Nicolson, 1956).

PRACTICAL
WORK

Techniques for collecting and preserving insects are given by the British Museum (Natural History), *Instructions for Collectors: Insects*; and Harold Oldroyd, *Collecting, Preserving and Studying Insects* (2nd edn) London: Hutchinson, 1973).

Several textbooks also give useful practical information, for instance, Borror and DeLong, *An Introduction to the Study of Insects* (revised edn) (New York, London: Holt, Rinehart and Winston, 1966).

A good introduction to practical work on beetles is given in *A Coleopterist's Handbook*, edited by Walsh and Dibb (London: The Amateur Entomologists' Society, 1954). This gives a great deal of useful information, including: collecting methods; where and when to collect; how to identify beetles and prepare a collection; information on larvae, life histories and rearing methods; and lists of beetles associated with particular plants.

FIELD WORK

The lives of even some of the common British beetles are still unknown or unrecorded in many respects, so there are still many gaps to be filled by field observations and other practical work. The sort of questions one might ask are:

What does a beetle feed on (particularly a predaceous beetle in its natural habitat), and what feeds on beetles?
What are the details of a beetle's life history, and are they the same in different places and different years?
How does a beetle normally protect itself?
How do its numbers vary from place to place and year to year?
When is it most active, and why?

As far as the last two questions are concerned, a particularly easy group of beetles to study are the surface runners, which can be caught by pitfall trapping as described in Chapter 6. The pitfall traps may be one pound jam-jars set flush with the surface. Alternatively, cheap plastic beakers are handy, for instance, the type used in tea or coffee machines. These beakers can be used in pairs, one inside the other, so that the inner one can be removed to extract its catch whilst the outer one remains in place, thus preventing the sides of the hole from collapsing. The traps may be examined at dawn and dusk, or every morning, or once a week, depending on how accessible they are. They can be set out in lines, or rectangles or circles – it will need some thought to decide what area is being trapped.

One obvious result of trapping will be to discover which beetles are common and which rare. It is also possible to make a rough estimate of the number of beetles active in your trapping area. This is not quite so simple as it may seem. If, in the traps, one Carabid is twice as common as another, it may merely mean that the first beetle is twice as active as the second. However, a population estimate can be made by using a simple sampling technique. When the traps are examined in the morning, mark the commonest species of beetles with a blob of cellulose paint (or nail varnish) on the elytra, and after drying, release the beetles nearby. The next morning, you may find that amongst the beetles trapped some are marked, and are therefore re-captures. If it is assumed that when you released the marked beetles the day before they mixed randomly with their fellows, your capture of marked and unmarked beetles is a small sample of the total number of marked and unmarked beetles in the whole population. For instance, if four out of twenty beetles are marked, then you assume that one fifth of the whole population is marked. But you know how many beetles you originally marked, so by multiplying this number by five you can calculate the total population. It must be emphasised, however, that this method of estimation is very rough; more refined versions of this have been explained by Andrewartha, *An Introduction to the Study of Animal Populations* (London: Methuen, 1961).

After catching your beetles, the main difficulty is in identifying them. It is most important that the species are correctly named, although if they can be consistently recognised as species A, B, etc., their identity can be established later. Museum entomologists and local natural history societies are always very helpful, and checking a species against an authoritatively named collection is the ideal means of identification, but of course this is inconvenient for day-to-day determinations. A great drawback is that the two major keys to British beetles, by Fowler and by Joy (see Further Reading), are out of print and very difficult to obtain through libraries. This is also true of Dibb's ecological key, whilst the fine series of Royal Entomological Society Handbooks is incomplete. Linssen's book in the Wayside and Woodland series unfortunately does not give specific keys, although it is well illustrated, and Bechyne's keys are useful, but were not originally intended for British beetles. Thus although experienced collectors have keys for identification, the beginner often has none. In order to try to bridge this gap, keys to some of the commonest beetles likely to fall into your traps are included in this appendix. They are taken from the Handbook of the North Western Naturalists' Union for 1963.

These keys apply particularly to woodland beetles, although the common species of gardens and meadows, etc., will often be included. Most of the less common species are omitted, and the species of more difficult genera are not keyed out; Joy or Fowler will have to be consulted for beetles which do not fit the keys. A series of keys to the species of larval Carabidae is being produced by Luff in the *Entomologist*, and van Emden's keys enable Carabid genera to be determined. Other keys have been mentioned under 'Further Reading'. A millimetre rule, a ×10 (at least) or ×15 lens, and a very bright light will be sufficient in almost all cases.

Colour: Beetles which have just emerged from the pupae are often very light in colour, i.e. white to brown. The normal coloration of the beetle may take from several hours to several days to develop.

Using the key. The following determination keys work in the same way as those found in most biology books. A key is a list of pairs of descriptive phrases which are numbered consecutively on the left hand side of the page. Each pair of descriptions consists of two alternatives, and you must choose the alternative which most clearly corresponds to your specimen. The number on the right hand side of your chosen description indicates which pair of alternatives must be considered next. You follow this procedure until you reach a name (family, genus or species) instead of a number on the right hand side of a description.

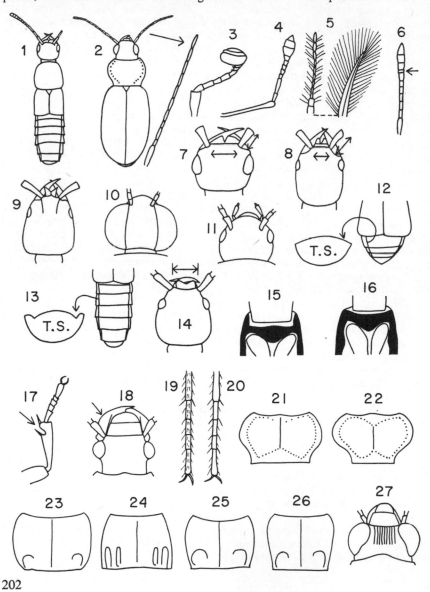

For example:

1 description A – (if A, go to pair number)   2
    description B – (if B, go to pair number)   3
2 description C – (if C, this is)   *species X*
    description D – (if D, this is)   *species Y*
3 description E   etc.
    description F   etc.

The words in parentheses are normally omitted. Figure numbers refer to the illustration on p. 202 and below.

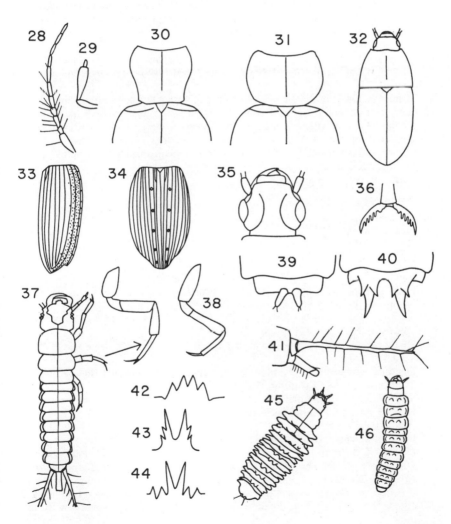

1. ADULTS: KEY TO FAMILIES

1. Elytra short, leaving 3–6 segments of abdomen exposed (fig. 1) Staphylinidae
   Elytra covering whole of abdomen, or all except last segment   2
2. Antennae long and thread-like; head with large jaws (fig. 2)   Carabidae
   Antennae clubbed, or slightly thickened with joint 8 smaller than 7 or 9
   (fig. 6); jaws small or difficult to see   3
3. Antennae with a club composed of plates (fig. 3); legs broad, with large
   spines (dung beetles)   4
   Not as above   5
4. Elytra quadrate or transverse, antennae 11-segmented. (Black, sometimes
   metallic, bulky, 11–26 mm)   Geotrupidae-*Geotrupes* spp.
   Elytra elongate, antennae 9-segmented (2·5–12 mm) Scarabaeidae-*Aphodius* spp.
5. Antennae clubbed, with an 'elbow', (fig. 4); head prolonged forwards into
   a short snout (Weevils) Curculionidae   6
   Not as above   7
6. 2·5–3·5 mm, black   *Barypithes araneiformis* (Schr.)
   5·5–8 mm, brown (black patches if scales rubbed off), *Otiorrhynchus singularis*
   (L.)
7. Minute (1 mm); antennae with long hairs, wings feather-shaped (fig. 5);
   elytra not covering last abdominal segment   *Acrotrichis* spp. (Ptiliidae)
   Small (2·5–5·5 mm); antennae slightly thickened towards apex, with joint 8
   smaller than 7 or 9 (fig. 6); oval, elytra covering abdomen, head with
   transverse keel at back   Anisotomidae–Catopinae (= Cholevidae) 8
8. Brown, 2·5–3 mm   *Nargus* spp.
   Black, or very dark (3·5–5·5 mm)   *Catops* spp.

STAPHYLINIDAE

8 mm or more in length   Key A
Less than 8 mm in length   Key B

KEY A

1. Head and thorax coppery, elytra dull bronze or brown, hind-body dark;
   centre of thorax with two rows of 4 or 5 punctures, 11–13 mm
   Philonthus decorus (Grav.)
   Not as above   2
2. Distance between base of antennae equal to, or greater than length of
   joint 1 (fig. 7)   3
   Distance between base of antennae less than length of joint 1 (fig. 8)   6
3. Thorax smooth and shining, with a few large punctures   4
   Thorax densely punctured   5
4. Sides of sternum (behind neck) meeting sides of thorax behind front angles
   (fig. 15), 8–14 mm   *Quedius* spp.
   Sides of sternum (behind neck) meeting sides of thorax at front angles
   (fig. 16), 8–14 mm   *Philonthus* spp.
5. 10–30 mm, stoutly built, large jaws   *Staphylinus* spp.
   (if black, 20–30 mm   *S.olens* (Muel.))
   8–9 mm, small jaws (fig. 14) (black with red legs) *Lathrobium brunnipes* (F.)
6. Elytra not overlapping; head widest in middle (fig. 8), (black with elytra

and legs reddish brown), 10–14 mm *Gyrohypnus* (=*Othius*) *punctulatus*
(Goeze)
Elytra overlapping; head triangular, widest at back (fig. 9), 8–13 mm
Xantholinus spp.

KEY B

1. Eyes very large (fig. 10), antennae with small club, 2–6 mm
Steninae–*Stenus* spp.
Eyes not so large, antennae not clubbed   2
2. Antennae placed on forehead (fig. 11); (usually less than 4 mm)
Aleocharinae
Antennae not placed on forehead   3
3. Side-borders of hind-body hardly raised (fig. 12); head often with two
ocelli between eyes   Omaliinae
Side-borders of hind-body strongly raised (fig. 13) and obviously angled
with middle part; no ocelli   4
4. Fish-shaped, with head and hind end much narrower than thorax
Tachyporinae   5
Not fish-shaped   6
5. 4·5–6·5 mm; black or nearly so; hairs projecting from sides of thorax
Tachinus signatus Gr. (= *T.rufipes* (DeG.))
2·5–4 mm; Head and most of hind-body black, thorax and palps yellow,
elytra reddish; no hairs at sides of thorax   *Tachyporus chrysomelinus* (L.)
6. Antennae inserted within outer margin of mandibles (figs. 7, 8, 9)
Staphylininae   7
Antennae inserted outside outer margin of mandibles (fig. 14), Paederinae
(e.g. 7–8 mm, black, red legs   *Lathrobium brunnipes* (F.))
7. Distance between base of antennae equal to, or greater than length of
joint 1 (fig. 7)   8
Distance between base of antennae less than length of joint 1 (fig. 8)   9
8. Sides of sternum (behind neck) meeting sides of thorax behind front
angles (fig. 15) (eyes often large); 4–8 mm   *Quedius* spp.
Sides of sternum (behind neck) meeting sides of thorax at front angles
(fig. 16); 4–8 mm   *Philonthus* spp.
9. Elytra not overlapping; head widest in middle (fig. 8); light brown to
dark brown, 4·5–7 mm   *Gyrohypnus* (= *Othius*) *myrmecophilus* (Kies.),
and *G.angustus* (Steph.)
Elytra overlapping; head triangular, widest at back (fig. 9), 4·5–8 mm
Xantholinus spp.

CARABIDAE

1. No notch in front tibia (over 6 mm)   2
Notch in inner side of front tibia (fig. 17); if difficult to see, length less
than 6 mm   12
2. 15 mm or more, hind body almost oval   3
13 mm or less, hind body not oval   6
3. 20–28 mm, head and thorax not very narrow   4
15–18 mm, head and thorax very narrow; (black, snail and slug eater)
Cychrus caraboides (L.) var. *rostratus* (L.)
4. Elytra black or blue-black   5

205

Elytra dark coppery (head and thorax black, sides of thorax and elytra sometimes reddish)   *Carabus nemoralis* Muel.

5. Elytral side-margin ('gutter') roughened, and shining blue-violet; surface of elytra rough   *C.problematicus* Hb. (= *C.catenulatus* Sp.)
Elytral side-margin smooth and very shining, coloured blue, green or red; elytral surface almost smooth   *C.violaceus* L.

6. Mandibles normal, sides of mandibles nearly straight (black 9–13 mm)   7
Mandibles expanded into side plates, with outer margins very rounded (fig. 18)   9

7. Antennae and palpi red, legs usually reddish   8
Antennae and palpi black, legs usually black (mountains and moorlands, etc.)   *Nebria gyllenhali* (Sr.)

8. Upper surface of hind tarsi with several pairs of fine whitish hairs, or pores, if the hairs are rubbed off (fig. 19) (woods, gardens, meadows, etc.)   *N.brevicollis* (F.)
Upper surface of hind tarsi smooth (fig. 20) (probably mainly in open country, edges of moorland, dunelands, etc.) *N.salina* Fair. (= *N.degenerata* Sch., = *N.iberica* Ol.)

9. Reddish (6·5–7 mm)   10
Bluish metallic   11

10. Head darker than thorax; hind angles of thorax diverging from base   *Leistus terminatus* (Hw.) (= *L.rufescens* (F.))
Head and thorax same colour; thorax strongly contracted at base (fig. 22)   *L.ferrugineus* (L.)

11. Bright blue; thorax only slightly contracted at base (fig. 21), 8–10 mm   *L.spinibarbis* F.)
Dark blue to nearly black; thorax strongly contracted at base (fig. 22), 7·5–8·5 mm   *L.fulvibarbis* Dj.

12. 14 mm or more (entirely black)   13
Less than 14 mm   17

13. Elytra smooth, with no pubescence   14
Elytra with fine pubescence (antennae and legs red, 14–16 mm)   *Harpalus rufipes* (DeG.) (= *Pseudophonus pubescens* (Muel.))

14. Hind angles of thorax rounded (fig. 23) (legs red or black, 14–17 mm)   *Pterostichus madidus* F. (= *Feronia madida* (F.))
Hind angles of thorax sharp   15

15. Hind part of thorax with two longitudinal depressions on each side (fig. 24), 18–22 mm   *Abax parallelopipedus* (P.&M.)
Hind part of thorax with one depression on each side   16

16. Thorax broadest at middle and evenly rounded (14–18 mm) (fig. 25)   *P.melanarius* (Il.) (= *P.vulgaris* (L.), = *F.melanaria* (Il.))
Thorax broadest near front, back part with nearly straight sides (fig. 26), 16–21 mm   *P.niger* Schal. (= *F.nigra* (Schal.))

17. Brilliantly shining with metallic reflection (brassy, green or purple)   18
Not brilliantly shining (black, brown or reddish)   27

18. Eyes very large (fig. 27), metallic bronze (4·5–5·5 mm)   *Notiophilus* spp.
Eyes not so large   19

19. Antennae with very long hairs on first five joints (fig. 28) (brassy, 7–8 mm)   *Loricera pilicornis* (F.)
Antennae without long hairs on first five joints   20

20. Last joint of maxillary palp very small (fig. 29)   *Bembidion* spp.
(e.g. 2·5–3·5 mm, brassy   *B.lampros* Hb.)
Last joint of palp not so small   21
21. Thorax much narrower than elytra (figs. 30 or 31)   22
Thorax not so much narrower than elytra   24
22. Sides of thorax S-shaped (fig. 30) (head and thorax bright green, elytra reddish with dark central patch, 6–7·5 mm)
Agonum (= *Anchomenus*) *dorsale* (Pp.)
Sides of thorax evenly rounded (fig. 31) (head and thorax green)   23
23. Elytra brassy (6–9 mm)   *A.mulleri* (Hb.)
Elytra green with sides yellow (8·5–10 mm)   *A.marginatum* (L.)
24. Characteristic oval shape (fig. 32), shining brassy, greenish or bluish   *Amara* spp.
Not with characteristic oval shape   25
25. Antennae reddish; sides of elytra with very many small punctures near outer margins (fig. 33), 7·5–10 mm (bronze, green or purple)
Harpalus aeneus (F.)
Antennae black, with joints 1 and 2 red; few punctures at sides of elytra (usually brassy or green, 10–13 mm)   26
26. Head with many small punctures
Pterostichus cupreus (L.) (= *Feronia cuprea* (L.))
Head with very few punctures   *P.versicolor* Sturm (= *P.coerulescens* (L.))
27. Last joint of maxillary palp very small (fig. 29) (2·5–6·5 mm)   *Bembidion* spp.
Last joint of palp not so small   28
28. Characteristic oval shape (fig. 32) (claws not toothed as in fig. 36)   *Amara* spp.
Not with characteristic oval shape   29
29. Thorax much narrower than elytra (fig. 30), black   30
Thorax not so much narrower than elytra   31
30. 10–12 mm, legs dark   *Agonum* (= *Anchomenus*) *assimile* (Pk.)
6·5–8·5 mm, legs very pale (edge of water) *A.albipes* (F.) (= *A. ruficorne* (Gz.))
31. A line of five punctures on each elytron near midline (fig. 34); brassy-black, 10–12 mm
Pterostichus oblongopunctatus (F.) (= *Feronia oblongopunctata* (F.))
Each elytron without a line of five punctures   32
32. Claws not toothed (6 mm or less)   33
Claws toothed (fig. 36) (6 mm or more)   35
33. Black, 5–6 mm (legs red)   *P.strenuus* (Pz.)
Reddish-brown, 2·5–5 mm, or if black, 2·5–3·5 mm   34
34. Forehead with deep impression (fig. 35)   *Trechus* spp.
Forehead without impression   *Bradycellus* spp.
35. Thorax not black   36
Thorax black   37
36. Thorax red (or partly red); head and elytra black, 6–8 mm
Calathus melanocephalus (L.)
Thorax, head and elytra light or dark brown; 6–9 mm (sandy coasts)
C.mollis (Marsh.)
37. Shoulders of elytra much broader than hind border of thorax (black, 7–11 mm)   *C.piceus* (Marsh.)
Shoulders of elytra of about same width as hind border of thorax   38
38. 7–8 mm (black, hind angles of thorax blunt)   *C.micropterus* (Df.)
9–13 mm (black)   39

39. Two longitudinal rows of pores near middle of each elytron (3rd and 5th
    interstices); 9–13 mm   *C.fuscipes* (Gz.)
    Only one row of pores on each elytron (3rd interstice); 9–11 mm; sandy
    places, especially near coast   *C.erratus* Sg.

2. KEY TO LARVAE

Beetle larvae have the head capsule and jaws well developed, and bear short
antennae. Legs are usually well developed, as in Carabidae and Staphylinidae,
but are very reduced in the Hydrophilidae–Sphaeridiinae, and are absent in weevil
larvae. Cerci – processes from the posterior end of the abdomen – are present in
many larvae.

1. Leg with five joints and claw (often two claws) (fig. 37)   Adephaga
    i.e., if terrestrial   Carabidae 2
    Leg with four joints or less (tibia and tarsus fused) (fig. 38)   Polyphaga 7
2. Cerci short and horn-like; body heavily built (broader than in fig. 37);
    upper surface blue-grey to black   3
    Cerci fairly long and slender, with hairs; body not heavily built   4
3. Cerci with one or two teeth or spines (fig. 40)   *Carabus* spp.
    Cerci very short and blunt (fig. 39); body very wide, as in a wood-louse
                              Cychrus caraboides (L.) var. *rostratus* (L.)
4. Cerci jointed at body; cerci slender, unsegmented and with long hairs
    (fig. 41)   5
    Cerci not as above (i.e. cerci fused to body, or if jointed at body, them-
    selves segmented)   other Carabidae
5. Front of head with four teeth, without large spines (figs 42 & 37) *Nebria* spp.
    Front of head with two large spines projecting forwards   6
6. Outer sides of spines bearing teeth (fig. 43)   *Leistus* spp.
    Outer sides of spines without teeth (fig. 44) (small and dark, to almost
    black)   *Notiophilus* spp.
7. Larvae with well developed legs and slender cerci (often two-seg-
    mented); large head and jaws, superficially like Carabid larvae
                                                                 Staphylinidae
    Not as above, more fleshy   8
8. Larvae with fleshy lobes projecting from the sides of the body (fig. 45);
    legs and cerci small or very reduced   Hydrophilidae
    Skin of larvae with velvety surface; legs not reduced; cerci absent (fig. 46)
                                                                  Cantharidae

GLOSSARY

Several words explained in context have been omitted.

n. – noun   a. – adjective   v. – verb   p. – plural

abdomen, n.   the third, legless region of the insect body

acclimation, n.   adaptation of an individual animal to a particular climate; rather like acclimatisation

aedeagus, n.   main part of the male genitalia of an insect

aestivate, v.   to become quiescent during a hot, dry period, usually the summer

aldehyde, n.   organic compound containing the —CHO group

algae, n.   a group of simple plants

allometry, n.   differential growth of part of an animal

antenna, n.   one of a pair of (usually) many-jointed sensory appendages on an insect's head (i.e. 'feeler')

anterior, a.   towards the front end

antibody, n.   protein produced in the blood serum of an animal when a foreign substance (antigen) is introduced to the body. It is part of the body's defence mechanism: the antibody is specific to the antigen, and combines with it

antigen, n.   introduced foreign substances causing the formation of antibodies

antiserum, n.   blood plasma containing antibodies

arboreal, a.   tree-living

arthropod, n.   a member of the group (phylum) of animals with jointed legs and an external skeleton; it includes insects, arachnids and crustacea

attractant, n.   chemical substance which attracts insects

Batesian mimicry, n.   mimicry in which a palatable insect mimics (q.v.) a protected model

buffer, v.   in a climatic sense – to tone down extreme conditions, thus making them less harsh

cambium, n.   the growth zone in the stem or trunk of a higher plant, lying just outside the wood zone

carnivore, n.   a flesh eater

cephalo-thorax, n.   a single region of the body formed by the head and thorax being fused together (e.g. in a female *Stylops*)

coxa, n.   the basal segment of the insect leg

crop, n.   a wide part of the foregut used as a food store

cryptic, a.   hidden, usually referring to coloration or habits

cuticle, n.   the outer, non-living covering or skeleton of an insect

defoliate, v.   to remove all the leaves from

diapause, n. or v.   a quiescent stage in insect development
dorsal, a.   towards the top

ectoparasite, n.   a parasite living upon the outside of its host
elytra, p.n.   the horny wing cases formed from a beetle's modified first pair of wings
endocuticle, n.   the innermost layer of the cuticle
endoparasite, n.   a parasite living inside its host
enzyme, n.   an organic catalyst which promotes most of the chemical reactions which occur in an organism
epicuticle, n.   the very thin, outermost layer of the cuticle
epipleuron, n.   the turned-down side border of an elytron
epithelial cells, p.n.   (e.g. of mammal sense organs) an outer layer of covering cells
exocuticle, n.   the layer of cuticle between the endocuticle and epicuticle which is often hardened by sclerotisation

femur, n. (p. femora)   the middle region of an insect's leg, often the largest
filiform, a.   (e.g. of antenna) thread like

galea, n.   the outer lobe at the tip of a maxilla
gall, n.   an abnormal swelling on a plant, often caused by an insect, a mite or a fungus
ganglion, n. (p. ganglia)   a swollen region of the insect nerve cord containing an accumulation of nerve cells
gene, n.   a unit character of heredity
genus, n. (p. genera, a. generic)   a group of closely related species
gizzard, n.   part of the foregut often adapted for filtering and/or grinding up the food

Habitat, n.   the particular place, or type of environment, which an animal inhabits
herbivore, n.   a plant-eating animal
hibernate, v.   to overwinter, a quiescent stage during a cold season
hormone, n.   a 'chemical messenger' circulated in the blood
hydrofuge, a.   water repellent, particularly of cuticle or hairs
hypermetamorphosis, n.   a complex series of stages in the development of an insect
hypopharynx, n.   a structure found on the dorsal side of the labium, at the entrance to the insect's mouth

inhibitor, n.   a substance which prevents or stops a particular activity, for instance, feeding
instar, n.   a period between moults, usually of a larva
interstice, n.   the space between two stria on an elytron

labium, n.   the most ventral, or posterior mouthparts; i.e. the 'lower lip'
labrum, n.   the 'upper lip' above the mandibles and mouth
lacinia, n.   the inner lobe at the tip of a maxilla
larva, n.   young, growing stage of an insect with complete metamorphosis
lateral, a.   towards the side

mandible, n.   the main jaw, usually the largest, of an insect with biting mouthparts
maxilla, n.   the second pair of jaws which underlies the mandibles

210

melanism, n.   the presence of dark forms in a species

mesosternum, n.   ventral sclerite of the mesothorax (q.v.)

mesothorax, n.   the middle thoracic segment

metamophosis, n.   the change from one form to another during an animal's life history, e.g. egg–larva–pupa–adult

metathorax, n.   the hindermost thoracic segment

microclimate, n.   climate of the minute region surrounding an insect

mimic, n.   an animal which copies the colour pattern and/or behaviour of a protected species

model, n.   the protected animal copied by a mimic

molar region, n.   basal region of a mandible

monogamous, a.   having a single mate

Mullerian mimicry, n.   mimicry in which there are several protected species which share a common colour pattern

mycelium, n.   vegetative part of a fungus usually forming a network of threads

niche, n.   the whole way of life, i.e. the 'job' done by one particular species, and no other

notum, n.   the dorsal sclerite of a segment

nymph, n.   young stage of an insect which lacks a pupal stage in its life history

olfactory, a.   concerned with smelling

palp, a.   sensory appendage of the maxilla or labium

parasitoid, n.   a parasitic insect which always kills its host before emerging

pharynx, n.   the most anterior part of the foregut, a muscular region into which the mouth cavity leads

plastron, n.   a coat of hairs on the surface of an insect which traps a layer of air to form a physical gill

pleuron, n.   the side of the body, the lateral region which lies between the sternal and notal regions

posterior, a.   towards the back end

predator, n.   an animal which captures prey for food; a carnivore

pronotum, n.   dorsal sclerite of the prothorax

proteolytic, a.   protein digesting (enzyme)

prothorax, n.   most anterior thoracic segment

proventriculus, n.   dilated region at the hind end of the foregut, sometimes a gizzard

pupa, n.   apparently quiescent life history stage in which the larva is transformed into the adult

pupation, n.   the act of becoming a pupa

pygidium, n.   the end of the abdomen which, seen from above, projects beyond the elytra

quinone, n.   a compound produced by oxidising a hydroquinone, which is an aromatic compound with two hydroxy groups

repellent, n.   a volatile chemical which repells insects

retina, n.   (or retinal cells) the part of the eye where light causes a chemical change, which in turn produces nerve impulses in the optic nerve

211

scale insect, n. a small, aphid-like insect (Hemiptera–Homoptera) which is protected dorsally by an all-enveloping carapace

sclerite, n. a hard, tanned region of the cuticle

sclerotised, a. hard and sclerite-like

serological, a. blood serum using (technique)

serrate, a. saw-like or toothed

species, n. (a. specific) a particular kind of animal or plant

spiracle, n. the 'breathing hole' in the side of an insect which allows air to enter the tracheal system

sternum, n. (or sternite, a. sternal) a ventral sclerite

stria, n. one of the longitudinal grooves on an elytron

stridulate, v. to regularly rub together two parts of the cuticle in order to produce a sound

suture, n. 1. a junction between two sclerites
2. more specifically, the longitudinal junction in the midline at which the two elytra meet

tarsus, n. the 'foot' region of an insect leg, with up to five segments in beetles

tergum, n. (or tergite) a dorsal sclerite

tibia, n. (p. tibiae) the part of the insect leg between the femur and the tarsus

trachea, n. (p. tracheae) an air tube, part of the insect's respiratory system

trachiole, n. small branch of a trachea

triungulin, n. (or triungulinid) the small, active first-stage larva of a beetle with hypermetamorphosis (q.v.)

trochanter, n. a small segment in the insect leg which forms the top of the femur, and articulates with the coxa

ventral, a. towards the underside

warning coloration, n. the coloration exhibited by a protected species, which advertises distastefulness, or a sting, etc

FURTHER READING

It is impossible to be completely comprehensive, so a selection of some of the most useful works is given.

KEYS: 1 *Adults*

BRITAIN

Handbooks for the Identification of British Insects (Royal Entomological Society of London) Vols IV, V, Coleoptera – a fine series, but incomplete.

BALFOUR-BROWNE, F., *British Water Beetles*, 3 Vols (London: Ray Society, 1940–1958) – the standard work; includes keys, figures and descriptions.

BECHYNE, J., *Beetles* (Open Air Guides) (London: Thames & Hudson, 1956), translated and edited by C. M. F. von Hayek from the German original – includes many common British species.

DIBB, J. R., *Field Book of Beetles* (London: Brown, 1948) – ingenious, based on ecological groupings; but one must decide on a habitat and a picture before reaching the keys.

Faune de France, Coléoptères (Paris: Lechevalier) – a series of volumes on Western European beetles, also including many British species; line drawings. In French.

FOWLER, W. W., *The Coleoptera of the British Islands*, 6 Vols (Vol 6 by Donisthorpe, H. St. J.) (London: Reeve, 1887–1913) – excellent coloured plates; some keys difficult. Out of print.

HINTON, H. E. *A Monograph of the Beetles associated with Stored Products* (London: The British Museum (Natural History), 1945) – a detailed study of many pests, including keys, figures and descriptions of both larvae and adults.

JOY, N. H., *A Practical Handbook of British Beetles*, 2 Vols (London: Witherby, 1932) – good line drawings; most keys reasonable. Out of print.

JOY, N. H., *British Beetles, Their Homes and Habits* (London: Warne, 1933) – a useful little book with keys to several common species and notes on their natural history. Out of print.

KLOET, G. S. and HINCKS, W. D. *A Check List of British Insects* (Stockport: Kloet & Hincks, 1945) – not a key, but essential for checking the correct name of an insect. A revised edition is in process of publication.

REITTER, EDMUND, *Fauna Germanica. Die Käfer des Deutschen Reiches*, 5 Vols (Stuttgart: Lutz, 1908–1916) – classic work on Central European beetles, which includes many British species; excellent colour plates. In German.

NORTH AMERICA

The North American Beetle Fauna Series. This is a new series which will consist of a set of regional manuals with keys to all the species occurring in the United States, adjacent Canada and adjacent Mexico. It will be produced by the North American Beetle Fauna Project, Director: Ross H. Arnett Jr., Dept. of Biology, Siena College, Loudonville, N.Y. 12211, U.S.A.

At present there is no complete key to all the 26,000-plus species, but there are keys to families and genera, and some regional keys.

Arnett, Ross H., *The Beetles of the United States* (*a manual for identification*), 1,112 pp. (Washington, D.C.: Catholic University of America Press, 1960–1962) – keys to all families and genera.

Blatchley, W. S., *An Illustrated and Descriptive Catalogue of the Coleoptera or Beetles* (*exclusive of the Rhynchophora*) *known to Occur in Indiana*, 1,385 pp. (Indianapolis, Ind.: Nature Pub. Co., 1910).

Blatchley, W. S. and Leng, C. W., *Rhynchophora or Weevils of North-eastern North America*, 682 pp. (Indianapolis, Ind.: Nature Pub. Co., 1916).

Borror, D. J. and DeLong, D. M., *An Introduction to the Study of Insects*, 819 pp. (Revised edition.) (New York: Holt, Rinehart & Winston, 1966) – keys to families and some subfamilies.

Dillon, E. S. and Dillon, L. S., *A Manual of Common Beetles of Eastern North America*, 884 pp. (Evanston, Ill.: Row, Peterson & Co., 1961).

Edwards, J. Gordon, *Coleoptera or Beetles East of the Great Plains*, 181 pp. (Ann Arbor, Mich.: J. W. Edwards, 1949).

Edwards, J. Gordon, *A Bibliographical Supplement to Coleoptera or Beetles East of the Great Plains, Applying Particularly to Western United States* (San Jose State College, San Jose, Calif.: J. W. Edwards, 1950), pp. 182–212.

Hatch, Melville H., *The Beetles of the Pacific North-west*, Parts I–IV (Seattle: University of Washington Press, 1953–1965) – keys to all families, subfamilies, genera and species.

Jaques, H. E., *How to Know the Beetles*, 372 pp. (Dubuque, Iowa: W. C. Brown Co. 1951).

Leech, H. B. and Sanderson, M. W., *Coleoptera*. In: *Fresh-water Biology*, ed. W. T. Edmondson (New York, N.Y.: John Wiley & Sons, 1959), pp. 981–1023.

KEYS: 2 *Larvae*

Keys to all the larvae of the British beetles are not likely to be available for many years.

For keys to families, refer to:

Böving, A. G. and Craighead, F. C., *An Illustrated Synopsis of the Principal Larval Forms of the Order Coleoptera* (reprint edition 1953) *Entomological Americana*, Vol. XI (n.s.) (New York: Brooklyn Entomological Society, 1931).

Crowson, R. A., *The Natural Classification of the Families of Coleoptera* (London: Nathaniel Lloyd, 1955).

Roberts, A. W. Rymer, 'A key to the principal families of Coleoptera in the larval stage', *Bull. Ent. Res.*, Vol. 21 (1930), pp. 57–72.

For generic and specific keys to particular groups, many different papers in the entomological literature must be consulted. But note particularly:

Van Emden, F. I., 'Larvae of British beetles,' Published in parts in *The Entomologist's*

Monthly Magazine, Vol. 75, pp. 257–73; Vol. 76, pp. 7–13; Vol. 77, pp. 117–27, 181–92; Vol. 78, pp. 253–72; Vol. 79, pp. 209–23, 259–70; Vol. 81, pp. 13–37; Vol. 83, pp. 154–71; Vol. 85, 265–83.

For Carabidae:

Luff, M. L. 'The larvae of the British Carabidae (Coleoptera)', I. Carabini and Cychrini, *Entomologist*, Vol. 102 (1969), pp. 245–63; II. Nebriini ibid., Vol. 105, pp. 162–79 – a series in process of publication.

Van Emden, F. I., 'A key to the genera of larvae Carabidae (Col.)', *Trans. R. ent. Soc. Lond.*, Vol. 92 (1942), pp. 1–99.

For Staphylinidae:

Kasule, F. K., (Keys to subfamilies and genera), *Trans. R. ent. Soc. Lond.*, Vol. 118, pp. 261–83; Vol. 120, pp. 115–38; Vol. 122, pp. 49–80 (1966–70).

Paulian, R. 'Les premier états des Staphylinoidea', *Mem. Mus. natn. Hist. nat. Paris*, Vol. 15 (1941), pp. 1–361.

Steele, W. O., (Genera of Omaliinae) *Trans. R. ent. Soc. Lond.*, Vol. 122 (1970), pp. 1–47.

GENERAL

Chauvin, R., *The World of an Insect* (Trans. H. Oldroyd) (London: Weidenfeld & Nicolson, World University Library, 1967) – insect life from an ecological viewpoint.

Fabre, J. H. His beetle writings have been collected into four books:

The Sacred Beetle and others (1918);
The Glow-worm and other Beetles (1919);
The life of the Weevil (1922);
More Beetles (1922).

All translated by A. Teixeira de Mattos (London: Hodder & Stoughton) – these are first-hand accounts of the lives of many beetles by the nineteenth-century pioneer of both insect natural history and its exposition to a wide readership. These books are fairly easy to obtain secondhand.

Imms, A. D., *Insect Natural History* (New Naturalist Series) (London: Collins, 1947) (3rd edition, 1971) – a classic, very readable.

Linssen, E. F., *Beetles of the British Isles*, 2. Vols (London: Warne, 1959) – no keys, but Fowler's plates are reproduced, half in colour; gives information on life histories, etc., for many species.

Mandahl-Barth, G., *Woodland Life*, edited in the English Edition by A. Darlington (London: Blandford, 1966) – one of a useful series; good for the identification of all the common woodland insects; no keys, but excellent colour illustrations.

Paulin, R., *Les Coléoptères. Formes – Moeurs – Rôle* (Paris: Payot, 1943) – a great deal of information on beetle biology. In French.

Wigglesworth, V. B., *The Life of Insects* (London: Weidenfeld & Nicolson, 1964) – an excellent, clear account of how insects work.

WORKS OF REFERENCE ON CLASSIFICATION, STRUCTURE AND FUNCTION

Borror, D. J. and DeLong, D. M., *An Introduction to the Study of Insects* (revised edition) (New York, London: Holt, Rinehart & Winston, 1966) – a North American textbook.

Chapman, R. F., *The Insects, Structure and Function* (London: English Universities Press, 1969) – excellent, modern account.

Crowson, R. A., *The Natural Classification of the Families of Coleoptera* (London: Nathaniel Lloyd, 1955) – a comprehensive, modern system of classification.

Crowson, R. A., 'The Phylogeny of Coleoptera,' *Annual Review of Entomology*, Vol. 5 (1960), pp. 111–34 – the evolution of beetles.

C.S.I.R.O., *Insects of Australia* (Division of Entomology, C.S.I.R.O., Australia: Melbourne University Press, 1970) – Coleoptera by E. B. Britton; A comprehensive Australian textbook.

Imms, A. D., *A General Textbook of Entomology* (9th edition revised by Richards and Davies) (London: Methuen, 1957) – a standard work on structure and classification.

Wigglesworth, V. B., *The Principles of Insect Physiology* (London: Methuen, 1953) – how insects work.

PICTURE BOOKS

All include a text with general information.

Bandsma, A. T. and Brandt, R. T., *The Amazing World of Insects* (London: Allen & Unwin, 1963) – fine photographs of New Zealand and Australian insects.

Bohac, V. and Winkler, J. R., *A Book of Beetles* (London: Spring Books, 1964) – good colour illustrations; good value for money.

Burton, J., and others, *The Oxford Book of Insects* (London: Oxford University Press, 1968) – good colour plates with an informative text.

Reitter, Ewald, *Beetles* (London: Hamlyn, 1961) – magnificent, large colour photographs; expensive.

Stanek, V. J., *The Pictorial Encyclopedia of Insects* (London: Hamlyn, 1969) – a large number of excellent insect photographs, including some in colour; excellent value for money.

BIBLIOGRAPHY

CHAPTER 2

Arnett, R., 'Present and future systematics of the Coleoptera in North America', *Ann. Ent. soc. Amer.* Vol. 60 (1967), pp. 162–70.

Arrow, G. J., *Horned Beetles: A Study of the Fantastic in Nature* (Ed. W. D. Hincks) (The Hague: Junk, 1951).

Britton, E. B., in C.S.I.R.O., *Insects of Australia* (Division of Entomology, C.S.I.R.O. Australia: Melbourne University Press, 1970).

Chapman, R. F., *The Insects, Structure and Function* (London: English Universities Press, 1969).

Crowson, R. A., *The Natural Classification of the Families of Coleoptera* (London: Nathaniel Lloyd, 1955).

Dethier, V. G., *The Physiology of Insect Senses* (London: Methuen, 1963).

Horridge, G. A., 'The flight of very small insects', *Nature*, Vol. 178 (1956), pp. 1334–5.

Horridge, G. A., 'The eye of the firefly *Photuris*', *Proc. Roy. Soc. B.*, Vol. 171 (1969), pp. 445–63.

Hughes, G. M., in M. Rockstein (Ed.), *The Physiology of Insecta* (New York & London: Academic Press, 1965), Vol. II.

Imms, A. D., *Insect Natural History*, New Naturalist Series (London: Collins, 1947) (3rd Edition, 1971).

Joy, N. H., *British Beetles, their Homes and Habits* (London: Warne, 1933).

Kloet, G. S. and Hincks, W. D., *A Check List of British Insects* (Stockport: Kloet & Hincks, 1945).

Reitter, Ewald, *Beetles* (London: Hamlyn, 1961).

Wells, M., *Lower Animals* (London: World University Library, Weidenfeld & Nicolson, 1968).

Williams, C. B., 'The range and pattern of insect abundance', *Amer. Nat.*, Vol. 94 (1960), pp. 137–51.

CHAPTER 3

Arrow, G. J., *Horned Beetles: A Study of the Fantastic in Nature* (Ed. W. D. Hincks) (The Hague: Junk, 1951).

Balduf, W. V., *The Bionomics of Entomophagous Coleoptera* (New York: 1935. London: E. W. Classey, 1969 reprint).

Buck, J. B., 'Synchronous flashing of fireflies experimentally induced', *Science*, Vol. 81 (1935), pp. 339–40.

Chapman, R. F., *The Insects, Structure and Function* (London: English Universities Press, 1969).

Davey, K. G., *Reproduction in Insects* (Edinburgh: Oliver & Boyd, 1965).

Emden, F. I. van, 'Egg-bursters in some more families of polyphagous beetles, and some general remarks on egg-bursters', *Proc. R. Ent. Soc. Lond. A.* Vol. 21 (1946), pp. 89–97.

Fabre, J. H., *The Sacred Beetle and Others*, Trans. A. Teixeira de Mattos (London: Hodder & Stoughton, 1918).

Gardiner, L. M., 'Egg bursters and hatching in the Cerambycidae (Coleoptera)', *Canad. J. Zool.*, Vol. 44 (1966), pp. 199–212.

Halffter, G. and Matthews, E. G., 'The natural history of dung beetles of the subfamily Scarabaeinae (Coleoptera, Scarabaeidae)', *Folia Entomologica Mexicana*, Vols 12–14 (1966), pp. 1–312.

Hinton, H. E., 'The "gin-traps" of some beetle pupae; a protective device which appears to be unknown', *Trans. R. Ent. Soc. Lond.* Vol. 97 (1946), pp. 473–96.

Imms, A. D., *A General Textbook of Entomology* (9th ed. revised by Richards and Davies) (London: Methuen, 1957).

Lewis, J. G. E., 'Protective devices in two species of African Coleoptera', *Proc. R. Ent. Soc. Lond. A.*, Vol. 39 (1964), pp. 50–2.

Ling, R. T., 'Burying beetles', *Countryside*, Vol. 18 (n.s.) (No. 2) (1957), pp. 58–64.

Mampe, C. D. and Neunzig, H. H., 'Function of the stridulatory organs of *Conotrachelus nenuphar* (Coleoptera, Curculionidae)', *Ann. Ent. Soc. Amer.*, Vol. 59 (1966), pp. 614–15.

Manee, A. H., see Arrow, G. J., *Horned Beetles*.

Ohaus, F., see Arrow, G. J. *Horned Beetles*.

Parker, G. A., 'Sperm competition and its evolutionary consequences in insects', *Biol. Rev.*, Vol. 45 (1970), pp. 525–67.

Paulian, R., *Les Coléoptères. Formes – Moeurs – Rôle* (Paris: Payot, 1943).

Pearse, A. S. et al., see Arrow, G. J., *Horned Beetles*.

Pringle, J. A., 'A contribution to the knowledge of *Micromalthus debilis* le C. (Coleoptera.)', *Trans. R. Ent. Soc. Lond*, Vol. 87 (1938), pp. 271–86.

Pukowski, E., 'Okologische Untersuchungen an *Necrophorus* F', *Z. Morp. Ökol. Tiere*, Vol. 27 (1933), pp. 518–86.

Robertson, J. G., 'Ovariole numbers in Coleoptera', *Canad. J. Zool.* (1961).

Schwalb, H. H., see Wickler, W. *Mimicry in Plants and Animals*.

Wickler, W., *Mimicry in Plants and Animals* (London: World University Library, Weidenfeld & Nicolson, 1968).

Wigglesworth, V. B., *The Life of Insects* (London: Weidenfeld & Nicolson, 1964).

Wood, D. L., Browne, L. E., Silverstein, R. M. and Rodin, J. O., 'Sex pheromones of bark beetles. I. Mass production, bioassay, source and isolation of the sex pheromone of *Ips confusus* (LeC.)', *J. Insect. Physiol.*, Vol. 12 (1966), pp. 523–36.

Zwölfer, H., 'Rüsselkafer mitunge wöhnlicher Lebenweise. Koprophagie, Brutparasitismus und Entomophagie in der Familie der Curculionidae', *Mitt. Schweiz. ent. Ges.*, Vol. 42 (1969), pp. 185–96.

CHAPTER 4

Arrow, G. J., *The Fauna of British India, including Ceylon and Burma. Coleoptera, Lamellicornia, Part III (Coprinae)* (London: 1931).

Bornemissza, G. F., 'An analysis of arthropod succession in carrion, and the effect of its decomposition on the soil fauna', *Australian J. Zool.*, Vol. 5 (1957), pp. 1–12.

Chrystal, R. N., *Insects of the British Woodlands* (London: Warne, 1937).

Clausen, C. P., *Entomophagous Insects* (New York & London: McGraw-Hill, 1940).

218

Crowson, R. A., *The Natural Classification of the Families of Coleoptera* (London: Nathaniel Lloyd, 1955).

Dempster, J. P., 'A quantitative study of the predators on the eggs and larvae of the broom beetle, *Phytodecta olivacea* (Forster), using the precipitin test', *J. Anim. Ecol.*, Vol. 29 (1960), pp. 149–67.

Dixon, A. F. G., 'An experimental study of the searching behaviour of the predatory coccinellid beetle, *Adalia decempunctata* (L.)', *J. Anim. Ecol.*, Vol. 28 (1959), pp. 259–81.

Ehrlich, P. R. and Raven, P. H., 'Butterflies and plants', *Scientific American*, Vol. 216 (June 1967), 105–13.

Evans, M. E. G., 'The feeding method of *Cicindela hybrida* L., (Coleoptera, Cicindelidae)', *Proc. R. Ent. Soc. Lond. A.*, Vol. 40 (1965), pp. 61–6.

Fabre, J. H., *The Sacred Beetle and Others*, Trans. A. Teixeira de Mattos (London: Hodder & Stoughton, 1918).

Fox, C. J. S. and McLellan, C. R., 'Some Carabidae and Staphylinidae shown to feed on a wireworm, *Agriotes sputator* (L.), by the precipitin test', *Canad. Ent.*, Vol. 88 (1956), pp. 228–31.

Fraenkel, G., 'The chemistry of host specificity of phytophagous insects', in Levenbrook (ed.) *Biochemistry of Insects* (London: Pergamon Press, 1959).

Green, J., 'The mouthparts of *Eurynebria complanata* (L.) and *Bembidion laterale* (Sam.) (Col., Carabidae)', *Ent. Mon. Mag.*, Vol. 92 (1956), pp. 110–13.

Halffter, G. and Matthews, E. G., 'The natural history of dung beetles of the subfamily Scarabaeinae (Coleoptera, Scarabaeidae)', *Folia Entomologica Mexicana*, Vols 12–14 (1966), pp. 1–312.

Jeannel, R., 'Coléoptères', in Grassé, P.-P., *Traité de Zoologie*, Tome IX (1965), Paris.

Landin, B. O., 'Ecological studies on dung beetles (Col., Scarabaeidae)', *Ent. Opuscula Suppl*, Vol. 19 (1961), pp. 1–228.

Laurence, B. R., 'The larval inhabitants of cowpats', *J. Anim. Ecol.*, Vol. 23 (1954), pp. 234–60.

Lloyd, J. E., 'Aggressive mimicry in *Photuris*: firefly femmes fatales', *Science*, Vol. 149 (1965), pp. 653–4.

Mohr, C. O., 'Cattle droppings as ecological units', *Ecol. Monographs*, Vol. 13 (1943), pp. 275–98.

Paulian, R., *Les Coléoptères. Formes–Moeurs–Rôle* (Paris: Payot, 1943).

Scott, H., see Chrystal, R. N.

Sharp, D., Insects Part II. *The Cambridge Natural History* (London: Macmillan, 1899).

Wallace, H., 'The ecology of the insect fauna of pine stumps', *J. Anim. Ecol.*, Vol. 22 (1953), pp. 154–68.

Zwölfer, H., 'Rüsselkafer mitunge wöhnlicher Lebenweise. Koprophagie, Brutparasitismus und Entomophagie in der Familie der Curculionidae', *Mitt. Schweiz. ent. Ges.*, Vol. 42 (1969), pp. 185–96.

Zwölfer, H. and Bennett, F. D., '*Ludovix fasciatus* Gyll. (Col. Curculionidae), an entomophagous weevil', *Ent. mon. Mag.*, Vol. 105 (1969), pp. 122–3.

CHAPTER 5

Aneshansley, D., et al., 'Biochemistry at 100°C.: Explosive secretory discharge of bombardier beetles (*Brachinus*)', *Science*, Vol. 165 (1969), pp. 61–3.

Beament, J. W. L., 'The rôle of physiology in adaptation and competition between animals', in *Symposia of the Society for Experimental Biology: XV. Mechanisms in Biological Competition* (1961).

Cloudsley-Thompson, J. L., 'The merkhiyat jebels: a desert community', in G. W. Brown (ed.), *Desert Biology* (New York & London: Academic Press, 1968), Vol. 1.

Cloudsley-Thompson, J. L., *The Zoology of Tropical Africa* (London: World Naturalist Series, Weidenfeld & Nicolson, 1969).

Crowson, R. A., *The Natural Classification of the Families of Coleoptera* (London: Nathaniel Lloyd, 1955).

Darlington, P. J., see Wickler, W., *Mimicry in plants and animals*.

Edney, E. B., 'The body temperature of Tenebrionid beetles in the Namib desert of Southern Africa', *J. exp. Biol.*, Vol. 55 (1971), pp. 253–72.

Edwards, J. S. and Tarkanian, M., 'The adhesive pads of Heteroptera: a re-examination', *Proc. R. Ent. Soc. A.*, Vol. 45 (1970), pp. 1–5.

Eisner, T., Kafatos, F. C. and Linsley, E. G., see Wickler, W., *Mimicry in plants and animals*.

Eisner, T., van Tassel, E. and Carrel, J. E., 'Defensive use of a "faecal shield" by a beetle larva', *Science*, Vol. 158 (1967), pp. 1471–3.

Evans, M. E. G., 'The jump of the click beetle (Coleoptera, Elateridae) – a preliminary study', *J. Zool. Lond.*, Vol. 167 (1972), pp. 319–36.

Evans, M. E. G., 'The prodigious jump of the click beetle', *New Scientist*, Vol. 55 (1972), pp. 490–3.

Gressitt, J. L., 'Epizoic symbiosis: the Papuan weevil genus *Gymnopholus* (Leptopiinae) symbiotic with cryptogamic plants, oribatid mites, rotifers and nematodes', *Pacific Insects*, Vol. 8 (1966), pp. 221–80.

Gressitt, J. L., 'Epizoic symbiosis: cryptogamic plants growing on various weevils and on a Colydiid beetle in New Guinea', *Pacific Insects*, Vol. 8 (1966), pp. 294–7.

Hinton, H. E., 'On the respiratory adaptations, biology, and taxonomy of the Psephenidae, with notes on some related families (Coleoptera)', *Proc. Zool. Soc. Lond.*, Vol. 125 (1955), pp. 543–68.

Hinton, H. E., 'On the spiracles of the larvae of the suborder Myxophaga (Coleoptera)', *Aust. J. Zool.*, Vol. 15 (1967), pp. 955–9.

Hughes, G. M., 'The co-ordination of insect movements, III. Swimming in *Dytiscus*, *Hydrophilus* and a dragonfly nymph', *J. Exp. Biol.*, Vol. 35 (1958), pp. 567–83.

Larsen, O., 'On the morphology and function of the locomotor organs of the Gyrinidae and other Coleoptera', *Opuscula Ent. Suppl.*, Vol. 30 (1966), pp. 1–242.

Lawrence, R. F., see Cloudsley-Thompson, J. L., *The Zoology of Tropical Africa*.

Lewis, J. G. E., 'Protective devices in two species of African Coleoptera', *Proc. R. Ent. Soc. Lond. A*, Vol. 39 (1964), pp. 50–2.

Lloyd, J. E., see Wickler, W., *Mimicry in Plants and Animals*.

Nachtigall, W., 'Locomotion: swimming (Hydrodynamics) of aquatic insects', in M. Rockstein (ed.), *The Physiology of Insecta* (New York & London: Academic Press, 1965), Vol. II.

Nutting, W. L. and Spangler, H. G., 'The hastate setae of certain dermestid larvae: An entangling defence mechanism', *Ann. ent. Soc. Amer.*, Vol. 62 (1969), pp. 763–9.

Roth, L. M. and Eisner, T., 'Chemical defences of arthropods', *Ann. Rev. Ent.*, Vol. 7 (1962), pp. 107–36.

Rothschild, M. and Lane, C., 'Exhibit of slides and oscillograms at R. ent. Soc. meeting', *Proc. R. Ent. Soc. Lond. C*, Vol. 29 (1964), p. 26.

Thorpe, W. H., 'Plastron respiration in aquatic insects', *Biol. Rev.*, Vol. 25 (1950), pp. 344–90.

Wigglesworth, V. B., *The Life of Insects* (London: Weidenfeld & Nicolson, 1964).

Wickler, W., *Mimicry in Plants and Animals* (London: World University Library Series, Weidenfeld & Nicolson, 1968).

Williams, C. B., 'Some bioclimatic observations in the Egyptian desert', in J. L. Cloudsley-Thompson (ed.), *Biology of Deserts* Symposium (London: Institute of Biology, 1954).

CHAPTER 6

Andrewartha, H. G., *Introduction to the Study of Animal Populations* (London: Methucn, 1961).

Birch, L. C., 'The mortality of the immature stages of *Calandra oryzae* L. (Small Strain) and *Rhizopertha dominica* Fab. in wheat of different moisture contents', *Aust. J. Exp. Biol. Med. Sci.*, Vol. 23 (1954), pp. 141–5.

Birch, L. C., Park, T. and Frank, M. B., 'The effect of intraspecies and interspecies competition on the fecundity of two species of flour beetles', *Evolution*, Vol. 5 (1951), pp. 116–32.

Bodenheimer, F. S., *Problems of Animal Ecology* (London: Oxford University Press, 1938).

Briggs, J. B., 'A comparison of pitfall trapping and soil sampling in assessing populations of two species of ground beetles (Col.: Carabidae)', *Rep. E. Malling Res. Sta*, Vol. 1960 (1961), pp. 108–12.

Browning, T. O., *Animal Populations* (London: Hutchinson, 1963).

Chauvin, R., *The World of an Insect*, trans. Oldroyd, H. (London: World University Library, Weidenfeld & Nicolson, 1967).

Coaker, T. H. and Williams, D. A., 'The importance of some Carabidae and Staphylinidae as predators of the cabbage root fly, *Erioschia brassicae* (Bouche)', *Entomol. Exptl. et Appl.*, Vol. 6 (1963), pp. 156–68.

Crombie, A. C., 'Interspecific competition', *J. Anim. Ecol.*, Vol. 16 (1947), pp. 44–73.

Danthanarayana, W. see Waloff, N.

Dempster, J. P., 'A quantitative study of the predators on eggs and larvae of the broom beetle *Phytodecta olivacea* (Forster), using the precipitin test', *J. Anim. Ecol.*, Vol. 29 (1960), pp. 149–67.

Elton, C. S., *The Ecology of Animals* (London: Methuen Monograph, Methuen, 1933).

Elton, C. S., *The Pattern of Animal Communities* (London: Methuen, 1960).

Evans, M. E. G., 'The surface activity of beetles in a northern English wood', *Trans. Soc. Brit. Ent.*, Vol. 18 (1969), pp. 247–62.

Fabre, J. H., *The Sacred Beetle and others*, Trans. A. Teixeira de Mattos (London: Hodder & Stoughton, 1918).

Fairhurst, J. M., 'Aspects of activity and density in some Carabidae', Ph.D. Thesis (University of Manchester: 1969).

Geiger, R., *The Climate near the ground* (Harvard: Harvard University Press, 1950).

Gilbert, O., 'The natural histories of four species of *Calathus* (Coleoptera, Carabidae) living on sand-dunes in Anglesey, North Wales', *Oikos* Vol. 7 (1956), pp. 22–47.

Greenslade, P. J. M., 'On the ecology of some British Carabid beetles with special reference to life histories', *Trans. Soc. Brit. Ent.* Vol. 16 (1965), pp. 149–79.

Luff, M. L., 'The abundance and diversity of the beetle fauna of grass tussocks', *J. Anim. Ecol.*, Vol. 35 (1966), pp. 189–208.

Maelzer, D. A., see Andrewartha, H. G., *Introduction to the study of Animal Populations*.

Murdoch, W. W., 'Life history patterns of some British Carabidae (Coleoptera) and their ecological significance', *Oikos*, Vol. 18 (1967), pp. 25–32.

Odum, E. P., *Ecology* (New York & London: Modern Biology Series, Holt, Rinehart & Winston, 1963).

Park, T., 'Experimental competition in beetles, with some general implications', in Cragg and Pirie (eds.), *The Numbers of Man and Animals*, Symposium of The Institute of Biology (Edinburgh: Oliver & Boyd, 1955).

Parnell, J. R., 'Observations on the population fluctuations and life histories of the beetles *Bruchidius ater* (Bruchidae) and *Apion fuscirostre* (Curculionidae) on broom (*Sarothamnus scoparius*)', *J. Anim. Ecol.*, Vol. 35 (1966), pp. 157–88.

Penney, M. M., 'Studies on certain aspects of the ecology of *Nebria brevicollis* (F.) (Coleoptera, Carabidae)', *J. Anim. Ecol.*, Vol. 35 (1966), pp. 505–12.

Penney, M. M., 'Diapause and reproduction in *Nebria brevicollis* (F.) (Coleoptera: Carabidae)', *J. Anim. Ecol.*, Vol. 38 (1969), pp. 219–33.

Pollard, E., 'Hedges IV. A comparison between the Carabidae of a hedge and field site and those of a woodland glade', *J. Appl. Ecol.*, Vol. 5 (1968), pp. 649–58.

Waloff, N., 'Studies on the insect fauna on Scotch broom *Sarothamnus scoparius* (L.) Wimmer', *Advances Ecol. Res.*, Vol. 5 (1968), pp. 88–208.

Williams, G., 'Seasonal and daily activity in Carabidae, with particular reference to *Nebria*, *Notiophilus* and *Feronia*', *J. Anim. Ecol.*, Vol. 28 (1959), pp. 309–30.

CHAPTER 7

Arrow, G. J., *The Fauna of British India, including Ceylon & Burma. Coleoptera Lamellicornia Part III* (*Coprinae*) (London: Taylor & Francis, 1931).

Bornemissa. G. F. and Norris, K. R., 'Using insects to improve pastures', Report in *Science Journal*, Vol. 2 (No. 5) (1966), p. 21.

Claridge, M. F., Blackman, R. L. and Baker, C. R. B., '*Haltica carduorum* Guerin introduced into Britain as a potential control agent for creeping thistle, *Cirsium arvense* (L.) Scop.', *Entomologist*, Vol. 103 (1970), pp. 210–12.

Creed, E. R., 'Geographic variation in the two-spot ladybird in England and Wales', *Heredity*, Vol. 21 (1966), pp. 57–72.

Hickin, N. E., 'The woodworm', *Science Journal*, Vol. 5 (No. 3) (1969), pp. 64–70.

Hingston, Major, see Arrow, G. J., *The Fauna of British India*.

Imms, A. D., *Insect Natural History* (London: New Naturalist series, Collins, 1947).

Legner, E. F. and Olton, G. S., 'The biological method and integrated control of house and stable flies in California', *California Agriculture*, Vol. 22 (No. 6), (1968), pp. 2–4.

Mellanby, K., *Pesticides and Pollution* (London: New Naturalist Series, Collins, 1967).

Melcalf, C. L., Flint, W. P. and Metcalf, R. L., *Destructive and Useful Insects. Their Habits and control* (4th ed.) (New York, London: McGraw-Hill, 1962).

Reay, R. C., *Insects and Insecticides*, Contemporary Science Paperbacks 39, (Edinburgh: Oliver & Boyd, 1969).

Reitter, Ewald, *Beetles* (London: Hamlyn, 1961).
Swan, L. A., *Beneficial Insects* (New York & London: Harper & Row, 1964).
Wigglesworth, V. B. 'Observations on the "furau" (Cicindelidae) of Northern
   Nigeria', *Bull. Ent. Res.*, Vol. 20 (1930), pp. 403–6.
Wright D. W. in *Rep. Nat. Veg. Res. Stn. Wellesbourne (1955)*, p. 47.

GENERAL INDEX

INDEX TO GENERA AND FAMILIES

230

231

Date Due